Multiethnic Literature and Canon Debates

Multiethnic Literature and Canon Debates

Edited by
Mary Jo Bona
and
Irma Maini

State University of New York Press

Cover illustration by Christine Perri, *detail* of *My Totem* (1999)

An earlier version of Chapter 4, "'But Is It Great?': The Question of the Canon for Italian American Women Writers" by Mary Jo Bona was published in *Breaking Open: Reflections on Italian American Women's Writing*, edited by Mary Ann Vigilante Mannino and Justin Vitiello, © 2003 Purdue University Press. Reprinted by permission.

Published by
State University of New York Press, Albany

© 2006 State University of New York

All rights reserved

Printed in the United States of America

No part of this book may be used or reproduced in any manner whatsoever without written permission. No part of this book may be stored in a retrieval system or transmitted in any form or by any means including electronic, electrostatic, magnetic tape, mechanical, photocopying, recording, or otherwise without the prior permission in writing of the publisher.

For information, address State University of New York Press,
194 Washington Avenue, Suite 305, Albany, NY 12210-2384

Production by Kelli Williams
Marketing by Michael Campochiaro

Library of Congress Cataloging-in-Publication Data

Multiethnic literature and canon debates / edited by Mary Jo Bona and Irma Maini.
    p. cm.
  Includes bibliographical references and index.
  ISBN 0-7914-6761-9 (hardcover : alk. paper) — ISBN 0-7914-6762-7 (pbk. : alk. paper)
1. American literature—Minority authors—History and criticism—Theory, etc.
2. Minorities—United States—Intellectual life.   3. Pluralism (Social sciences) in literature.   4. Ethnic groups in literature.   5. Minorities in literature.   6. Ethnicity in literature.   7. Canon (Literature)   I. Bona, Mary Jo.   II. Maini, Irma, 1958–

PS153.M56M847   2006
810.9'920693—dc22

2005018999

10 9 8 7 6 5 4 3 2 1

Contents

Foreword   vii
  John Lowe

Acknowledgments   xiii

Introduction: Multiethnic Literature in the Millennium   1
  Mary Jo Bona and Irma Maini

PART I
HISTORICAL CONSIDERATIONS

Chapter 1	From the Road not Taken to the Multi-Lane Highway: *MELUS*, The Journal *Veronica Makowsky*	23
Chapter 2	On the Trail of the Chicana/o Subject: Literary Texts and Contexts in the Formation of Chicana/o Studies *Aureliano Maria DeSoto*	41
Chapter 3	"A House Made with Stones / Full of Stories": Anthologizing Native American Literature *Kristin Czarnecki*	61

PART II
TEXTUAL READINGS

Chapter 4	"But is it Great?": The Question of the Canon for Italian American Women Writers *Mary Jo Bona*	85
Chapter 5	Racial Politics and the Literary Reception of Zora Neale Hurston's *Their Eyes Were Watching God* *Stephen Spencer*	111
Chapter 6	De-Centering the Canon: Understanding *The Great Gatsby* as an Ethnic Novel *Joe Kraus*	127
Chapter 7	An Exile's Will to Canon and Its Tension with Ethnicity: Li-Young Lee *Wenying Xu*	145

PART III
POPULAR CULTURE

Chapter 8	Canon-Openers, Book Clubs, and Middlebrow Culture *June Dwyer*	167
Chapter 9	From the Boardroom to Cocktail Parties: "Great" Books, Multiethnic Literature, and the Production of the Professional Managerial Class in the Context of Globalization *Sarika Chandra*	183
Chapter 10	It's Just Beginning: Assessing the Impact of the Internet on U.S. Multiethnic Literature and the "Canon" *Patricia Keefe Durso*	197
Contributors		219
Index		223

Foreword

John Lowe

Mary Jo Bona and Irma Maini in *Multiethnic Literature and Canon Debates* have given us an extremely useful overview of what some have termed the "triumph" of ethnic studies in the American academy over the past few decades. As the title of this study indicates, however, the battle is far from won; indeed, signs of counterattack are everywhere on campuses around the nation, and not just from reactionary forces. Critical fashions wax and wane, and some of the recruits we mustered for the so-called canon wars have moved on to newer, sometimes trendy issues and approaches. Ethnic studies programs—including African American studies—have recently experienced diminished budgets, and some have even been shrunk from departments into programs, or from programs into minors. Perhaps more ominously, the crisis in academic publishing has meant that books proposed on unknown or marginal ethnic writers are less attractive than surer bets, such as another book on Ernest Hemingway or Henry James. In trade publishing, many ethnic writers are going out of print, making the construction of syllabi more difficult, and forcing students to search diligently on the Internet for used copies.

This process has been exacerbated by the increasing involvement of state legislatures in the heretofore sacrosanct precinct of college and university curricula matters. Following national leaders like Lynne Cheney and Edward Bennett, legislators are mustering campaigns to restore the "classics" to prominence, which all too often gets translated into elimination of ethnic literature courses and programs, rather than adding new sections of Shakespeare or Milton.

We need to do a better job of disseminating knowledge about what has actually been accomplished through the teaching of ethnic literature. The impressive progress we have made in the academy toward the publishing, reading, and critical analysis of ethnic American writers has invigorated many students and teachers, and has not surprisingly also strengthened our understanding of the more established, "canonical" writers—most of them white—who long reigned without competition on English department reading lists and in anthologies. Reading Abraham Cahan's immigrant saga, *Yekl*, for example, certainly casts new light on Henry James's *The American Scene*; similarly, Charles Chesnutt's African American plantation tales naturally lead to a reconsideration of white Southern writers such as Thomas Nelson Page and William Faulkner. Understanding our cultural diversity as an essential nutrient of democratic society can only lead to a better sense of cultural richness and proud, but tolerant, democratic solidarity. The clear excellence of American ethnic writing provides prima facie evidence of how immigration has richly contributed to our national culture, especially in the arts, but in many other areas as well, as the various narratives of immigration, acculturation, and democratic debate reveal. Further, the rather different experiences of Native Americans and African Americans fosters a much keener understanding of the tragedies of Manifest Destiny and slavery, but also of what W. E. B. Du Bois meant when he predicted that the great issue of the twentieth century would be the "color line." These several traditions, it must be said, have not been solely comprised of tales of suffering and victimization. Works such as Native American writer James Welch's *Fools Crow*, Langston Hughes's African American "Simple" stories, and Italian American Jerre Mangione's *Mount Allegro* have taken us inside the community, warming us with folktales, ethnic humor, and a sense of the buoyant creativity fostered by dynamic ethnic cultures.

Native Americans, African Americans, and immigrants to this country have all been shaped by international as well as national and local vectors. One of the critical fashions that at times has seemed to be eclipsing ethnic studies is transnationalism. Ultimately, to follow Homi Bhabha's observations on the local and the global, this valuable new area can only lead back to a fresh appreciation of the value of ethnic literary study, for the trans-Atlantic, pan-Pacific connections can best be explored through the most obvious links, namely, between the old country (China, for example), and the immigrants to specific ethnic conclaves within our own nation (such as New York or San Francisco's early "Chinatowns"). Diasporan studies—Jewish, black, Latino—while necessarily transnational in nature, also need to be built on the solid foundation of prior ethnic literary studies of discrete American ethnic traditions.

These advances have been most notable in anthologies. An earthquake hit the publishing field when *The Heath Anthology of American Literature* first appeared in 1989, as Bona and Maini indicate. I was part of the original group of scholars who met in Yale in 1982 to plan such an anthology, and edited the Faulkner section, so I have followed the trajectory of this great work closely over the years. Although it is true that the right pilloried the volumes, the *Heath* quickly became the anthology of choice for thousands of teachers, and firms such as W. W. Norton & Company, Inc., took notice. Almost immediately, they and their mainstream competitors began to revamp their own anthologies, including writers never seen in such collections before. Today, although the always innovative *Heath* still maintains an edge in the inclusion of the best ethnic writers, its competitors continue to pay it the ultimate compliment of mimicry. How long, however, will this continue? My best comfort is that our leading graduate schools continue to teach this material, and so our new professors will probably do so as well, but if the market conditions touched on above and in the pages that follow continue, this could gradually change. It is not enough to teach ethnic literature—we need to better educate the general public and our legislators about the value of doing so. We need to get more people *outside* the academy excited about ethnic authors. All too often those who mount criticism of the inclusion of ethnic texts on a syllabus have never read a word of the narratives they scorn.

The essays in this collection tackle these problems and opportunities in a variety of ways. The cost of the struggle to get ethnic studies on the map emerges clearly in Veronica Makowsky's engrossing history of MELUS, and the journal it publishes under the same name. As the leading organization for ethnic studies, and the force behind much of the ethnic revival, its story proves inspiring, and should go a long way toward educating younger scholars and students about the academic pioneers whose work has made today's projects possible.

The discrete essays that follow on Chicana/o, Italian American African American, Native American, and Asian American literature illustrate in each of these areas the principles set down in the introduction and in the other, more general essays that have governed the development of ethnic literary studies. We learn how key texts came into view, were praised, examined, critiqued, and popularized in the academy. But we also see the myriad lines of connections between apparently separate ethnic communities, which of course are daily being knit together through intermarriage, new cultural formations, and the day-to-day operations of our democracy. The concluding essays on book clubs, reading canonical texts through the lens of ethnicity, and the global and national consequences of expanding the American literary canon, usher us into a more theoretical, complex, and often troubling realm, where we receive a storm warning about the dangers ahead for future writers, teachers, and students of ethnic literature; all must navigate over the shoals of commodification, conservative ideologues, the pressures of the academic/publishing marketplace, and the politics of the academy and its surrounding communities. Ethnic texts can be claimed, as the contributors to this volume do, as "cultural capital," but they can just as easily be jettisoned as mere academic ballast by those who want to direct our cultural ship of state. The Internet, as the concluding essay here indicates, is already the "next" battleground for these issues, as students, readers, and scholars too unfortunately count electronic prominence as a gauge of excellence and importance, bypassing the hard work of individual reading and evaluation. Clearly, those of us who care about the study of ethnic literature must equip ourselves for this new battlefield, and train our students to avoid its booby traps and mines. All these hazards, however, can be mapped, alongside the bolder outline of the territories we have been charting for students and readers for several decades. As we continue our vital work in a new century, we will return again and again to these sustaining essays, which arm, protect, sustain, and inspire a new generation of academic warriors.

Acknowledgments

Collaborations are delicious. Like a basket of sweets, no piece is insufficiently pleasing, just differently flavored, but equally savory. Our project was auspicious, since it emerged from sundry conversations over luncheons and dinners at various venues of the MELUS conference, the Multiethnic Literature of the United States Association. From the Pike Street Market in Seattle to Biga on the Banks in San Antonio, our conversations about the intersection between canonicity and multiethnic literature grew more and more urgent. We both finally agreed to this pressing fact: the canon debate ain't over yet, and we knew others would be interested in contributing their ideas to the mix. We were not disappointed. *Multiethnic Literature and Canon Debates* is the fruit of several years of conversation and connection with distinguished and emerging scholars around the country. We are grateful to our contributors for sharing their knowledge about the history of multiethnic literature and its relation to "canonical" American literature, the classroom, and popular culture. Their excellent work increased our appreciation of the complexity of canonical texts and lesser-known works and revealed a richness of interpretation when strenuous debate and rigorous scholarship are applied.

In the spirit of collaboration, we also must thank James Peltz of State University of New York Press, whose enthusiasm for our project enormously supported our efforts toward its completion. In that regard, we also extend warm thanks to Katy Leonard, Allison B. Lee, Kelli Williams, Lani M. Blackman, Michael

Campochiaro, and Carol Inskip, whose editorial expertise sharpened our book and eased a difficult process. Finally, we both thank our families, whose patience and goodwill made the completion of this book a joy to experience.

Introduction

Multiethnic Literature in the Millennium

Mary Jo Bona and Irma Maini

In a 1999 article in the *Chronicle of Higher Education*, Scott Carlson discusses the implementation of "Great Books" programs in eleven colleges, with support from the National Association of Scholars, the Princeton-based group "known for its crusades against multiculturalism and political correctness" (18). In a subsequent report, "Losing the Big Picture: The Fragmentation of the English Major since 1964," the National Association of Scholars were aghast to learn that Toni Morrison and Zora Neale Hurston are now more frequently cited in course descriptions than Pope, Swift, Twain, and Poe (Eakin). In their attempt to offer students what they believe constitutes a solid foundation in Western thought, faculty members involved in such programs apply the Arnoldian maxim on criticism—"to know the best that is known and thought in the world"—to the teaching of the Great Books. In fact, some professors refuse to acknowledge political motivations undergirding the work of writers such as Thucydides and Machiavelli, promulgating a noncritical response to richly political works. Spouting the oft-heard reactionary response to recent literary criticism, one professor at Wright College in Chicago proclaims that "'ideologies have no place as a dominant, controlling lens through which to see literature. . . . Literature has to do with the soul, not with political movements'" (qtd. in Carlson).

Disingenuous and alarming, such proclamations potentially suggest that examining literature cannot be a polysemous experience for students, whose souls may be inspirited by political engagement. According to the Readers' Guide to the Great Books of the Western World from *Encyclopedia Britannica*, an author's work must be more than fifty years old to be included on the list of books worthy to be read. Certainly in the past fifty years, the landscape of the American academy has undergone fundamental changes in its constituencies. Undergraduate female students now outnumber males, women and minority faculty members have been hired to teach in traditional English departments, and the study of American literature has been revitalized through republication and anthologizing of noncanonical works. Some Great Books programs have extended their study of Western works to include non-Western writers from Africa, East Asia, and South America (Carlson), but not surprisingly, multiethnic U.S. literature is excluded from consideration. Unfortunately, the cultural conflict about what constitutes literature worthy of examination is oversimplified, clearly dividing conservatives and liberals, as though no overlap exists. Many of us teaching multiethnic literature were raised on Shakespeare and Eliot, and have gladly taught many of the European-descended writers of the past. However, campus revivals of Great Books, criticism against multiculturalism, and excoriation of contemporary literature strongly compel those of us devoted to the dissemination and examination of multiethnic literature to revisit the ongoing debate on the expansion of the literary canon. As William Cain points out, "the 'canon' controversy not only involves choices among books, but also impels people to make decisions about the degree to which America's diverse population will be represented in institutional life" (3).

If the 1960s was characterized as a decade of social movements for change and justice, then the 1970s was surely the decade that witnessed the first fruits of those struggles. In the context of academia, scholarship, and teaching, many radical changes began to take place. One of the most significant tasks in the 1970s was the recovery of "lost" or "forgotten" texts by scholars. Feminist scholars in particular played a pivotal role in unearthing and republishing works like Rebecca Harding Davis's "Life in the Iron Mills" ([1861]1971), Charlotte Perkins Gilman's "The Yellow Wallpaper" ([1892]1973), Harriet Jacobs's *Incidents in the Life of a Slave Girl, Written by Herself* ([1860]1973), Zora Neale Hurston's *Their Eyes Were Watching God* ([1937]1978), and scores of others. Other than reiterating the existence of women's and blacks' literary traditions, republishing these works also brought into focus the social and sexual politics that had been largely responsible for the demise of these works in the past. Similarly works by writers of color like John Okada's *No-No Boy* ([1957]1976), D'Arcy McNickles's *The Surrounded* (1978), Jean Toomer's *Cane* ([1923]1975), and Jose Antonio Villarreal's *Pocho* ([1959]1970) among others were given attention and republished. It was critical to establish the presence of these works as the process of redefining American literary history began in earnest.

In an ongoing effort to produce, distribute, and make available works by contemporary women and writers of color, and works that had been ignored or silenced in the past, academics and scholars put together several new anthologies. Keenly aware of the nexus of publication and accessibility of texts, scholars saw the importance of anthologies and rightly believed that in many ways anthologies were key to bringing about change in syllabi and reading lists. Some of the most significant anthologies in the 1970s were: Abraham Chapman (ed.) *New Black Voices: An Anthology of Contemporary Afro-American Literature* (1972); Luiz Valdez and Stan Steiner (eds.) *Aztlán: An Anthology of Mexican American Literature* (1972); Frank Chin, et al. (eds.) *Aiiieeeee! An Anthology of Asian American Writers* (1974); Mary Helen Washington (ed.) *Black-Eyed Susans: Classic Stories by and about Black Women* (1975); and Alan Velie (ed.) *American Indian Literature: An Anthology* (1979). Each of these anthologies contributed to the growing need and demand for a body of literature that was conspicuously absent in the influential and popular *Norton Anthology* through much of the 1970s. For instance, only one African American writer, Le Roi Jones (Amiri Baraka) was given the last two pages of the 1,906 page *Norton Anthology* (Hemenway 65), thus underscoring the relationship between hegemonic control and distribution of knowledge.

Gradually, publishers both large and small started publishing more works by minority writers, some who have gained canonical status today. Toni Morrison's *The Bluest Eye* (1970), *Sula* (1973), and *Song of Solomon* (1977), Maxine Hong Kingston's *The Woman Warrior: Memoirs of a Childhood Among Ghosts* (1976), Leslie Marmon Silko's *Ceremony* (1977), and Ernest Gaines's *The Autobiography of Miss Jane Pittman* (1972) were published by major houses like A. A. Knopf and Random House. On the other hand, several small and independent presses like The Feminist Press and Broadside Press dedicated themselves to publishing works by minority writers. Quinto Sol publishers did much to promote Chicano literature and published Tomás Rivera's *. . . y no se lo tragó la tierra / And the Earth Did Not Part* (1971); Rudolfo A. Anaya's *Bless Me, Ultima* (1972); and Rolando Hinojosa's *Estampas del valle y otras obras: Sketches of the Valley and other Works* (1973). These authors later came to be known as the "Chicano Big Three."

With the publication of a large number of works by women and ethnic writers, it was inevitable that there would be a growth in the scholarship and research of these writers and their works. The 1970s saw the emergence of new critical methodologies as scholars questioned the validity of imposing so-called universal critical paradigms on works by "minority" writers. Recognizing the patriarchal and/or Eurocentric assumptions as well as the underlying hegemonic structures of many of these tools of inquiry, critics sought to formulate diverse strategies that would allow them to take into account differences in gender, race, ethnicity, class, culture, location, and sexual preference. Some of the groundbreaking work in this area began with theorizing vernacular and oral traditions, narrative and language, folklore and myth, genre and form. Addison Gayle's *Black Aesthetic* (1971), and Robert Stepto's *From Behind the Veil: A Study of Afro-American Narrative* (1979) started this process, which gained momentum in the 1980s with Houston Baker's *Blues, Ideology, and African American Literature* (1984), and Henry Louis Gates Jr.'s *The Signifying Monkey: A Theory of African American Literary Criticism* (1988). Critical anthologies of essays like Joseph Sommers and Tomas Ybarra-Frausto (eds.) *Modern Chicano Writers: A Collection of Critical Essays* (1979), and Charles R. Larson (ed.) *American Indian Fiction* (1978) helped theorize and contextualize works by Chicano and Native American writers.

Scholars and academics who were engaged in the rereading and reinterpreting of canonical works as well as analyzing and theorizing contemporary works needed the network and support of academic organizations. However, instead of lending support, premier organizations like the MLA used highhanded tactics to silence the demands of its "radical" members to present their research and ideas. A case from the annals of MLA convention history comes to mind: one of the foremost leaders in the movement to bring to the academic table issues on the Vietnam War and the repression of students and blacks, Paul Lauter (along with Louis Kampf and Florence Howe among others) disrupted the 1968 MLA convention. Seeking an expansion of focus which included discussion of the Vietnam War and the repression of authors Eldridge Cleaver and Octavio Paz, Lauter and others fought the MLA stalwarts of the organization to include the establishment of a Commission on the Status of Women and a reconsideration of the practice of aestheticism to include analysis of black, Chicano, and women writers. As Kampf and Lauter attested, "literature and literary practice, in spite of the intentions of the practitioners of aestheticism, are weapons in maintaining or transforming the received order of social relations" (*The Politics of Literature* 41).

Eventually in 1976, the MLA established a Committee on Minority Literature and organized a series of seminars in African American literature and Native American literature that "began the process of 'decentering' the canon, redefining American literature and literary history" (Singh et al. 4). This also led to the publications of four important volumes by the MLA: Dexter Fisher (ed.) *Minority Language and Literature* (1977); Dexter Fisher and Robert Stepto (eds.) *Afro-American Literature: The Reconstruction of Instruction* (1979); Houston A. Baker, Jr. (ed.) *Three American Literatures: Essays in Chicano, Native American, and Asian American Literatures for Teachers of American Literature* (1982); and Paula Gunn Allen (ed.) *Studies in American Indian Literature* (1983) (Singh et al. 14). Meanwhile several academic organizations and groups like MELUS (Multiethnic Literature of the United States), AAAS (Association for Asian American Studies), and AIHA (American Italian Historical Association) were formed and established. Likewise there was a spurt of new scholarly journals and periodicals like *Amerasia, Callaloo, African American Review, Journal of Ethnic Studies, Studies in American Indian Literature, Revista Chicano-Riqueña, MELUS,* and others that provided space for scholars in these fields to publish their research.

Demands to make curricula, syllabi, and reading lists more democratic, inclusive, and pluralistic gained currency in the 1970s though arguments about canons became a national debate primarily in the 1980s. Critics and academics questioned the criteria used to determine literary value, criteria that usually included vague notions of aesthetic excellence and universality. They asked: "What is excellence?" "Who determines it?" "Whose reality/truth is universal?" Urging a redefinition of the criteria and the evaluative process, scholars grappled with the difficult and complex task of deciding which works should be studied and taught, researched and critiqued. Paul Lauter asserts that the questions of the 1960s: "Where are the blacks?" "Where are the women?" shifted to "Whom do you want to replace?" in the 1970s (*Canons* 7–8). This was a potent question, particularly for those who saw this as an attempt not to replace but to displace "canonical" writers. Despite changes in reading lists and scholarship, literature by women and writers of color was by and large separated and ghettoized in much of the 1970s. Most academics did not see this literature as an integral part of the mainstream curriculum and preferred to relegate it to "specialty" courses or programs. Others attempted to include a token writer or two in their reading lists, usually to be taught at the end of the term. More than just the practical reason that not many professors were trained to teach these "new" works, this marginalization of minority literature was yet another way to dismiss and invalidate it on the grounds that it lacked aesthetic value and had a purely political and ideological agenda.

Nevertheless, the small and big gains of the 1970s unsettled a large group of people—both inside and outside of academia—and caused enough alarm among them that brought about a backlash in the 1980s, spearheaded by the publication of Alan Bloom's *The Closing of the American Mind*, and E. D. Hirsch's *Cultural Literacy*. Intellectuals in academia did not anticipate the far-reaching effects of such books, but conservatives working in the 1980s for the Reagan Administration, including the head of the National Endowment for the Humanities, Lynne Cheney, and formerly William Bennett, who became secretary of education under Reagan, advocated a return to the classics, "defending a body of knowledge that should constitute a stable curriculum, expressing humanistic wisdom—expressing, indeed, the highest aspirations of the Western tradition—against the onslaughts of the new barbarians" (Gilbert and Gubar xiv, xv). An approach to literature that was committed to established classics—an immutable canon—was debated in many venues, "From *Newsweek* and *Time* to *The New Criterion* and *The American Scholar*, low-, middle-, and high-brow magazines featured articles caricaturing or lambasting an academy we hardly recognized from our own experience" (Gilbert and Gubar xii). For academics committed to opening the canon and introducing students to marginalized literary cultures, the culture wars of the 1980s—"these war whoops"—as Gilbert and Gubar describe them, "were impinging on our lives as writers, readers, and teachers, no matter how we tried to ignore them" (xii).

Undoubtedly, canon debates came into vogue in the 1980s. Many in academia engaged strenuously in debates about *the* canon, a topic not of much interest until movements for social change in the 1960s and 1970s shifted and diversified the academic landscape. Professors in literature departments seemed divided on the issue of canons. Did expanding the canon mean that *the* masterpieces would remain untaught? On one side of the divide were the canon expanders, who wanted to consider the "transformation of perception" that occurs when a "traditional category is shattered by adding a range of different works to prior accounts of it" (Lauter, *Reconstructing* xxiii). On the other side were advocates of a Hirschian "cultural literacy," placing faith in an objective reality of greatness, which included a cultural canon already ensconced.

Alongside the debates about literary canons in the American academy came important attempts to define the critical term itself. According to Wendell Harris, citing a biblical parallel when discussing literary canons is inappropriate despite the word's core meaning of "rule" or "measure," "and by extrapolation, 'correct' or 'authoritative,' . . . the process of biblical canonizing was toward closure, whereas literary canons have always implicitly allowed for at least the possibility of adding new or revalued works" (110, 111). In his analysis of the canon and the Hebrew Scriptures, however, Gerald Bruns reminds us that the biblical canon is not "a literary category but a category of power" (81). Ongoing heated discussion ensued regarding considerations of *the* literary canon, especially during the 1980s. Such conversations often resulted in polemics rather than "critical colloquy" (Harris 112). Suggesting that feminist challenges to the literary canon have been intrinsically but refreshingly polemical, Lillian Robinson also put forth the radical idea that including women's writing "alters" our view of the traditional canon (213).

John Guillory has described the canon debate as an argument for opening the canon, or the liberal critique, and the argument for preserving the canon, or the conservative critique. Lost in both arguments, according to Guillory, is historical context. Believing that the question of judgment, of aesthetic value, is the wrong question to raise with regard to canons, Guillory reminds readers that "an individual's judgment that a work is great does nothing in itself to preserve that work, unless that judgment is made in a certain institutional context, a setting in which it is possible to insure the *reproduction* of the work, its continual reintroduction to generations of readers" (237). Those of us in academia know that the institution of the school has organized and regulated our practices of reading (Guillory 239). And perhaps the best description of the word "canon" comes from an awareness of the social function of the academy and its distribution of knowledge (Guillory 240). Paul Lauter has sought to understand canon formation in its historical context, recognizing the relationship between the history of the school and literacy itself. Awareness of what is "central" and what is "marginal" to literary study is a basic function of canonization, argues Lauter, but *who* decides these categories determines "who studies, who teaches, and who has power in determining priorities in American colleges" (*Canons and Contexts* ix). Like the biblical canon, therefore, the literary canon is about power.

Offering a definition of the word "canon," is never a neutral undertaking. Lauter's definition continues to be useful after the canon wars of the 1980s have been putatively laid to rest because a "classic" text continues to be a category that is reinforced by academics in power. Keeping in mind Lauter's working definition of canon allows those of us teaching ethnic literature and multicultural works in English departments and programs such as Women's Studies and Ethnic Studies to remember that such books less than a generation ago were not considered worthy to teach. Lauter writes, "by 'canon' I mean the set of literary works, the grouping of significant philosophical, political, and religious texts, the particular accounts of history generally accorded cultural weight within a society. How one defines a cultural canon obviously shapes collegiate curricula and research priorities, but it also helps to determine precisely whose experiences and ideas become central to academic study" (*Canons and Contexts* ix). Such a definition has serious import for the future of the academy and for the teaching of multiethnic literature. Lillian Robinson earlier recalled that the whole effort of maintaining a traditional literary canon has been hardly a conspiracy by the academic elite. Nonetheless, people in academia use power consciously, and defenders of a traditional canon reinforce the status quo by teaching primarily white and masculine works. Moreover, if we think of the traditional literary canon as a "gentlemanly artifact" then we recognize that the process of expanding it has as much to do with diversifying academe as it has to do with textbook availability (Robinson 213).

Entering the controversy about the canon during the height of the literary culture wars of the 1980s, Carey Kaplan and Ellen Cronan Rose admitted that they could not predict "who will be tomorrow's canon-makers and common readers, only that they will surely contest each other's right to own, and define, culture" (xix). Citing a 1987 position paper issued by the National Endowment for the Humanities (authored by Lynne Cheney) on the grim situation in the nation's public schools, Kaplan and Rose illuminate the dichotomous nature of the culture debate between the conservatives and the liberals, in effect echoing the concerns of Lauter and others at the 1968 MLA convention. The conservative authors of the NEH document, according to Kaplan and Rose, "are committed to timeless, eternal 'classics' that institutionalize and ossify the world they already control" (3). Recognizing that reevaluating the canon is "neither revolutionary nor unprecedented," Kaplan and Rose reiterate a basic premise of canon reformation: it is an "organic and ongoing process" (10). As such, multiethnic literature, like women's literature, challenges the "academic establishment to examine its ideological premises and alter existing power relations" (13).

Meanwhile the 1980s saw a huge influx of works by women, writers of color, and voices that had been silenced or ignored over the years, including gay/lesbian writers. It is no exaggeration to state that Alice Walker's *The Color Purple* (1982), which won the Pulitzer the following year, "placed the entire group [of black women writers] within a new dimension in the national consciousness" (McKay 249). In fact, 1987 and 1988 were enormously auspicious years for black writers, several of whom won the Pulitzer: August Wilson for his play, *Fences* (1987); Rita Dove for her poetry collection, *Thomas and Beulah* (1987); and Toni Morrison for her novel, *Beloved* (1988). In addition, the National Book Critics Circle awarded its annual prize to Louise Erdrich's *Love Medicine* (1984), and Bharati Mukherjee's *The Middleman and Other Stories* (1988). Not only did works like these make it to the *New York Times* best seller list but those like Amy Tan's *Joy Luck Club* also remained on the list for forty weeks. The year 1988 also saw the immense popularity of David Hwang's play *M. Butterfly*, which won the Tony that year and was selected as a finalist for the Pulitzer in 1989. The public appetite for more multiethnic works paralleled the student demand for changes in syllabi and curriculum across campuses. Not coincidentally, Werner Sollors published his landmark study *Beyond Ethnicity: Consent and Descent in American Culture* in 1986, furthering a wide-ranging exploration of "the origins and ambiguities of the term 'ethnicity,'" itself, thereby reinforcing the pluralistic origins of American literary culture (18). In addition, one of the major publishing events that further helped to propel this appetite for multiethnic works was the first edition of *The Heath Anthology of American Literature* in 1989. The first anthology to include a multiplicity of voices and genres, the *Heath* played a pivotal role in canon expansion and transformation. Greeted with both cheers and jeers, the *Heath* added more fodder to the raging cultural wars of the 1980s. It aroused the ire of Roger Kimball, the editor of the *New Criterion*, who declared it to be "a shabby production, intellectually shallow, politically tendentious" and asserted that "it deserves the scorn of everyone who cares about the preservation and transmission of American literature" (qtd. in Cain 8).

The process of decolonizing the literary canon gained further momentum with the growth of postcolonial studies in the late

1980s and much of the 1990s. As Salah Hassan points out, "Postcolonial studies, notably in the form of colonial discourse analysis, formulated a critique of the canon by exposing the traces of empire and the construction of a colonial object in canonical texts" (300). Though Edward Said's *Orientalism* (1978) had brought into focus the hegemony of the colonial discourse in literature and Salman Rushdie's *Midnight's Children* had won the Booker prize in 1981, it was only after the publication of *The Empire Writes Back* (1989), by Bill Ashcroft, Gareth Griffiths, and Helen Tiffin, that postcolonial studies took off. Even as critics and scholars continued to wrestle with the term 'postcolonial,' theorists like Gayatri Spivak, Homi Bhabha, among others, laid the groundwork for postcolonial theory and discourse that not only challenged underlying assumptions of current theories, but also showed new and interesting ways of analyzing literature.

Discussions of sexuality and identity also gained momentum, spearheaded by pioneering anthologies such as *This Bridge Called My Back: Writings by Radical Women of Color* (1981), edited by Cherríe Moraga and Gloria Anzaldúa, and *Nice Jewish Girls: A Lesbian Anthology* (1982), edited by Evelyn Toron Beck, to name just two. Such collections, as Martha Vicinus explains, "problematized the contemporary relationship between a lesbian identity and a racial identity in the United States" (433). Reading about sexual identity necessitated an awareness of the various and complicated ways in which sexuality intertwined with cultural identity, social class, and regional background. In their collection, Anzaldúa and Moraga not only called attention to racism within the feminist movement, but they also paved the way for future writers to expand on concepts of feminism, queerness, and multiple identities. Creating a mixed-genre work such as her 1987 *Borderlands—La Frontera: The New Mestiza* testified to Anzaldúa's construction of a generic montage that deepened an understanding of marginalized identity be it national, racial, linguistic or sexual, centralizing borderlands writing in critical discourse. Committed to collective subjectivity, many gay/lesbian writers create works that complicate the intersection between sexual and cultural identities. For example, Norman Wong's 1994 collection of short stories *Cultural Revolution* portrays several generations of immigrants, and Carole Maso's 1986 debut novel *Ghost Dance* explores the multiple ethnic roots of her protagonist's family. Both works redefine multiethnicity, and challenge readers and scholars alike to explore the relationships between narrative experimentalism—genre mixing—and issues of cultural hybridity, sexual difference, and national identity.

Despite the radical developments in scholarship, perhaps because of them, the two previously mentioned jeremiads *The Closing of the American Mind* by Allan Bloom, and *Cultural Literacy* by E. D. Hirsch became best sellers in the 1980s. Each advocated educational reform through a "revival of a conservative system of education" (Simonson ix). In response to Bloom and Hirsch, the editors of *Graywolf Annual* collected essays that were mostly written before the appearance of either Bloom's or Hirsch's books, by such writers as James Baldwin, Paula Gunn Allen, Gloria Anzaldúa, and Wendell Berry. In doing so, these editors reinforced the fact that for many years authors have thought and written about "issues of multiculturalism, the history of civilizations, feminist literature and culture, ethnicity, and the literature and histories of non-White and non-European cultures" (Simonson xiiii). Perhaps the reason why "cultural literacy" quickly gained such wide currency in the 1980s was because "it seem[ed] to offer a simple solution to urgent problems. As with all quick fixes, this promise [was] deceptive" (Armstrong 29). Such urgent problems as reading deficiencies in elementary school children and a weak economy could not be solved by requiring students to learn a "national vocabulary" as promulgated by E. D. Hirsch in the 1980s (qtd. in Armstrong 27). Rather than focus solely on finding common ground based on memorization of vocabulary (as important as that is), Paul Armstrong suggests that we teach competing narratives in order to learn "what to do [linguisitically] when we find an absence of commonality" in a pluralistic society (32). Certainly the nation's schools in the 1990s and beyond are still suffering from lack of resources and unequal distribution of funding sources that leave the nation's poorest students unable either to memorize or to make meanings of their own.

The new millennium has brought a mixed bag in terms of literary culture. The resurgence of book clubs (Oprah's club of the

1990s being the most popular and powerful) compelled a rethinking about the common reader and literary novels. The resurgence of Great Books courses and its accompanying audiotapes in contrast reinforced the idea of a transcendent notion of greatness. Alongside these two divergent responses to literature aimed at a reading public outside academe, inspiring literary events took place inside the academy. The fourth edition of *Heath Anthology* was published. The most multiethnic of all the American literary anthologies, *Heath* continues to define American literature through the lens of multiethnic voices. John Alberti, one of the editors of the *Heath*, asserts "revising the canon of American literature and developing multicultural curricula . . . represent not just a rethinking of what texts to include on a syllabus, or the simple replacement of one group of privileged texts with another, but a fundamental re-examination of the purposes and practices of literary study as a whole and of American literature in particular" (Pedagogical xv). Further, this rethinking, Alberti points out is also necessary in examining the different pedagogical strategies in teaching multiethnic literatures (*Canon* xii)

Though traditionally more conservative, the *Norton Anthology* has also refocused its energies in recent editions by including voices of many cultures alongside the formerly dominant Anglo-American culture. While recognizing the significance of the material conditions of the distribution of a work, Susan Gallagher argues for the primacy of the "'pedagogical canon': texts that are taught in college and university settings," (54) over an "imaginary canon," a term she borrows from Guillory's *Cultural Capital: The Problem of Literary Canon Formation*. Asserting that "the literary canon is a loose, baggy monster, a fluid movement of ebbs and flows, ins and outs," Gallagher asks: "Will untaught texts eventually disappear from the imaginary canon? Can a text be canonical if no one teaches it?" (66). However, the process of what remains in the canon and what gets taught is a complex one as Judith Fetterley points out in her important anthology of early American women writers. Works gain cultural credence through ceaseless discussion and through publication in various forums. Such evidence includes a "nutrient mass of critical books and articles, scholarly biographies, exhaustive bibliographies, special and regular MLA sessions, hundreds of discussions in hundreds of classrooms, cheap and accessible paperback editions, richly elegant coffee-table editions, government-funded standard text editions." Such apparatus, Fetterley explains, testifies to the presumed worthiness of such texts to be fed (34).

Increasingly books that are now available in many editions and boast a generous scholarly response are multiethnic in content. Since the mid-to-late 1980s works such as Harriet Jacobs's *Incidents in the Life of a Slave Girl*, Zora Neale Hurston's *Their Eyes Were Watching God*, Toni Morrison's *Beloved*, and Maxine Hong Kingston's *The Woman Warrior* have become household names in English departments. In fact, these works, and others like them, are reprinted in multiple venues, including the canon-shaping anthology, *Heath* and the highly expanded, *Norton*. Scholars who teach multiethnic literature are instrumental in shaping the future of this body of texts.

Recognizing the shift in focus in canon debates in the 1990s, Gregory Jay explains that "revisionists now face many thorny questions about what to do in the wake of the end of consensus and the advent of multiculturalism" (6). Recent critical discourse about multiethnic literature has enriched the conversation about literary value, offering current formulations on such issues as contact zones, borderlands, and hybridity that supports the idea that all texts have contexts and all of them are about cultural contact with other modes of being and behavior. Both unsettling and exciting is the fact that those newly entering the debate on canonicity in the millennium are inheriting canon reform, not necessarily making it. Those new to the field of multiethnic literature are encouraged to enhance recent scholarship by examining such concerns as the category of identity itself, which gains further resonance in texts that focus on cultural hybridity, racial and ethnic crossing, and sexual identification.

The ten scholars represented in this book present useful and innovative ways to examine literary works in various stages of canonization. Recognizing the significance of studying the social, political, and literary history of multiethnic literatures, writers in part I of the anthology critically examine the reception and dissemination of ethnic literatures in their essays. In her essay, "From the Road not Taken to the Multi-Lane Highway: *MELUS:* The

Journal," Veronica Makowsky examines the development of multiethnic literature from the perspective of one of the preeminent academic journals in the discipline, *MELUS* (Multiethnic Literature of the United States). Evaluating the increasingly complex theoretical approaches used to introduce and discuss multiethnic literature, Makowsky is able to assess the wide-ranging diversity of the field thirty years after its inception. Aureliano Maria DeSoto's essay "On the Trail of the Chicana/o Subject: Literary Texts and Contexts in the Formation of Chicana/o Studies" traces the role of cultural and identity politics in the history of Chicana/o studies and the canonization of Chicano texts within the context of the polemics of the Chicano movement of the mid-1960s as well as the feminist, lesbian, and gay critique in the mid-1970s to the present. DeSoto argues that the current debate about the status of Chicana/o studies is a sign of healthy and productive involvement of Chicana/o activists, scholars, and intellectuals that points toward a more discursive and dialectic approach. A critical overview of the absence of Native American literature in popular anthologies since 1891 to the end of the 1980s is the subject of Kristin Czarnecki's essay "'A House Made with Stones / Full of Stories': Anthologizing Native American Literature." Drawing on theories of cultural capital and the production and distribution of literature, Czarnecki examines the impact of the exclusion of Native American works in anthologies until the publication of the *Heath* in 1989 and the subsequent revision of the *Norton Anthology*.

The essays in part II of the anthology analyze the issue of canonization of specific texts within the context of the politics of literary, aesthetic, and/or social value. Mary Jo Bona's essay, "'But is it Great?': The Question of the Canon for Italian American Women Writers" places Italian American women writers into the larger context of American literature by examining the development of the American literary canon in the early twentieth century. Introducing those critics responsible for placing Italian American writers on the literary map, Bona explores texts and themes that resonate an *italianità* distinct to this cultural group but also reverberating with other American works. In his essay, "Racial Politics and the Literary Reception of Zora Neale Hurston's *Their Eyes Were Watching God*," Stephen Spencer discusses the checkered history of Hurston's now famous novel. Despite the racial and gendered controversy surrounding Hurston's work, Spencer's essay shows the remarkable manner in which feminist and cultural critics retrieved the text and contributed to the current canonical status of the novel. Joe Kraus's essay "De-Centering the Canon: Understanding *The Great Gatsby* as an Ethnic Novel" engages a canonical text and reinterprets it by using theories and tools traditionally used to study ethnic texts. Focusing largely on the issue of "outsiderness," on "real" or perceived differences between the terms immigrant, ethnic, and American, Kraus's essay reveals the complex and deep connections between these markers of identity. In her essay "An Exile's Will to Canon and Its Tension with Ethnicity: Li-Young Lee," Wenying Xu examines Chinese American poet, Li-Young Lee, whose disavowal of ethnic community in favor of an identification with American transcendentalism is his effort to will himself—as the poet of exile—into the canon of American poetry. Despite his positioning as displaced and homeless, Li-Young Lee invokes, as Xu demonstrates, his Asian culture's foodways and stories.

Any discussion of multiethnic literature must necessarily address its place and status in popular culture. No longer can academia be the proverbial ivory tower separated from the concerns of the outside world. In fact, one might argue that multiethnic literature has been largely responsible for bridging the gap between "high brows" and "low brows." June Dwyer addresses this issue in her essay "Canon-Openers, Book Clubs, and Middlebrow Culture" in the third section of this anthology. Historicizing the existence of book clubs, Dwyer's essay examines the role of popular book clubs like Book-of-the-Month club and Oprah's book club in opening up the traditional literary canon. Sarika Chandra examines the question of a literary canon from a totally different perspective in her essay "From the Boardroom to Cocktail Parties: 'Great' Books, Multiethnic Literature, and the Production of the Professional Managerial Class in the Context of Globalization." Drawing on theories of Pierre Bourdieu and John Guillory, Chandra's essay examines the marketing of literary texts, "Great Books" as well as multiethnic works, to the professional managerial class and its effect on the literary canon. In her essay, "It's Just

Beginning: Assessing the Impact of the Internet on U.S. Multiethnic Literature and the 'Canon,'" Patricia Keefe Durso analyzes the way the Internet is dramatically reshaping literary and critical texts. Seeing a convergence between the web-based paradigm of multilinearity, multivocality and the text based nonlinear, nonhierarchical paradigm in multiethnic works, Durso's essay contends that the Internet is, perhaps, an ideal medium for the dissemination of multiethnic literature. As the innovative fiction writer Carole Maso explains, "electronic writing will help us to think about impermanence, facility, fragility, and freedom, spatial intensities, irreverences, experimentation, new worlds, clean slates. Print writing will allow us new respect for the mark on the page, the human hand, the erasure, the hesitation, the mistake" (173). Multiethnic literature—electronic and print—portrays American identities in multiple contexts and enriching complexity. Providing fruitful discussion about this literature paves the way for future canonization, which such scholarship encourages, but with clear-sighted awareness of the changing nature of canon formation itself.

Throughout the decade of 2000, issues about the value and necessity of disseminating multiethnic literature persist. Negative attitudes regarding the teaching and reading of ethnically diverse American writers continue to inspire heated discussion about the literary value of multiethnic works. Though Jessica Munns dramatically declares: "the canon is dead: long live pick and mix" (26), the debates go on. In fact, canon debates are certainly not meant to be resolved. As Susan Gallagher succinctly states, "canon formation is an imprecise process" (54). Engaging in strenuous debates on the efficacy of multiethnic literature in a time of conservative ideals suggests that "The Little Bourgeois Cultural Revolution of MLA 1968" that Paul Lauter and his cohorts initiated needs to be revitalized in the millennium (*The Politics of Literature* 34). In order to challenge a narrow understanding of what we read and how we read it, readers of multiethnic literature in America recognize that literature—all of it—must be read in all its complex contexts. The essays that follow show us how to do it: to read literature soulfully and mindfully, in tandem.

Works Cited

Alberti, John, ed. *The Canon in the Classroom: The Pedagogical Implications of Canon Revision in American Literature*. New York: Garland Publishing, Inc., 1995.

———."Pedagogical Introduction." *Instructor's Guide. The Heath Anthology of American Literature*. 4th ed. Ed. John Alberti. New York: Houghton Mifflin, 2002. xv–xviii.

Armstrong, Paul B. "Pluralistic Literacy." *Profession* (1988): 29–32.

Bloom, Allan. *The Closing of the American Mind: How Higher Education Has Failed Democracy and Impoverished the Souls of Today's Students*. New York: Simon & Schuster, 1987.

Bona, Mary Jo. "Gay and Lesbian Writing in Post-World War II America." *A Concise Companion to Postwar American Literature and Culture*. Ed. Josephine G. Hendin. Malden, MA: Blackwell Publishing, 2004. 210–237.

Bruce-Novoa, Juan. "Canonical and Noncanonical Texts: A Chicano Case Study." *Redefining American Literary History*. Eds. A. LaVonne Brown Ruoff and Jerry W. Ward, Jr. New York: MLA, 1990. 196–209.

Bruns, Gerald L. "Canon and Power in the Hebrew Scriptures." *Canons*. Ed. Robert von Hallberg. Chicago: University of Chicago Press, 1983. 65–83.

Cain, William E. "Opening the American Mind: Reflections on the 'Canon' Controversy." *Canon vs. Culture: Reflections on the Current Debate*. Ed. Jan Gorak. New York: Garland Publishing, Inc., 2001. 3–16.

Carlson, Scott. "A Campus Revival for the Great Books." *Chronicle of Higher Education* 19 (November 1999): A18–.

Eakin, Emily. "More Ado (Yawn) About Great Books." *The New York Times* 8 April 2001: 4A.

Fetterley, Judith, ed. *Provisions: A Reader from 19th-Century American Women*. Bloomington, IN: Indiana University Press, 1985.

Gallagher, Susan VanZanten. "Contingencies and Intersections: The Formation of Pedagogical Canons." *Pedagogy* 1.1 (2001): 53–67.

Gilbert, Sandra M., and Susan Gubar. *Masterpiece Theatre: An Academic Melodrama*. New Brunswick: Rutgers University Press, 1995.

Graff, Gerald. *Beyond the Culture Wars: How Teaching the Conflicts Can Revitalize American Education*. New York: W. W. Norton & Company, Inc., 1992.

Guillory, John. "Canon." *Critical Terms for Literary Study*. Eds. Frank Lentricchia and Thomas McLaughlin. Chicago: University of Chicago Press, 1990. 233–249.

Harris, Wendell V. "Canonicity." *PMLA* 106 (1991): 110–121.

Hassan, Salah D. "Canons after 'Postcolonial Studies'." *Pedagogy* 1.2 (2001): 297–304

Hemenway, Robert. "In the American Canon." *Redefining American Literary History*. Eds. A. LaVonne Brown Ruoff and Jerry W. Ward, Jr. New York: MLA, 1990. 62–72.

Hirsch, E. D. Jr., *Cultural Literacy: What Every American Needs to Know*. Boston: Houghton Mifflin, 1987.

Jay, Gregory S. *American Literature and the Canon Wars*. Ithaca: Cornell University Press, 1997.

Kampf, Louis and Paul Lauter, eds. Introduction. *The Politics of Literature: Dissenting Essays on the Teaching of English*. New York: Pantheon Books, 1972. 3–54.

Kaplan, Carey and Ellen Cronan Rose. *The Canon and the Common Reader*. Knoxville, TN: University of Tennessee Press, 1990.

Lauter, Paul. *Canons and Contexts*. New York: Oxford University Press, 1991.

——, ed. *Reconstructing American Literature: Courses, Syllabi, Issues*. New York: Feminist Press, 1983.

Maso, Carole. *Break Every Rule: Essays on Language, Longing, & Moments of Desire*. Washington, D.C.: Counterpoint, 2000.

McKay, Nellie. "Reflections on Black Women Writers: Revising the Literary Canon." *Feminisms: An Anthology of Literary Theory and Criticism*. Eds. Robyn R. Warhol and Diane Price Herndl. New Brunswick: Rutgers University Press, 1991. 249–261.

Munns, Jessica. "Canon Fodder: Women's Studies and the (British) Literary Canon." *Canon vs. Culture: Reflections on the Current Debate*. Ed. Jan Gorak. New York: Garland Publishing, Inc., 2001. 17–27.

Robinson, Lillian S. "Treason Our Text: Feminist Challenges to the Literary Canon." *Feminisms: An Anthology of Literary Theory and Criticism*. Eds. Robyn R. Warhol and Diane Price Herndl. New Brunswick: Rutgers University Press, 1991. 212–226.

Simonson, Rick and Scott Walker, eds. Introduction. *Multi-Cultural Literacy*. St. Paul: Graywolf Press, 1988. ix–xv.

Singh, Amritjit, Joseph T. Skerrett, Jr., and Robert E. Hogan, eds. Introduction. *Memory, Narrative, and Identity: New Essays in Ethnic American Literatures*. Boston, MA: Northeastern University Press, 1994. 3–25

Sollors, Werner. *Beyond Ethnicity: Consent and Descent in American Culture*. New York: Oxford University Press, 1986.

Vicinus, Martha. "'They Wonder to Which Sex I Belong': The Historical Roots of the Modern Lesbian Identity." *The Lesbian and Gay Studies Reader*. Eds. Henry Abelove, Michèle Aina Barale, and David M. Halperin. New York: Routledge, 1993. 432–452.

PART I

HISTORICAL CONSIDERATIONS

Chapter 1

From the Road Not Taken to the Multi-Lane Highway

MELUS, The Journal

Veronica Makowsky

The history of the journal *MELUS* (*Multi-Ethnic Literature of the United States*) is at once exemplary and unique. It has simultaneously initiated, modified, reflected, and guided trends in American literary history. In many ways, MELUS is a product of the racial, ethnic, and identity politics and antiauthoritarianism of the early 1970s that arose from the civil rights movement and protests against the Vietnam War. At the same time, though, the journal was a shaping force in itself, founding a new and evolving canon of American literature by examining ethnic writings with a scholarly rigor that demonstrated their worth. Although the founders explored the road not taken, their successors experienced the rigors of construction work, as that barely trodden path became a multilane highway. This article attempts to chart that development in the routes of ethnic literature through examining the form and content of the journal from 1973 to the present, and to consider some possibilities for future construction, changes of direction, and improvements.

1974–1978: Foundings

MELUS is the publication of the Society for the Study of Multi-Ethnic Literature of the United States. That society was founded at the 1973 annual Modern Language Association Conference, but MLA can only be awarded backhanded and reluctant credit. When denied panels for ethnic literature by MLA, the founders, led by Katharine Newman, decided to hold sessions in the hotel corridors. In other words, the initial tactic of MELUS was to seize some of the main arteries to the canonical major destinations, the MLA sessions on canonical literature, insuring that literary scholars could not bypass developments in ethnic literature.

This oppositional, in-your-face strategy persisted in the first issues of the society's publication, an unbound newsletter from 1974–1978, growing to four issues a year; it consisted of brief book and film reviews, short articles (several paragraphs) on ethnic literature, bibliographies, guides, informational resources, the activities of members, plans for MLA sessions (as an affiliated society since 1974), an ethnic guide to MLA, and discussion and reports of the Society's business. Over these four years, the publication became less and less like a learned society's newsletter and more and more like a journal, with longer, scholarly articles, but the sense of establishing a mission and challenging boundaries was consistent.

Although the heyday of the New Criticism was passing, literature that espoused anything other than aesthetic or formal greatness was suspect. In the early issues, writers were greatly concerned with reacting to what they believed to be the current contempt toward and/or ignorance of ethnic literature since ethnic texts considered social, cultural, and political questions (and often the necessity for reform) as vital to the interrogation of ethnic works. As Sanford Pinsker pointed out: "At best we are characterized as people of bumbling goodwill, as second-rate minds absorbed by third-rate questions, as laborers in a highly suspect vineyard" (4.2, 1977: 7). Uday Naval condemned the blindly canonical by implication as he described what MELUS is: "MELUS has open-mindedness, catholicity of outlook, absence of rigidity, and amenability to all worthwhile suggestions—all qualities making for strong growth" (1, 1974: 2). The founders of MELUS saw themselves as path breakers on the literary frontier while the high priests of the canon, still mainly Anglo males, considered them well-intentioned fools, harming only themselves as they wandered lost in the wilderness of uncultivated and worthless writings, not "literature" since that was found in the well-tended groves of academe. Writers who questioned social hierarchies, like James Baldwin and Frank Chin, were, by implication and often explicitly, threatening the professional credentials and right to canonical power of many members of the established professoriate.

In what became characteristic of the first decades of *MELUS*, not only critics, but also creative writers told of the rigors of establishing new literary outposts. According to African American novelist Ishmael Reed, ethnic writers were not regarded as brave pioneers but more like the howling savages of the Puritan view of the American landscape, as if the American literary canon were moving backward instead of forward in time: "At a time in history when the term 'American' isn't interchangeable with rudeness, grossness, and provincialism, but stands for a society where all of the cultures of the world may co-exist, and in which cultural exchange thrives, non-white American writers are still seen as a threat, and as even a terror. This is truly sad" (2). With his characteristic bluntness, Reed posits that the "Ugly American," according to the literary establishment, is not offensively wending his or her way through Europe but is found within U.S. territory in the person of the ethnic writer, a classic act of displaced anxiety and shame.

Asian American playwright Frank Chin was (and remains) a consistently confrontational challenger of ostensible literary "truisms" and values. In an early issue of *MELUS*, Chin expressed his frustration at being forced into the role of a hardy and experienced scout guiding a bunch of tenderfoots through a frontier that they were incapable of understanding or appreciating:

> Before I could talk about our literature, I had to explain our sensibility. Before I could explain our sensibility I had to acquaint them with our history. Before I could acquaint them with our history I had to dispel the stereotypes they carried in their systems like antibodies to the yellow truth. Before I could dispel the stereotypes I had to convince them they held stereotypes about yellows. I didn't like working for free trying to do the impossible only to make a fool of myself again. (3.2, 1976: 14)

Why should he do all the work while literary tourists gape and pretend to see and appreciate? He asserts:

> The whites have wiped out our history to make themselves look good. My work will never be understood, much less appreciated, till whites start calling themselves white people instead of just people, "universal man" and all their other white supremacist titles they've taught us to call them to make them feel exalted, mysterious and cosmically powerful. (3.2, 1976: 17).

Chin is calling for a realignment of the literary landscape. Instead of a "white" center surrounded by ethnic provinces, he wants a landscape of interlinked regions with no margin and no center. For Chin, "civilization" requires as much exploration and explanation as the ostensible wilderness of ethnicity.

The contributors to the early newsletters also successfully prophesied some of the journal's avenues of scholarly inquiry. There were demands for textbooks that featured ethnic literature (2.3, 1975: 2). Ruth Keenan called for a change of name to MELA with the 'A' standing for America to show that there was more to ethnic American literature than was contained within U.S. borders (2.3, 1975: 2). Foreshadowing what we would now call cultural studies, John Zebrowski wanted to call it MES, with the 'S' for Studies, to make it interdisciplinary. Thomas Inge raised the question of aesthetics, one that persists to this day. Is a work of ethnic literature really literature and worthy of study if it does not meet the highest aesthetic standards, and who gets to determine those standards? Inge comments, "to study only such works that also aspire to the aesthetic standards of a Shakespeare or a Faulkner is to practice cultural snobbery of the worse sort" (3.1, 1976: 7). Like Chin, these writers want a re-mapping and re-zoning of the literary landscape, as described by Brom Weber:

> It is ironic that American literary studies has the possibility of becoming international even though its focus will be American. The day may yet arrive when an Americanist who can read, write and speak Chinese will be studying the

literature of Chinese Americans and perhaps visiting China as a Fulbright lecturer in American literature. Comparative literary studies conducted competently may become an everyday affair for Americanists. It should be obvious that multi-lingualism and multi-culturalism are but one future direction for American literary studies. Its growth will make possible a genuine universalism inspiring respect for its inclusiveness rather than pathos for its provincial neglect of the imagination, thought, and experience present in ethnic American literatures. (2.1, 1975: 17–18)

Weber prescribes and predicts a literary map in which provinces and center are reversed, and clinging to the old centers of the canon would be considered, as it is today, "provincial."

1978–1981: The Newman Years

Under Katharine Newman of the University of Southern California, *MELUS*, in 1978 with volume 5, became a bound, scholarly journal of about one hundred pages between an array of pastel covers. It contained full-length scholarly articles as well as news of the MELUS society. In this case, we can judge the book by its professional looking covers, for Newman was formulating a professional study of ethnic literature whose credo she announced in the last issue of the newsletter version. It was professional in the sense of knowledgeable, but not in the sense of exclusive, or, of course, *ivory* tower. It was to be, she envisioned,

> *scholarly-readable*, with the accent on the second term. . . . Anyone interested in American literature is invited to join MELUS, but only those who are already sensitive to social issues and concerned about the moral climate of America will want to. So when you write your article for MELUS remember that we are a very special audience. Give those specific facts which you have researched, those precise theories that you have developed from your professional needs. Be clear. Be explicit. Write so that specialists in the

field will say, "This is new work," and yet people outside of the area will say, "I am glad to learn this." Write for yourself, on your own level of sophistication. Don't sing to the choir. Remember, you are part of it yourself. (4.2, 1977: 18)

MELUS was to exemplify the best in multiethnic studies: consideration for the needs of those who want to learn about an ethnic literature, but with no dumbing-down of scholarly and theoretical standards. Like the writers of the early newsletters, Newman neither refuses to apologize for ethnic literature, nor to justify an existence on the margins. Scholars of ethnic literature are not commenting from the sidelines of the canon, but "are part of it yourself." In terms of style, Newman's emphasis on clarity and accessibility has been and remains a hallmark of the journal to this day, for how can your content be inclusive, if your style is obfuscating and repellent, welcoming only to a caste of specialists?

The contents of the Newman issues of *MELUS* are broad. Today's ethnic literature is often considered synonymous with "racial" groups (African American, Asian American, Latino/a, and Native American), identified as people who look different from dominant Anglo stereotypes and often referred to as "people of color." These first issues included articles on a much wider array of European American literature than one would find today: Norwegian, Greek, French, Scandinavian, Portuguese, and Czech. The identity of individual ethnic groups was less important than mounting a multiethnic and multicultural challenge to the prevailing Anglo-dominated American literary canon. Writers did not stick to their own ethnic groups, or indeed to ethnic writers. African American critic (and later *MELUS* editor) Joseph Skerrett wrote on black characters in a white author, James Purdy (6.2, 1979); African American poet Marilyn Nelson (then surnamed Waniek) considered two Jewish American writers (7.1, 1980), while Luther Luedtke considered the founding father of the traditional American literary canon in "Ralph Waldo Emerson Envisions the 'Smelting Pot'" (6.2, 1979). Some issues of the journal had similarly broad topics, covering what we would now consider the obvious tropes of ethnic American literature, but which were not at all obvious then: "The Smelting Price," Oppression and Ethnic Literature (guest edited by Raymond

Paredes), "Ethnic Women Writers," and "New Writers and New Insights." Newman also began the tradition of *MELUS* interviews with creative writers with Gerald Vizenor.

With these broad and inclusive topics and articles, the editor and authors of these issues of *MELUS* were rewriting the literary map. Emerson was a valuable center or destination, but one of many. No writer was confined to a "ghetto" of his or her own ethnic group but was free to rove about the literary landscape and comment, appreciate, and evaluate. In addition to the re-valuation of the literary map, the Newman issues contained foundational articles on ethnic literatures, in other words, the roads not taken: an issue devoted to the evolution of Chicano literature (5.2, 1978) and articles on forgotten works, such as a 1901 play by African American Joseph Cotter, *Caleb the Degenerate*. Ethnic writers and critics could be informed and insightful spectators and pathfinders, not merely the spectacles at "exotic" destinations by literary dilettantes who considered themselves at the center.

Katharine Newman and John M. Reilly, in these early issues, make the study of ethnic literature as complex and sophisticated as the study of canonical literature was believed to be. Newman wrote: "People who have not read much ethnic literature prate (and the less they have read, the more do they prate) that it is *only* protest literature and that there is always 'a whining tone'" (5.3, 1978: 1). Through the study of ethnic literature, John M. Reilly wanted to move beyond simplistic approaches in two ways. He wanted to elaborate the traditional American narrative of the movement from ostensibly nonliterary forms to *belles lettres*. He indicted traditional narrative because

> it fails to acknowledge the presence in the United States of literary languages other than English. It fails to allow for the ways some ethnic groups have sustained oral and written forms well beyond the time when they disappear from the canon of Anglo-American writing. It fails to provide an important place to genres such as slave narratives and immigrant stories that are outside Anglo-American experience. And it fails to include as literary motive and artistic choice the identity many Americans find in ethnicity. (6.3, 1979: 2)

Further, Reilly, like Newman, questioned the common view of ethnic literature as uncomplicated and transparent protest literature from a homogeneous ethnic identity:

> Rather, ethnic literature can only be fully explained by an approach that studies writing as the expressions of the cognitive orientations of the authors. Ethnicity is a constant among these orientations, but it is as varied and modified by authorial disposition, assumptions about social and personal relationships, self-image, and assumptions about the way the natural and social world works. The differences among authors can become apparent within ethnic groups as well as between authors of different backgrounds. In fact, I should add to the critical agenda implied in this essay the task of studying why some ethnic groups find a literary voice at a different time than others, and the related task of explaining why shifts occur within the writing of a single ethnic group from plots varying toward victimization to plots resolved by self-growth of the protagonist. (5.1, 1978: 12)

Newman and Reilly's hope that ethnic literature would be approached as rich, complex, and challenging was realized as the history of *MELUS* continued to unfold. There were trees out there, as well as a forest, and the intricacies of the species and their relationships would be explored as *MELUS* continued to respond to and initiate the formation of an innovative multiethnic literary canon.

1982–1985: The Miller Years

Under the editorship of Wayne C. Miller of the University of Cincinnati, *MELUS* continued to map a literary terrain with more topics as destinations and greater complexity of critical routes. Miller initiated his editorship with praise of Katharine Newman for her embrace of multiplicity, as he echoed Whitman: "She is large, she contains multitudes, but she does not contradict herself" (9.1, 1982: 4). Within the pale blue covers of Miller's issues, he broke new ground by expanding the coverage of genres with music and film reviews, some creative writing, and issues on ethnic literature and music and on ethnic biography and autobiography. Topics of single issues became increasingly specialized: Native American Literature ("first ever to be dedicated to a single ethnic group," 12.1, 1985:1), American Southwest literature (11.4, 1984, guest edited by Marcos Portales), the Ethnic novel (10.4), Ethnic Images in Popular Genres and Media (11.3, guest edited by Joseph Skerrett), and European Perspectives (12.4, guest edited by Dorothy Burton Skårdal). Miller's editorship began the increasingly scholarly specialization within *MELUS*. Just as the traditional American literary canon had specialists in the American Renaissance or the twentieth-century drama, *MELUS* scholars would provide a similar depth of research and interpretation for periods, regions, ethnic groups, and genres.

Miller also continued Newman's coverage of ethnic women writers in two issues, 9.3 and 12.3, but was chary of deflecting the *MELUS* focus from ethnicity: "It is not the editorial policy of the journal to necessarily foster or promote either the study of women writers or the criticism of women scholars. We do think, however, that we know at least part of the reason why women scholars wish to publish with us and why they frequently choose ethnic writers, female and male, as their subjects" (9.4, 1982: 1). Miller's somewhat defensive tone indicates how feminist scholarship was perceived in 1982: necessary for the completion of ethnic literary canons but a potential threat to ethnic literature by deflecting the focus to the concerns of women (who represented more than half the population) and away from relatively small ethnic groups. *MELUS*, however, was necessary to women scholars since it provided a venue where their work would be valued, not regarded with disdain or suspicion as it still was in many canonical journals, and Miller continued to provide space for the nurturance of women scholars as well as the consideration of ethnic women writers for his relatively brief tenure as editor. When he moved to the University of Houston at Clear Water in 1985, the promised support for *MELUS* failed to materialize due to "problems in the Texas economy" (12.3, 1985: 1), and the journal needed to find a new home.

1985–1999: The Skerrett Years

With the editorship of Joseph Skerrett of the University of Massachusetts at Amherst, *MELUS* realized its promise as the atlas of ethnic American literature, or, to cite Skerrett's own metaphor, "Once happy plying otherwise unknown waters, *MELUS* as an enterprise is now swept into midstream and its members are sought for leadership" (14.2, 1987: 1). The journal as a physical artifact became similarly authoritative as it attained not only a thoroughly professional, but also an elegant and compelling appearance. The vestiges of a newsletter were gone. The dark red covers feature art work, photographs, and graphics of great distinction that highlight the topic of each issue. A playful and engaging, yet serious, example is a crossword puzzle with the names of theorists that illustrates the cover of an issue titled "Intertextualities" (19.4). The number of pages increased, and so did their look of crispness and confidence. In other words, while still remaining innovative and challenging, *MELUS* looked canonical.

Skerrett saw his mission as sustaining the original goals of *MELUS* while relating ethnic literatures to current critical and theoretical concerns. In 1987, he wrote:

> The cultural theorizing of the last decade or so, which has been at pains to demonstrate, among other things, the impact of power relations on forms of cultural expression, the pervasive relevance of gender relations and the interrelated importance of reader-response and cultural reception, has begun to inform and reshape how we write about ethnic literature. While some portion of our work as scholars of ethnic literature will always be concerned with recovering lost or neglected texts and submitting them to close and careful reading, our work is becoming more diversified as we respond to new ideas about literature and culture. (14.2, 1987: 1)

Contributors to the journal increasingly employed selected theoretical constructs, a sometimes awkward process since much theory, such as deconstruction, harkened back to the New Critical emphasis on deauthored texts as autonomous entities. The author was dead, and the audience was in a state of flux because they were in a constant process of (de)constructing their identities as endless performative acts. Critics of ethnic literature, embedded in history and identity politics, could not wholeheartedly embrace a deracinated approach to texts. Scholars had to pick and choose from the theoretical tool kit for the instruments that would illuminate particular authors and works without removing them from their contexts.

The range of articles on European American literature became less broad and numerous, and continued the identification of "ethnic" with "racial" or visibly different, as was particularly evident in Ethnic Women Writers V (15.1). Some issues, though, did explore the terrain of a single European ethnic group, such as Italian American (14.3–4) and Irish American (18.1). Reflecting on the diminution of submissions on European American literature, the guest editor of the Irish American issue, Charles Fanning, commented: "I believe that students of ethnicity need occasionally to be reminded of the continued vitality and usefulness of the literature of European immigrants and ethnics" (18.1, 1993: 1). Skerrett also published an innovative and controversial issue on traditionally opposed ethnic groups, "Of Arabs and Jews" (15.4).

Within larger ethnic groups, Skerrett looked for depth of coverage of more specific literatures or genres, as in traditional canonical literature where increased specialization was a mark of scholarly seriousness and acceptance. For example, there was an issue that now focused only on Chinese American literature (20.1), not the broader Asian American literature. Interestingly, this issue was dominated by articles on Maxine Hong Kingston, illustrative of the way the entry of an ethnic literature into the literary canon is facilitated by a critically and popularly dominant text, in this case, Kingston's *The Woman Warrior*. One issue was devoted to Native American fiction (17.1), reflecting the dominance of fiction as a genre in critical writing about ethnic literature. There was an issue on African American literature (24.1), which Skerrett called "the broadest and best charted stream of writing in the literary continent" (24.1, 1999:1). African American literature, however, was placed in specific literary historical contexts in "Black Modernism and Post-Modernism" (17.4). In his editor's preface to the Latino/a issue, Skerrett hoped for more specialization in this literature as well, so that its worth for serious scholarship would be recognized: "We would much rather be able to devote whole issues to Puerto Rican Literature, or Cuban American Literature, or Brazilian American Literature" (23.1, 1998: 1).

Skerrett introduced current topics that cut across ethnic groups but had been neglected in much scholarship on ethnic literature. Many of these were guest-edited: Ethnic Humor by John Lowe (21.4); Folklore and Orature by Arlene Elder (16.1); Ethnicity and Pedagogy by Edward Ifkovic (16.2); and Ethnic Theater by Roberta Uno (16.3); Skerrett himself assembled issues on Popular Literature and Film (22.2); Religion, Myth and Ritual (24.2); and Ethnic Sexualities (22.1). What unites these seemingly disparate topics is an increased concern with ethnicity as performed, not essential, and the uses to which writers could put such performances as in "Maskers and Tricksters" (20.4). Although, as Skerrett points out, "we never succumbed to the 'death of the author syndrome' that briefly dominated in some critical venues," these issues of *MELUS* are indicative of critical trends that regard literary works as texts, malleable performances more removed from historical and cultural contexts, while never entirely relinquishing them, as exemplified in the issue on "Theory, Culture and Criticism" (23.4, 1998: 1).

Skerrett was particularly successful in addressing the most neglected genre in ethnic literature, poetry, in three issues of the journal (18.3, 21.1, and 23.3). In his prefaces to these issues, he speculated on the reasons for this critical disregard. In 1993, he posited: "The poet—more than the fictionist, more than the dramatist—refuses to be captured by the categories most in evidence in the criticism of ethnic literature. The subjectivity of the poet always overlaps some other territory of the heart, making the poet's ethnicity seem somehow more diffuse, making the critic's work more daunting and difficult" (18.3, 1993: 1). Ethnic poetry runs contrary to our expectations for ethnic literature and for its relation to its audiences:

> The focus of the poet in our time is often personal and psychological, whereas our notions of ethnicity revolve around communal and historical issues. The idea of eth-

nic poetry, then, to some readers suggests contradiction, contrary motion, paradox. The tensions that reside in the ethnic writer's relation to the double audience, which so often calls forth a rhetoric of explanation or cultural translation, put a real strain on lyricism as exaltation. (21.1, 1996: 1)

Critics, he comments, are in the delicate position of attempting "to put poetic practice into social, cultural, and intellectual contexts without bruising the poetry" (23.3, 1998: 1). In an ironic sense, ethnic poetry is consonant with the dominant or traditional American poetry canon. Many write poetry, but it is difficult to publish and sell, and critics and university professors and their students prefer to read prose, leading to the prominence of nonfiction ethnic prose, usually autobiographically based, such as Kingston's *The Woman Warrior* and Jerre Mangione's *Mount Allegro*.

Skerrett placed the traditional mission of *MELUS*, the study of the ethnic literatures of the United States, in a wider context, reflective of the way the field of American Studies no longer referred to interdisciplinary studies about the United States alone. In "Other Americas" (21.3), Skerrett wrote:

The current issue quite purposefully steps beyond our normal perimeters to approach writers from Canada, Mexico, and the Caribbean. In doing so, *MELUS* acknowledges the broadened understanding of American Studies that has been developing over the last decade or so. We are all of us Americans, whatever nation we inhabit on this side of the Atlantic. It is important to examine one another's felt experience of common issues such as slavery, racial oppression, ethnicity and immigration as it is to listen to a brother or sister. We relax the ordinary boundaries on this occasion as an acknowledgement of this family occasion. (21.3, 1996: 1)

Multiethnic literature of the United States was no longer on the periphery of the literary map as in the era of Katherine Newman. It had become a center that needed to embrace the margins, break down the distinction between center and margins, and once again rechart the literary terrain, but now it did so as a leader, not an interloper or challenger. *MELUS* was now a creator and certifier, as well as a reflector, of an increasingly prominent but evolving ethnic literary canon.

2000 to the Future

In 2000, *MELUS* moved to the University of Connecticut, and I, Veronica Makowsky, became the editor. UConn wanted to support the journal as evidence of its support for diversity and multicultural education and as a means of drawing students and faculty who would contribute to this effort. UConn won the journal in a competition to provide the most resources for the journal, as well as editorial competence. In short, *MELUS* was no longer an unwelcome interloper in the corridors of MLA and academe. It had arrived as a valued and desirable journal that lent institutional prestige, as also indicated by MLA's recent decision to digitalize *MELUS* as one of the first journals in its JStor project.

My first task as editor was to capitalize on this increased support to ensure the journal's efficiency and stability by modernizing submissions, subscriptions, ads, claims, and production, as well as putting the journal on a sound, even prosperous, financial basis. I have succeeded in those aims; we are fully computerized, we no longer operate on a shoestring, and, indeed, we even have money for improved production and more office help. Although we are now a thoroughly professional operation, we have paradoxically increased our financial well-being and retained our scholarly independence by one seemingly counterprofessional act. *MELUS* still publishes itself; it is not published by a large corporation or a university press. We do not pay middle men, nor do we answer to them.

As I struggled with administrative and financial issues for the first two years, I had the luxury of a backlog of fine articles that were accepted by my predecessor, Joseph Skerrett. I had the pleasure of sorting, arranging, and rearranging these articles into issues on special themes and groups: "Jewish American Literature"(25.1); "Latino/a Identities" (25.2); a double issue on "Revising Traditions" (25.3/4); a mélange of topics from detective fiction to letters to creative writing in "Varieties of the Ethnic Experience" (26.1); "Identities" (26.2); "Confronting Exiles" (26.3); "African American Literature" (26.4); "Contested Boundaries" (27.1), and "Native American Literature" (27.3). As I look back on these topics, I see not only the continued vitality of individual ethnic literatures, but also a preoccupation with revision: of identities, traditions, places of residence (physical and psychic), and boundaries. New authors like Native American Sherman Alexie enter the canon while "old" topics, like African American literature continue to be redefined by new authors like science fiction writer Octavia Butler and new relationships, for example, with Caribbean literature.

I will continue to publish issues on special topics, like the two guest-edited issues that have already appeared. "Multi-Ethnic Children's Literature," the first *MELUS* issue on this subject, was edited by Katharine Capshaw Smith and Margaret R. Higonnet and appeared in the summer of 2002 (27.2); it featured articles on children's literature from a variety of ethnic groups, including Native American, African American, Thai American, Chinese American, and Latino/a American. "Multi-Ethnic Literature and the Idea of Social Justice" appeared in the spring of 2003 and was guest-edited by Gaurav Desai, Felipe Smith, and Supriya Nair. Oddly enough, these late issues of *MELUS* involved a reconsideration and revision of the thematic issues confronted by the founding editors. According to Smith and Higonnet: "Children's literature allows readers a means to reconceptualize their relationship to ethnic and national identities. Telling stories to a young audience becomes the conduit for social and political revolution" (27.2, 2003: 1). Similarly, as they address the law's relationship to ethnic literature, Desai, Smith, and Nair contend, "in these essays, multiethnic literature also serves as a space for the resolution of social inequities, not by virtue of a fantastic projection into an unproblematic future, but by a determined impulse to set the record straight about the lived experiences of Americans" (28.1, 2003: 7).

In addition to these recapitulations and revisions of the early themes of *MELUS* as social, political, and literary activism, I will continue to publish issues on specific ethnic groups, such as Italian American in 28.3, edited by Mary Jo Bona, but with some new (at least to literary criticism) ethnic groups, such as Filipino American, edited by Rocio Davis in 29.1. We recently revisited our founding mother through a special issue (29.3/4) devoted to Katharine Newman's memory and accomplishments, edited by Amritjit Singh and C. Lok Chua. We have continued our vital interest in the teaching of ethnic literature in an issue (30.2) entitled "Pedagogy, Praxis, Politics, and Multiethnic Literatures," edited by Bonnie TuSmith and Sarika Chandra. A new departure will be a special issue on multiethnic literature and disabilities.

I would like to explore some new currents in multiethnic literature. There is increasing discussion of hybridity since many authors, such as Louise Erdrich, no longer claim just one ethnicity. Aesthetic considerations are receiving new prominence; while I doubt that we will return to the days of the New Critics, technique, structure, and other formal considerations will come increasingly to the forefront. In the early days of *MELUS*, the problem was to get ethnic literature taught at all; now we are beginning to examine improved techniques for teaching it and raising the many and uncomfortable questions about our own ideas and prejudices and those of our students that ethnic literature evokes. We are also seeing more scholarship on "whiteness" as an identity, no longer the dominant background for everything else, and this is initiating a return to consideration of European American works and a move away from ethnicity as denoting what is in common parlance called race.

From the road not taken to the multilane highway, *MELUS* has come a long way in professionalism, scholarly, critical and theoretical attainments, and literary stature. But what *MELUS* means to me and to many current members and contributors is not much different from what it meant to our founder, Katharine Newman, as she edited her last issue in 1981:

> This issue is the fulfillment of my personal dream. I have had the joy of combining, within these sixteen issues, the work of scholars dealing with nearly thirty different cultures. In my case, my father was also the father of my American Dream; when I was four, he formed one of the first Boy Scout troops in America, down in the slums of Philadelphia where the immigrants settled. He organized

a camp in some fields nearby, and there I lived with my parents, summer after summer. When we all sat around the campfire or gathered for Dad's interface religious service, I believed that this was the way America was. I learned better—bitterly—over the years, but in *MELUS* I see again the world of diversity, dignity, and fellowship. (8.4, 1981:1)

While we have, in many ways, achieved the world that Newman longed and worked for, we now face the challenge of continuing to innovate and of avoiding the inertia, rigidity, and defense of privilege that characterizes established institutions. *MELUS* has transformed ethnic literature from a single road not taken to well-maintained, multilane highways, but in order to succeed, it must always focus on the journey, with no final destination sought or reached. While *MELUS* has achieved canonical status, it must continue to define the canon, not as a fixed hierarchy of revered texts, but as an ever-evolving and always-contested process of seeking and studying the best in American literature.

Chapter 2

On the Trail of the Chicana/o Subject

Literary Texts and Contexts in the Formation of Chicana/o Studies

Aureliano Maria DeSoto

From its initial founding in the late 1960s, Chicana/o Studies as a field and the Chicana/o intellectuals gathered loosely under its umbrella have not only endeavored to radically intervene in the social and cultural conditions of Mexican Americans, but also to bring such radical practice into the halls of academe. One of the principle pursuits of the field has been tracing the emergence and articulation of a Chicana/o subject grounded in the principles of the Chicano Movement, the social and civil rights struggle of Mexican Americans. It is arguable that the legacy of the Chicano Movement is the most influential factor in contemporary Mexican American life. The benefits of the Movement, such as increased access to education and economic opportunity, have been widely embraced by all sectors of Mexican American society. The empowerment mantras of the Movement, echoing larger trends in American society, have propelled Mexican Americans into government, society, media, capital, and academe in unprecedented numbers. Most importantly, the Movement determined the primary academic aesthetic and political approaches to representing Mexican American culture and identity in literary and cultural forms.

Since the 1960s, the study of Mexican Americans has moved away from a broad based sociopolitical movement to the realm of cultural and academic politics, resulting in myriad theoretical, aesthetic, and ideological responses to the problem of classifying *lo chicano*, that which constitutes the Chicana or Chicano subject.

Particular ideas about Mexican American identity which have been dominant in specific historical moments have given way to other aspects of communal and individual identification that have displaced, but not quelled these earlier manifestations of thought. The result is that competing and sometimes contradictory ideals of the Chicana/o subject exist side by side, jostling for space in an increasingly diverse theoretical space.

Because of the role cultural politics and aesthetics play in discussions of the history of Chicana/o Studies, literary and cultural articulations are a particularly useful place to consider the changing ideas of Chicana/o identity and community and the move from rigidity to fluidity over the last thirty years. In particular, literature has been regarded as the tactile trace of a transformative consciousness that has been so important to Chicanas and Chicanos inspired by the politics and polemics of the Chicano Movement of the 1960s and 1970s. The cycling of texts within and without of the putative Chicano canon remains a process in formation, one dependent on the cultural and aesthetic politics of both the moment and practitioner, that reflects specific political moments in Chicana/o Studies. As the field enters the new century, it is characterized by a contestation played out over texts and the meanings assigned to them.

The zeitgeist of the field has gone through three distinct phases since the Chicano Movement's emergence in the mid-1960s: the years of pronounced Movement activism (1965–1975); the initial Chicana Critique of the 1970s (1970–present); and a post-1970s fragmentation informed by poststructuralist theory and a continuing emergence of marginalized subjects: feminists, lesbians, and gay men (1980–present). I have separated out these phases for narrative clarity and brevity of argument, while in reality they overlap and inform each other in ways that are not strictly linear. Additionally, although I have given chronological time spans for these periods, in reality the literature that has become indicative of these moments occurred in some cases before or after the initial period of activism, revealing the long historical pull or subsequent influence of each particular period of thought. As I argue for a certain historical progression, the Chicano Movement remains a vivid legacy in Chicana/o scholarship and cultural production. It has not been simply left behind by theories of the "post-."

Chicanismo Rising:
The Movement's New Mexican American

The Chicano Movement (1965–1975), which informs the contemporary development of Mexican American identity, was a multifaceted social and political phenomenon that sought to bring together arts, politics, and activism towards a specific vision of empowerment for Mexicans in the United States. Chicana/o Studies began in earnest in the early 1970s as the academic arm of this larger social movement for civil rights, rectification of historical discrimination, and the acknowledgement of the social, historical, and linguistic fact of Mexican Americans in the Southwest. One of the primary goals of early Chicana/o Studies was the canonization of a body of literature that reflected the goals of the Chicano Movement and its radical principles of cultural nationalism.

Mirroring the general tendency towards increased social radicalism in American society of the 1960s, the Chicano Movement was the *force majeure* in the social and political development of thousands of Mexican Americans, especially students. Social organizations for Mexican Americans in the 1940s and 1950s were oriented more towards legal and social reforms that would guarantee Mexican American participation in mainstream American society. These overtures were invariably accommodationist and assimilationist in tone and reflective of the general tenor of the times, arguing for greater Mexican American participation and access to Anglo-American middle-class values and practices. The Chicano Movement was a break from these earlier movements, with a radical version of a new cultural nationalism for Mexican America that entailed an identification with indigenous roots and a reification of the sociocultural dimensions of Chicana/o specificity. These sociocultural traits included an acknowledgement of the bicultural and bilingual character of Chicana/o experience and an adoption of the cultural politics of *mestizaje* that had informed the Mexican Revolution of the early part of the twentieth century. The new Chicano subject was specifically antiassimilationist, resistant, and oriented towards an introspective, community-based notion of subjectivity and identity. The Movement sought to define a third space of *Chicanismo* between the American hegemon and Mexico that addressed the particular experience of Mexican Americans who were neither valued nor respected in Mexico or the United States.

The Chicano Student Movement, developing after a series of 1968 high school strikes, called "blowouts," was the vanguard of the move to this new cultural nationalism. The student organization *El Movimiento Estudiantíl Chicano de Aztlán* (MEChA) was instrumental in organizing actions on university and high school campuses. A prime component of university reform was the institution of Chicano Studies programs and courses in bilingual and bicultural education. The rubric of *Chicanismo*, a radical consciousness that elevated community, the family, and race above assimilation, ethnicity, and capitalism, became the prominent aesthetic model among students and cultural producers. This rejection of Anglo-American cultural values is reflected in the turn away from the assimilationist "Mexican American" towards Chicano, where the nomenclature of self-description also becomes a signature of one's political perspective. Another key concept that emerged in this period is of *Aztlán*, a mythological homeland for Chicanas and Chicanos that reflected the spiritual and cultural values of a Chicano-centered reality.

Student activists took aim at the university, especially at the power of the university to define, label, and therefore affect, the Mexican American community. Students visualized the establishment of specific, Chicano-oriented programs, which would radically transform the academy. The student movement sought to harness the knowledge production engine of the university to its pursuit of radical politics. Student leaders fervently believed in a breakdown of the traditional boundaries between the university and the community as a key not only to political indoctrination, but also in fundamentally transforming a hegemonic institution. A key aspect of this was the nurturing of new aesthetic responses to the changed consciousness of Chicanas and Chicanos in various media as well as scholarship.

Following this, varied texts in different media (dramaturgy, literature, poetry, manifesto, performance art) of the Movement period sought to engrain the radical values of the new Chicano. This cultural nationalism became a characteristic departure point of both cultural production and scholarly analyses of Mexican American culture. Some examples of this productive time are

Rudy Acuña's *Occupied America: The Chicano's Struggle Toward Liberation* (1972); Armando Rendon's *Chicano Manifesto* (1971); Albert Camarillo's *Chicanos in a Changing Society* (1979); and Evangelina Enríquez and Alfredo Mirandé's *La Chicana: The Mexican American Woman* (1979). The journals *El Grito* (1969) and *Aztlán* (1970) became leading forums for emergent Chicana/o literature and scholarship. Anthologies of Chicano literature organized around Movement themes included: *The Chicanos: Mexican American Voices* (1971); *We Are Chicanos* (1973); *Festival de flor y canto* (1976); and critical volumes like *Literatura Chicana: texto y contexto* (1972).

The literary works that became most associated with the Chicano transformation of consciousness were those that actively reflected the values of the Chicano Movement. Works like Tomás Rivera's *. . . y no se lo tragó la tierra / . . . And the Earth Did Not Part* (1971), Ernesto Galarza's *Barrio Boy* (1971), Rudolfo Anaya's *Bless Me, Ultima* (1972), Rodolfo "Corky" Gonzales' *I Am Joaquin / Yo Soy Joaquin* (1972), Oscar Zeta Acosta's *Autobiography of a Brown Buffalo* (1972), Raymund Barrio's *The Plum Plum Pickers* (1970), along with the dramaturgy of Luis Valdez, and the poetry of Alurista, joined earlier works like Jose Antonio Villarreal's *Pocho* (1959, rpt. 1970), and Américo Paredes' *With His Pistol in His Hand* (1958) to become touchstone texts for what was quickly becoming a Chicano canon. Overall, this work foregrounded a particular Chicano subject, based in traditional cultural foundations of Mexican American life: the patriarch and patriarchal family, community, and the linkage of these to the health and well-being of the Chicano cultural nation of Aztlán. What emerged here is an essential, organic Chicano subjectivity that reflected the Chicano Movement's ideological goals and Utopian promise of a self-loving, powerful, and politically radicalized Mexican American.

This ideological work found support in the work of early Chicano scholarship. The historical and sociological texts of 1970s Chicano scholarship sought to define and label particular social and historical phenomena to typify the Chicano "experience" and the Chicano subject. The space of the subject became the *barrio* or the farm field. The Spanish language and agrarian culture of the farm worker were a great influence on young Chicanos and Chicano cultural producers, often writing predominantly in English and living in cities and seeking a greater authenticity of experience untainted by Anglo-American cultural corruption. Cultural nationalist scholarship became characteristic of analyses of Mexican American culture, as academics searched for the sociohistorical evidence to support the cultural and political claims of the Chicano Movement. These texts relied heavily on positivist subjectivity in their representation of an organic Chicano subject, rooted in the strength of family, the community, and cultural nationalism.

La Nueva Chicana: The Feminist Intervention

One of the prominent limitations with the initial formation of the Chicano canon was that it was almost exclusively focused on male experience, and the central role of the family and community in many early Chicano texts left unexamined the gendered aspects of those very structures. It was through the lens of both race and gender that Chicana feminists began in the late-1960s to craft a specifically feminine (and later feminist) politics as it related to the structures of Mexican American experience. Prominent themes of Mexican American life and Chicano Movement ideology, such as the family, marriage, and religion emerged quickly in the early critiques of Chicana feminists. These were areas of life that were experienced by both Chicanos and Chicanas, but with very different interpretations. The pronounced differences in the ways in which men and women were treated within Movement organizations, with men assigned leadership positions and women given largely domestic duties, caused many Chicanas to question these hierarchies of gender.[1]

And while Chicana feminism was articulated initially within the forum of the Chicano Movement, it was also undoubtedly fueled by the larger questioning of sexual roles and gender happening at the time, represented by second-wave feminism. The journal *Encuentro feminil*, the anthology *Women: New Voice of La Raza* (1971), the *Conferencia de Mujeres por La Raza* (1971), and a flurry of "special issues" in *Movimiento* publications marked the beginnings of a feminist articulation that, while critical, still proclaimed a loyalty to the *Movimiento* (Enríquez and Mirandé, 235–36).

This, however, was a problematic relationship. Feminist Chicanas faced pointed opposition among Movement Chicanos and

Chicanas. These Chicanas were often criticized for dividing the Movement and exalting the individual over the collective. This reaction was fueled by many factors, among which were the widespread impression that equated feminism with Anglo women, confusion among Chicanas themselves over the roles they should assume in a moment of great social change, and male intransigence and sexism in granting women an equal position in Movement organizations. This situation led to the alienation of many Chicana feminists from Movement organizations, the division of activist Chicanas between "feminists" and "loyalists," with the labeling of feminist Chicanas as traitors to their race. The rhetorical baggage of feminism was so great that at the First National Chicano Student Conference (1969), Chicana loyalists declared, "the Chicana woman does not want to be liberated" (qtd. in Córdova, 176).

The Chicana feminist critique of the sexist structure of the family was one of the primary reasons for the malevolent reaction of Chicanos and loyalist Chicanas. The family was regarded as the symbol of cultural survival in the face of assimilation, the locus within which Chicano values were preserved, and presided over by a typology of Chicana womanhood with the traditional manners and mores of femininity. As Alma García (1989) has noted: "[T]he Chicano family represented a source of cultural and political resistance. . . . At the cultural level, the Chicano Movement emphasized the need to safeguard the value of family loyalty" (419). This use of the family not only referred to the actual biological unit, but also served as a metaphor for the relationship that Chicanos sought between themselves as an element of racial unity. Importantly, early Chicana feminists correctly identified that the idea of unity in the face of Anglo power and culture could not be used to deform and subsume women's concerns. If anything, such a singular strategy would only serve to reinforce the subjugation of Mexican American women under a purportedly progressive program. By their insistence on an understanding of the gendered differences between Chicano men and Chicana women, nascent Chicana feminist thought was one of the first challenges to a uniformly definable Chicano identity.

Chicanas sought to ground their work in the radical praxis advocated by the Movement (that is, an acknowledgment of a working class/subaltern perspective), but with a decidedly feminist flavor. They also worked to distance themselves from white feminism, a direction influenced by the feminist baiting of Chicano nationalists who thought of feminists as *vendidas* ("sellouts"). By the mid-1970s, Chicana feminists had produced a remarkable number of texts, published in Movement journals or Chicana newsletters that articulated their social, cultural, and political concerns as racialized women distinct from both white women and Chicano men. The work of Bernice Rincón, Mirta Vidal, Enriqueta Longeaux Vasquez, and Anna NietoGomez, among others, published in small newsletters such as *Regeneración*, *El Grito del Norte*, and *Hijas de Cuauhtemoc*, implicitly advocated for the formation of *La Nueva Chicana*, or the New Chicana, a renaissance of Chicana writing that would determine, through the Chicana voice, the conditions and concerns of Mexican American women.

This formative period was a time in which Chicana feminists began articulating what would become foundational elements in the genre of Chicana writing. Among these would be the mother-daughter relationship, a reconstruction of notions of the family, an interest in gender and its attendant inequalities in culture and society, issues connected with reproduction rights and the body (abortion, forced sterilization, family planning). But perhaps the most powerful element of the new feminist paradigms for Chicana identity was the figure of the traitor in the lives of Mexican American women, specifically through the figure of Malintzín/Malinche.[2] Chicana feminists began to reimagine their relationship to Malintzín, and hence to Chicano history.[3] By turning the epithet of traitor on its head, Chicana feminists imagined a space of agency that directly undermined patriarchal social notions of female sin and moral limitation.

In general, Chicana feminism embraced an understanding of Chicana identity as amorphous and multiple, in an effort to address the different material and social conditions between Chicanas. This contingency of identity is a key aspect of contemporary Chicana feminism, allowing it to embrace a rhetoric of inclusion that has, theoretically, expanded the frame of Chicana identity in an acknowledgment of multiple subject positions. This legacy has enabled Chicana/o Studies as a field and more progressive elements of the Chicano intelligentsia to encompass, theoretically, the diverse elements of Mexican America.

As Chicana feminism began to grow into a cultural and institutional presence at the beginning of the 1980s, its victories in establishing itself as a legitimate and potent critical force were still somewhat tenuous. Many of the critical paradigms that Chicana feminists had begun to explore in the 1970s were ignored by many Chicano (male) scholars and cultural producers as irrelevant. Additionally, Chicana feminists were still encountering great difficulty in forcing Chicano professional organizations, like the National Association for Chicano Studies, Chicano academic journals, and cultural forums, like *teatro* and community galleries, to account for their concerns. In spite of these difficulties, Chicana feminist thought produced a profound shift in attitudes towards the study of Mexican Americans. Gender, and to a more limited extent sexuality, became integral to any study of the culture, social mores, and politics of Mexican Americans.

Building upon the antecedent Chicana feminism of the 1970s, scholars and cultural producers of the 1980s extended their critiques through anthologies, novels, memoirs, and monographs with a focus on Chicana experience. As well, they went from being outsiders to essential players within university departments and programs. This was due to the theoretical sophistication of many Chicana scholars as much as for the agitation that accompanied the challenges of feminists to the masculine-centered nature of Chicana/o Studies at the time. Although Chicana/o Studies was in many ways in its infancy as a field of inquiry, Chicana feminism demanded a shift that was by and large successful, at least at the larger or more liberal institutions in California and Texas. Increasingly, gender had to be addressed on syllabi and in course discussions.

Through the 1980s, the work of Chicana feminist writers became common aspects not only of Chicana feminist class reading lists, but also in more general courses on Chicana/o identity. Sandra Cisneros' *House on Mango Street* (1983), Ana Castillo's *The Mixquiahuala Letters* (1986), Lorna Dee Cervantes' *Emplumada* (1981), Helena Maria Viramontes' *The Moths and Other Stories* (1985), Cherríe Moraga's *Loving in the War Years: lo que nunca pasó por sus labios* (1983), and Gloria Anzaldúa's *Borderlands/La Frontera*

(1987) begin a process of creative production which continues, both from these authors and with new writers. This shift towards feminist and woman-centered cultural production displaced the initial canon of Chicano literature, and students and scholars spent less time reading Rivera's *And the Earth Did Not Part*, and more time on Cisneros' *House on Mango Street*. This shift split Chicana/o Studies and its approach to its canon among different political factions that were marked by gender as well as ideology. The rise of Chicana feminist literature in some ways made the Movement's canon irrelevant precisely because it had so fully ignored the gendered elements of Chicana/o culture and society.

Mario García (1989) has attempted to understand the struggles between political generations of Mexican American activists by observing that "each period possesses a distinct spirit, mentality, or Zeitgeist. Each era or generation to one degree or another, as Feuer suggests, 'deauthorizes' the previous one" (18). García's identification of differing generational zeitgeists is especially relevant in considering the tensions between different, opposed, and/or overlapping historical and discursive periods. The deauthorization of Movement aesthetics by Chicana feminism is reflected in approaches to literature and an expansion of what could possibly constitute a canon of Chicana/o literary, visual, and poetic texts. However, as Chicana/o Studies has continued to develop, there is never one, singular deauthorization process, but rather multiple, competing, and often contradictory voices.

The Sexual Outlaws:
Rodriguez, Moraga, and Anzaldúa

The bildungsroman became a central genre form to Chicana/o Studies from its initial period, for obvious reasons. The bildungsroman gives the illusion of transparency in tracing the political and social maturation of the subject, and the early work of Villarreal, Galarza, and Gonzales lend themselves to the genre. However, beginning in the 1980s, the bildungsroman is used by three writers in particular to upset the narrative structure of progressive Chicana/o social development in ways that mirror that inclusion of feminist texts within new canons of Chicana/o literature and in other ways depart from it. Two writers in particular mark the departure from the Movement and its body of literary and aesthetic values at the beginnings of the 1980s: Cherríe Moraga and Richard Rodriguez. Along with Gloria Anzaldúa, discussed below, Rodriguez and Moraga form a triad of the most influential Chicana/o polemicists of the last twenty years, and a decided shift not only onto the terrain of gendered, but also sexualized differences from the Chicana/o organic subject of the Movement.

Moraga has, since the beginning of the 1980s, produced two anthologies of essays, an extensive collection of dramaturgy, coedited several influential anthologies, and is active in supporting writing symposia in the San Francisco Bay Area, where she makes her home. Her work has been embraced by academic feminists, and has slowly become more intertwined in course syllabi as representative of the gendered critique of masculinist paradigms of Chicano experience. From her ground breaking first book, *Loving in the War Years: lo que nunca pasó por sus labios* (1983), to her most recent works (*The Last Generation* [1992], *Heroes and Saints and Other Plays* [1994], *Waiting in the Wings* [1997], and *Watsonville: Some Place Not Here* [2002]), Moraga has captured the sexual, social, and racial fissures of Mexican Americans in her passionate and polemic prose. She is, above all, a highly politicized writer, for whom writing is a tool against oppression. Certainly, her polemics have fueled her prominence in the left wing of Chicano Studies (and the nascent focus area of Chicana Studies).

Her fiery defenses of *Chicanismo* from the forces of assimilation and acculturalization appeal to students and radical professors, and Moraga has been embraced for the articulately political dimension of her work, as well as the prominence of being one of the first Chicana writers to write extensively on family, mixed-parentage, race, skin color, lesbian identity, and gender. From being a little-known writer in the early 1980s, she has been transformed into a canonical figure in the more progressive sites of Chicano Studies and cultural production.[4] Her extreme identification with *Chicanismo*, in spite of her unmarked, light-skinned body and the assumption of the privilege that could mean, is one aspect of what draws Chicanas and Chicanos to her work. The one vital theme running through Moraga's work as a whole is the project of creating a Chicana/o identity supple enough to encompass a variety of differences (gender, homosexuality, racially unmarked bodies, and those of mixed parentage), while retaining a radical political vision with an explicitly liberatory edge.[5]

On the opposite end of the political spectrum, Richard Rodriguez has, over the course of his thirty years of public writing, become one of the most conspicuous voices of Mexican America and one of its most controversial. His 1982 autobiography *Hunger of Memory: The Education of Richard Rodriguez* has garnered reviews, essays, and opinion pieces that in turn laud and denounce both it and its author.[6] The volume elicited a firestorm of controversy among Chicana/o critics for its neoliberal individualism, criticism of bilingual education and affirmative action, and embrace of assimilation as a legitimate strategy for Mexican Americans. He remains marked by these controversies, engendered by his first autobiography, and as such is an important parameter of Chicana/o identity. His discord with Chicana/o intellectuals has not stopped his mainstream success from blossoming: Rodriguez writes regularly for the *Los Angeles Times*, is an editor at Pacific News Service, an on-air commentator for PBS's *Newshour with Jim Lehrer*, and works regularly with the broadcasting companies of the larger anglophone world. Additionally, he has published two well-received volumes since *Hunger of Memory*: 1992's *Days of Obligation: An Argument With My Mexican Father* and 2002's *Brown: The Last Discovery of America*. In his role as televisual and print interlocutor, he is by far the most prominent Mexican American journalist in the global anglophone media, and therefore represents, for better or worse, the face of Mexican America for audiences both Latino and Anglo. Certainly an aspect of this success is Rodriguez's talent with language, which both in form and content stamp him as perhaps the best Mexican American writer in English today. In fact, part of the intense opposition to him among the Chicano intelligentsia is due to his wide circulation, and hence influences, outside the academy. The paradox of Rodriguez's mainstream prominence and the almost universal loathing of his work among Chicana/o intellectuals and cultural producers is indicative of the battle over who defines Chicana/o identity, and how such an identity is understood both within Chicano communities and by the public at large.[7]

Both Rodriguez and Moraga contested the foundations of Movement aesthetics and their grounding in narrative and experience by foregrounding their experiences as gendered and sexualized outsiders. Moraga's outsider status ultimately led back into the radicalism of the Movement through a neo-nationalist stance, but Rodriguez was a strange return of the repressed, a voice from before the Movement period, reflecting earlier reformist values of assimilation and accommodation, and as such was so completely alien to the project of Chicana/o Studies as to be incomprehensible. Remarkably, this has not stopped him from being a central player in the drama of Chicana/o literature and aesthetics, and *Hunger of Memory* remains one of the most discussed and debated texts in Chicana/o Studies, the subject of innumerable articles, critical pieces, and reviews.

Taken together, Moraga and Rodriguez rupture the field and, along with the increased prominence of feminist writing in courses on Chicana/o literature and experience, effectively open the field up to new possibilities. This process worked both within the professoriate and outside of it, producing a cross-pollination of effort that was mutually influential. Alongside and often times intertwined with these feminist interventions, the 1980s and 1990s saw an expansion of the theoretical paradigms fomented by poststructuralist and postmodern critique. The popularity of "post" studies in Chicana/o Studies matched the general academic trend in the humanities. From being narrowly defined by the search for a universal paradigm in the 1970s, by the 1990s Chicana/o Studies was embracing a variety of theoretical techniques to understand Mexican America, including most prominently borderlands models of sociocultural analysis.[8] Fomented by the artistic and theoretical work of Guillermo Gómez-Peña, D. Emily Hicks, and Gloria Anzaldúa, borderlands theory emerges from the desire to figure new relationships in light of the limitations of foundational texts grounded in organic, essential identities that were so important to the Movement.

Gloria Anzaldúa's *Borderlands/La Frontera: The New Mestiza* (1987) is widely regarded to be one of the foundational texts of borderlands theory. Anzaldúa offers a holistic broadening of

Chicana/o identity through her articulation of the borderlands as the home of the "new *mestiza*": a reconceived Chicana(/o) subject based in an alchemic mixture of *indigenismo*, progressive sexual politics, and a feminist reappraisal of *mestizaje*. By grounding the borderlands within a developing gender politics and a recasting of Movement typologies (*indigenismo, mestizaje*), Anzaldúa, like other Chicana feminists, attempts here to shift discursive practice. Anzaldúa renames a cultural state of cross-frontier connections obfuscated by Movement ideologies of Chicano specificity and Aztlán nationalism. Because of this, *Borderlands/La Frontera* has become one of the most important texts in the field. Anzaldúa's particular interpretation was grounded in several phenomena. Her strong identity as a Chicana lesbian feminist deeply informed her desire to break open rigid distinctions between nations and within ethnic groups.

Her marginalization on the edges of traditional Movement discursive strategies (the family, heterosexuality, and patriarchy) enabled her to construct an alternative paradigm to the cultural nationalism of the Movement that was in tune with the larger Chicana feminist project. It is also clear that Anzaldúa's paradigm is based on life experience in the Mexico-U.S.A. border region along the Texas-Chihuahua-Nuevo Leon frontier, the Rio Grande Valley. As such, it reflected at once the specifically Texan qualities of Mexican American identity and the particularisms of the Rio Grande Valley, which is marked by a highly interconnected social and cultural structure between Mexicans and Mexican Americans across the border. This structure is not only one of food, language, and geography, but also of pronounced violence. Especially in her poetic entries, Anzaldúa makes explicit the brutal aspects of the borderlands via intimate and state violence alike. The hazards of the borderlands tend to be elided in favor of its more holistic qualities of cross-cultural pollination, something Anzaldúa militates against in the volume.

The power of Anzaldúa's formulation was its recognition that Chicanos and Chicanas were polymorphous in their linguistic, social, political, and most importantly, gendered and sexual dimensions. This apperception, paired with the critical emergence of Chicana feminism and coming at a moment of fragmentation engendered by poststructuralism, has also deeply attracted Chicana/o critics. This is precisely because borderlands theory offered a paradigm that implicitly acknowledged and affirmed the fact of intra-Chicana/o differences, while maintaining the sociocultural connections so important to the Chicano Movement.

Many Paradigms:
Chicana/o Studies Into the 21st Century

The work of Anzaldúa, Moraga, and Rodriguez form a front of literary critique that, while sharing broad outlines of similarity with initial works of the Chicano canon, depart significantly from the themes of cultural and communal preservation within the rigid organic model of the Movement period. This departure, however, has not managed to eclipse completely the previous literary efforts at canonicity pursued by earlier generations of Chicana/o cultural producers and scholars. Indeed, some critics have struck back at the trend towards feminist and theoretical innovation from the position of the Movement's foundational principles.[9] Rather, it has contributed to a state of productive cacophony among Chicana/o scholars, activists, and cultural producers that reveals a living, invested process of canon formation and textual evaluation and meaning.

What these struggles over the role and meaning of the study of Mexican America indicate is the vibrant nature of Chicana/o intellectualism. This critical richness is a legacy of the Chicano Movement, and while certain tenets of the Movement have proven to be obsolete, the creation of an intellectual practice predicated on the study of Mexican America, is a profound contribution to American letters. The contestations over identity and praxis by Chicana/o scholars and activists from the moment of the Movement's emergence testify to a robustness of dialogue that is healthy and, ultimately productive. Additionally, the theoretical sophistication of Chicana/o scholars counters the reactionary criticism from outside the field that Ethnic Studies programs are grounded not in academic rigor but exclusively in a simplistic kind of identity politics.

Chicana/o critics of the last thirty years have been active in attempting to offer answers, however contingent, to both the pressing political questions confronting Mexican America as well as plumbing the depths of its complex inner life. It can be expected that the critical apparati for assessing Mexican America will continue to grow and subdivide, and that the discursive approach of Chicana/o intellectuals shall reflect this. As Juan Bruce-Novoa (1990), an early advocate of Chicana/o diversity, has described, Chicana/o identity is one that is non-monological, dialectic, diatactical, and "in process" (39). The discursive history of Chicana/o intellectuals signifies the prescience of this observation through their responses to the challenges of Mexican American identity formation, one always already in process.

Notes

1. Many have noted the subservient relationship of Chicanas to Chicanos in Movement organizations (García [1989]; Córdova [1994]; Gutiérrez [1993]), often being relegated to clerical work, cooking, running errands, and serving the sexual needs of Chicano activists. Gutiérrez relates a particularly compelling piece of evidence in this regard, noting a 1970 visit of Corky Gonzalez, an important Movement figure, to San Diego State University. The Chicana chair of the campus Chicano organization was asked, and agreed, to recuse herself from the proceedings as it was felt inappropriate to welcome such an important personality with female representatives (47–48).

2. Octavio Paz (1961) has discussed the role of Malintzín in the cultural politics of gender in Mexico, one that is decidedly negative, as she was considered to have betrayed her (indigenous) people in favor of the Spanish conquerors. The paradox is that this betrayal resulted, theoretically, in the birth of the modern Mexican, which is a *mestizo* identity. For Mexican and Chicana women, Malintzín is the negation of goodness and virtue, which is represented by the Guadalupe, patron saint of the Mexican people, and by extension for *mestizos* everywhere (e.g. Chicanas/os).

3. This was a process in both the literary and critical dimensions of Chicana feminists, one that was deeply informed by Moraga's work of the period (1981; 1983). For succinct discussions of Malintzín and her effect on Chicana feminism, see Norma Alarcón (1981) and Mary Louise Pratt (1993).

4. Deena González (1997) offers an interesting disquisition on how Moraga's texts become the sole presence of Chicana lesbianism on

course syllabi, functioning both as recognition and tokenism simultaneously. She urges, correctly, against collapsing all of Chicana lesbian-feminist theorizing into Moraga's oeuvre. Her observations, however, speak to the canonical role that Moraga has assumed, in that her work is so well known that it may now circulate as "the" representational text of Chicana lesbian identity.

5. Yvonne Yarbro-Bejarano (2001) offers the most extensive analysis on Moraga's work.

6. For an exhaustive survey of critical literature on Rodriguez, see Randy A. Rodríguez (1998).

7. For an intriguing argument as to why the Chicano intelligentsia opposes Rodriguez, see José Limón (1998).

8. For an excellent overview of Chicana/o critical thought in the 1980s, see Angie Chabram (1989).

9. Two of the most pointed examples are Ignacio M. García (1996) and Rodolfo F. Acuña (1998).

Works Cited

Acosta, Oscar Z. *The Autobiography of a Brown Buffalo*. San Francisco: Straight Arrow, 1972.

Acuña, Rodolpho. *Occupied America: The Chicano's Struggle Toward Liberation*. San Francisco: Canfield, 1972.

Acuña, Rodolfo F. *Sometimes There Is No Other Side: Chicanos and the Myth of Equality*. Notre Dame: University of Notre Dame Press, 1998.

Alarcón, Norma. "Chicana's Feminist Literature: A Re-Vision Through Malintzin/ or Malintzin: Putting Flesh Back on the Object." *This Bridge Called My Back: Writings by Radical Women of Color . . .* Ed. Cherríe Moraga and Gloria Anzaldúa. Watertown: Persephone, 1981. 182–190.

Alurista [Alberto H. Urista], et al., eds. *Festival de flor y canto: an anthology of Chicano literature*. Los Angeles: University of Southern California Press, 1976.

Anaya, Rudolfo. *Bless Me, Ultima*. Berkeley, CA: Quinto Sol, 1972.

Anzaldúa, Gloria. *Borderlands/La Frontera: The New Mestiza*. San Francisco: Aunt Lute, 1987.

Barrio, Raymund. *The Plum Plum Pickers*. Sunnyvale, CA: Ventura Press, 1970.

Bruce-Novoa, Juan. *Retrospace: Collected Essays on Chicano Literature*. Houston: Arte Público, 1990.

Camarillo, Albert. *Chicanos in a Changing Society: From Mexican Pueblos to American Barrios in Santa Barbara and Southern California, 1848–1930*. Cambridge, MA: Harvard University Press, 1979.

Castañeda Shular, Antonia, et al., eds. *Literatura chicana: texto y contexto*. Englewood Cliffs, NJ: Prentice-Hall, 1972.

Castillo, Ana. *The Mixquiahuala Letters*. Binghampton, NY: Bilingual Press, 1986.

Cervantes, Lorna Dee. *Emplumada*. Pittsburgh: University of Pittsburgh Press, 1981.

Cisneros, Sandra. *The House on Mango Street*. Houston: Arte Público, 1983.

Chabram, Angie. "Chicano Critical Discourse: An Emerging Cultural Practice." *Aztlán* 18.2 (1989): 45–90.

Córdova, Teresa. "Roots and Resistance: The Emergent Writings of Twenty Years of Chicana Feminist Struggle." *Handbook of Hispanic Cultures in the United States: Sociology*. Ed. and intro. Félix Padilla. Houston: Arte Público, 1994. 175–202.

Enríquez, Evangelina, and Alfredo Mirandé. *La Chicana: The Mexican American Woman*. Chicago: University of Chicago Press, 1979.

Galarza, Ernesto. *Barrio Boy: The Story of a Boy's Acculturation*. Notre Dame: University of Notre Dame Press, 1971.

García, Alma M. "The Development of Chicana Feminist Discourse, 1970–1980." *Gender and Society* 3.2 (1989): 217–238. Rpt. in *Unequal Sisters: A Multicultural Reader in U.S. Women's History*. Ed. Ellen Carol DuBois and Vicki L. Ruiz. New York: Routledge, 1990. 418–431.

———, ed. *Chicana Feminist Thought: The Basic Historical Writings*. New York: Routledge, 1997.

García, Ignacio M. "Juncture in the Road: Chicano Studies Since 'El Plan de Santa Bárbara.'" *Chicanas/Chicanos at the Crossroads: Social, Economic, and Political Change*. Ed. David R. Maciel and Isidro D. Ortiz. Tucson: University of Arizona Press, 1996. 181–204.

García, Mario T. *Mexican Americans: Leadership, Ideology, Identity, 1930–1960*. New Haven: Yale University Press, 1989.

Gómez-Peña, Guillermo. "Border Brujo." *TDR* 35.3 (1991): 48–66.

Gonzales, Rodolfo. *I Am Joaquin / Yo Soy Joaquin: An Epic Poem*. New York: Bantam, 1972.

González, Deena J. "Chicana Identity Matters." *Aztlán* 22.2 (1997): 123–138.

Gutiérrez, Ramón A. "Community, Patriarchy and Individualism: The Politics of Chicano History and the Dream of Equality." *American Quarterly* 45.1 (1993): 44–72.

Hicks, D. Emily. *Border Writing: The Multidimensional Text*. Theory and History of Lit. 80. Minneapolis, MN: University of Minnesota Press, 1991.
Limón, José. "Editor's Note on Richard Rodriguez." *Texas Studies in Language and Literature* 40.4 (1998): 389–95.
Longeaux Vasquez, Enriqueta. "The Women of *La Raza*." *García* (1997) 29–31.
Ludwig, Ed, and James Santibanez. *The Chicanos: Mexican American Voices*. Baltimore: Penguin, 1971.
Moraga, Cherríe. *Heroes and Saints and Other Plays*. Albuquerque: West End, 1994.
———. *The Last Generation: Prose and Poetry*. Boston: South End, 1993.
———. *This Bridge Called My Back: Writings by Radical Women of Color*. Watertown, MA: Persephone, 1981.
———. *Loving In The War Years: lo que nunca pasó por sus labios*. Boston: SouthEnd, 1983.
———. *Waiting in the Wings: Portrait of a Queer Motherhood*. Ithaca: Firebrand, 1997.
———. *Watsonville: Some Place Not Here*. Albuquerque: West End, 2002.
Mujeres en Marcha. "Chicanas in the 80's: Unsettled Issues." *García* (1997): 253–64.
NietoGomez, Anna. "*La Chicana*: Legacy of Suffering and Self-Denial." *García* (1997): 48–49.
Orozco, Cynthia. "Sexism in Chicano Studies and the Community." *García* (1997) 265–269.
Ortego y Gasca, Philip D., ed. *We Are Chicanos: An Anthology of Mexican American Literature*. New York: Washington Square Press, 1973.
Paredes, Américo. *"With His Pistol in his Hand": A Border Ballad and its Hero*. Austin: University of Texas Press, 1958.
Paz, Octavio. *The Labyrinth of Solitude: Life and Thought in Mexico*. Trans. Lysander Kemp. New York: Grove, 1961.
Pratt, Mary Louise. "'Yo Soy La Malinche': Chicana Writers and the Poetics of Ethnonationalism." *Callaloo* 16.4 (1993): 859–873.
Rendon, Armando B. *Chicano Manifesto*. New York: MacMillan, 1971.
Rincón, Bernice. "La Chicana: Her Role in the Past and Her Search for a New Role in the Future." *García* (1997): 24–28.
Rivera, Tomás. . . . *y no se lo tragó la tierra / . . . And the Earth Did Not Part*. Berkeley, CA: Editorial Justa, 1971.
Rodríguez, Randy A. "Richard Rodriguez Reconsidered: Queering the Sissy (Ethnic) Subject." *Texas Studies in Language and Literature* 40.4 (1998): 397–423.

Rodriguez, Richard. *Brown: The Last Discovery of America*. New York: Viking, 2002.

———. *Days of Obligation: An Argument with My Mexican Father*. New York: Viking, 1992.

———. *Hunger of Memory: The Education of Richard Rodriguez*. Boston, MA: Godine, 1981.

Valdez, Luis y El Teatro Campesino. *Actos*. San Juan Bautista, CA: Menyah Productions, 1971.

Vidal, Mirta. *Women: New Voice of La Raza: Chicanas Speak Out*. New York: Pathfinder, 1971.

Villarreal, Jose Antonio. *Pocho*. Garden City, NY: Anchor, 1970.

Viramontes, Helena Maria. *The Moths and Other Stories*. Houston: Arte Público, 1985.

Yarbro-Bejarano, Yvonne. *The Wounded Heart: Writing on Cherríe Moraga*. Austin: University of Texas Press, 2001.

Chapter 3

"A House Made With Stones / Full of Stories"

Anthologizing Native American Literature

Kristin Czarnecki

"Coyote, it seems / you can tempt the rain, / call it by its true name, / make its meaning change, / in a house made with stones / full of stories," writes Shaunna McCovey, Karuk/Yurok activist, scholar, and poet. The prevalence of multiethnic American literature in today's classrooms reflects McCovey's perception of stories as crucial to cultural strength and survival. Colleges and universities offer programs of Native American, African American, and Asian American studies, among others, as well as core curricula inclusive of ethnic American works. In September 2004, nearly one hundred new open positions in English posted on the Modern Language Association's on-line *Job Information List* called for specialists in multiethnic literary studies, and current anthologies include an array of multiethnic works. Such was not always the case, however, as history exhibits the academy's persistent dismissal of minority writing. Not until the late 1960s did the professoriate admit the merits of ethnic literature, that writing by Euro-Americans and Anglo-Saxons (whites) constitutes only a fraction of America's oeuvre. Tracing the development of twentieth-century anthologies and their stances toward Native American literature in particular, I address the prejudice enacted upon multiethnic works and the academic and social climates that fostered change in mainstream education. If, as Paul Lauter says, "The question of what we teach cannot be separated from what we value" ("Cultural Boundaries"

183), then a multiethnic canon is paramount to ensuring the cultural and literary survival of all Americans.

A sampling of late-nineteenth-century anthologies reveals the Puritan emphasis prevalent in American education at the time. In 1891, the editor of *Masterpieces of American Literature* selected texts based largely on the morals they extolled, on whether they were "inspiring and uplifting [. . .] in their influence upon life and character" (*Masterpieces of American Literature* iii). Additionally, the preface states, an anthology should serve as a proficient "reading-book in the school sense [. . .] to be used for improvement in the art of oral reading as well as for studies in literature" (*MAL* iv). The editor includes a variety of prose and poetry by Euro-American men. Presumably he selected the works of Washington Irving, Benjamin Franklin, and Nathaniel Hawthorne because they inspire, uplift, and promote eloquent recitations among schoolboys nationwide. In *Achievement in American Poetry, 1900–1950* (1951), Louise Bogan observes that by 1900, the "active, though hidden, force of moral criteria [. . .] was soon to become more and more apparent" in literary studies (Bogan 3). Instilling moral fortitude in pupils supersedes recognizing minority writing or narrative innovation. Arnold Krupat also finds that up until the mid-nineteenth century, "all litterature [. . .] was required to be pedagogical to the extent at least that it traditionally was expected to play a role in instructing our reason in how to be the kind of citizens valued by our particular societies" (*The Voice in the Margin* 39). In the 1800s, the valued American citizen was white, male, and Christian.

Interestingly, turn-of-the-century collections often included folktales and examples of the "negro spiritual," such as Edmund Clarence Stedman's *American Anthology* of 1900 (Bogan 2). Early twentieth-century anthologies, however, privilege the works of white men. *The Spirit of American Literature* (1911) contains sixteen chapters on sixteen white males, while *An Introduction to the Study of American Literature*, revised in 1911, "focuses fifteen chapters on individual white men and then devotes one to 'other writers,' including Whitman and Stowe" (Lauter, "Race and Gender" 22). With the 1920s came a conservative coterie of professors, "college-educated white men of Anglo-Saxon or northern European origins" whose anthologies reflected their own limited forays into

American letters (Lauter, "Race" 28). *American Poetry and Prose: A Book of Readings, 1607–1916*, published in 1925, includes works by more than sixty white men, two white women, and no writers of color. Editor Norman Foerster selects the poetry and plays he finds most representative of America's relation to Europe and the profound effect upon early Americans of nature and frontier life. The "Americanism of American literature," Foerster writes, lies in its "pioneer psychology" (v). Alfred Kreymborg's *Lyric America* (1930) contains poetry by seven African American males, yet this was an exception to the pervasive practice of omitting ethnic American and women writers from the canon (Lauter, "Race" 25).

Charles Lee, editor of *North, East, South, West: A Regional Anthology of American Writing* (1945), takes a unique approach to text selection by imagining "anthology" as a living, albeit not too intelligent, creature: "*Homo anthologus* [. . .] is the perfect product of his imperfect times of uncritical material abundance, of increasingly seductive entertainments. I think it would be fair to place him in a setting of magazine digests, book club announcements, vitamin pills, and newspaper headlines" (Lee 1). The primary function of *A Regional Anthology*, Lee says, is to charm the general public. He cheerfully acknowledges his collection's lack of critical depth, touting brevity and wit as more important characteristics. Gearing his anthology toward the nonspecialist, Lee taps into important, indeed ancient debates on the fundamental purpose of literature. Plato viewed poetry and writing as dangerous for weakening the mind, for depicting only a semblance of wisdom, and for spurring youth to imitate its deviance. Literature can only attempt to imitate life; in Plato's estimation, it often fails in this attempt. An Aristotelian stance posits literature not as dangerous but as a natural facet of the human condition, capable of revealing universal truths in a "conjoint attempt to teach and delight" (qtd. in Krupat, *Voice* 42). Lee is not averse to sparking his readers' intellectual curiosity, yet he wishes above all to provide them with a pleasant diversion.

Nevertheless, Charles Lee is among the first anthologizers to strive for representation, an "ideological and literary assessment of [. . .] the country as a whole" (Lee 2). He therefore organizes American literature according to the geographical regions from which it comes: New England, the Middle Atlantic States, the South, the Midwest, and the Far West. He encourages the reader to hop, skip, and jump through the various sections, thereby displaying "anthological tendencies of his own" (Lee 2). Lee calls *A Regional Anthology* an "American sampler" reflecting "the character of our country and its literature in a generally accurate way" (2), yet of the collection's two hundred works by one hundred fifty writers, only a few are by people of color. Lee furthermore presumes a predominantly white male readership, assuring the reader that works by Melville, Dickinson, and Longfellow "will echo from his past" (Lee 4). Despite indigenous Native Americans, the four hundred year presence of Africans and African Americans, and three centuries of immigration to the United States, Lee's anthology of regional American literature contains only a cursory recognition of nonwhite writers. In 1945, the concept of representative literature was still largely undeveloped.

In compiling his collection, Lee selects or rejects works according to practical concerns of "space, of design, of personal taste, of pertinence to the work at hand" (Lee 6–7). His approach resonates with contemporary debates over anthologizing American literature. In *Cultural Capital: The Problem of Literary Canon Formation* (1993), John Guillory argues that "the construction of a syllabus begins with selection; it does not begin with a 'process of elimination.' What is excluded from the syllabus is not excluded in the *same way* that an individual is excluded or marginalized as the member of a social minority, socially disenfranchised" (Guillory 33). Guillory ascribes the problems of canon formation not to individual academics' personal biases but to the "problem in the constitution and distribution of cultural capital, or more specifically, a problem of access to the means of literary production and consumption" (Guillory ix). A multiethnic canon therefore "question[s] the cultural order, and thus the social boundaries, upon which that process of marginalization has been based" (Lauter, "Cultural Boundaries" 183). The process of text selection is complicated more by societal issues, racial bigotry among them, than by concerns over formatting and numbers of pages, as Charles Lee suggests. Lee's methodology neglects the impact of ethnic voices not only in the American literary canon, but also in society. As Arnold Krupat notes, "most commentators on American culture generally have managed to proceed as though there were no relation between the two, white and red, Euramerican and Native American, as if absence rather than avoidance defined the New World" (*Voice* 3). With the 1949 publication of *American Life in Literature*, editor Jay B. Hubbell enacts the avoidance that mars—and contributes to—canon formation.

Emphasizing early American literature's debt to European predecessors, Hubbell disregards the overwhelming influence of ethnic sensibilities upon American texts. According to Hubbell, "Until the nineteenth century our literary fashions came from overseas, and since that time they have often been determined by developments in Europe" (xv). Hubbell is only partly right, for while many writers adhered to European formal models, early American and European texts differ greatly in content. Contemporary scholars locate America's literary origins in colonial encounters with Native Americans, Africans, and African Americans rather than in efforts to replicate European schemes. "From the first days of settlement," states Krupat, "Americans sought to establish their own sense of American 'civilization' in opposition to some centrally significant Other, most particularly to the Indian 'savage'" (*Voice* 3). While Hubbell lauds white writers for "doing their utmost to create an indigenous literature" (Hubbell xv), Krupat and others recognize indigenous and ethnic Americans as the true catalysts of American letters. In *Playing in the Dark: Whiteness in the Literary Imagination* (1991), for instance, Toni Morrison demonstrates how early American fiction reflects white colonial response to the "darkness" of Africans and African Americans.

Into the mid-twentieth century, scholars persisted in valuing writing by whites only. In the critical study *The American Novel and its Tradition* (1957), Richard Chase appraises the originality and "Americanness" of novels like *The Scarlet Letter*, *Moby-Dick*, and *The Portrait of a Lady*, echoing Hubbell in pointing out English literature's influence upon them. He commends Melville for depicting American intellectuals' "radical skepticism about ultimate questions" (Chase x), overlooking race relations as one of them, evident, as Toni Morrison reveals, in Melville's obsession with images of black and white (Morrison 37). Chase also extols American literature for formulating "moral truths of universal validity" (xi). Given his selection of white writers only, "universal" to Chase evidently means Western and male. Similarly, he uses the term "native tradition" to describe America's contribution to the romance novel, rather than the literary production of indigenous peoples. Ironically, Chase describes early American literature that diverges from European forebears as fragmented, ironic, and abstract—terms useful in describing ethnic American works. Their referents for Chase, however, are the techniques of white male writers, indicating a biased view of what constitutes noteworthy writing.

Another critical study of 1957, *The Cycle of American Literature*, by Robert E. Spiller, reiterates narrow concepts of representation in sections titled "The First Frontier" and "The Second Frontier." The divide between them arises circa 1870, Spiller explains, with "the conflict between the agrarian idea of Jefferson and the industrial ideals of Hamilton, [. . .] the plantation gentility of the South and the commercial gentility of the North, and [. . .] a culturally mature East and a raw and expanding West" (Spiller 92). Using the word "frontier" to explicate an American literary genre, Spiller displays the imperialism so devastating to ethnic American cultures and dismissive of ethnic writing. North America was not "'virgin land,' empty, uninhabited, silent, dumb until the Europeans brought the plow and the pen to cultivate its wilderness" (Krupat, *Voice* 3), but home to aboriginal people for millennia, "between 20,000 and 28,000 years" (Ruoff, "American Indian Literatures" 280). Here, too, the ill-defined specter of literary merit arises, as Spiller disparages folk ballads and legends and "minor authors who were faithful to the moods of their times" (Spiller viii). Such writing may be vigorous and authentic, he concedes, but "seemed to lose its character as art" (Spiller ix). Critics today level similar arguments against incorporating ethnic works into the American literary canon, suspecting social or political agendas at the forefront of text selection.

Spiller adopts a more critical stance in the introduction to "The First Frontier," in which he rues European contempt for Native American orature as shortsighted arrogance that destroyed a "rich culture" (15). He sets the word "savages" in quotation marks, denounces the settlers' view of Native Americans as childlike, and acknowledges that Indians were "pushed back, despoiled, and exploited for three hundred years" (Spiller 15). His own prejudice emerges, however, as he notes approvingly that John Smith "makes King Powhatan and his daughter Pocahontas into reasoning human beings" (Spiller 15), implying that without the white man's influence, they would have remained *childlike savages*. He takes the extinction of Native Americans for granted, referring to them in the past tense and praising the American Indian for having "accepted his place in the physical universe, and with it his place in his own limited society" (15). Spiller nevertheless realizes that the Indian of early American literature bears little resemblance to the Indian of fact, which is more than may be said of Moses Coit Tyler in his 1927 work, *A History of American Literature: 1607–1738*. In chapter two, "New England: Its Nature and Its People," Tyler discusses colonial writings of encounters with Native Americans. William Wood, writing in 1634, mentions the "mirth and laughter" the Indians inspired in the colonists, describing their physical attributes meticulously and referring to their bodies as "tawny hides" (Tyler 39). Almost three hundred years later, Tyler echoes Wood's racism in discussing Native American savages and "the contact of English culture with the mental childhood of the Indians" (Tyler 39). Even Spiller's equivocal nod to Native American orature is an improvement over Tyler's bigotry.

The slant of early anthologies is better understood in light of prevailing attitudes toward English and American letters. Throughout the 1940s and 1950s, scholars struggled to legitimize the teaching of American literature in the academy. "In 1944, the journal *American Literature* was only fifteen years old," Richard Ruland explains. "The next two decades produced *American Renaissance* and *LHUS* [*Columbia Literary History of the United States*] and led directly to the founding of *American Quarterly* in 1951," a remarkable feat given the academy's insistence on valuing English over American works (Ruland 355). As late as the early 1960s, critical studies espousing Euro-American male writers were part of an ongoing "effort to begin defining a national literary tradition where it seemed least vulnerable" (Ruland 356). The preface to *Major Writers of America* (1962), for instance, notes the brief literary history of the United States—put at seventy-five years—and the urgency of establishing a canon of high literary quality. General editor Perry Miller calls for the rigorous selection of literary pieces that resists capitulation "merely to local (or, to what is worse, regional) patriotism" (xviii). He therefore selects only white males for *Major Writers*: Emerson, Hawthorne, Melville, James, and Twain.

Similarly, the 1967 edition of *The American Tradition in Literature* presents a "fresh view" of American letters, as "the writers of our Colonial and Federalist periods were more complex men than earlier critics supposed" (Bradley xxvii). The anthology includes more selections by Edward Taylor, Jonathan Edwards, and Benjamin Franklin, while a "greater range" of poems by Ezra Pound, Wallace Stevens, and William Carlos Williams "gives them the same significance as Edwin Arlington Robinson, Robert Frost, and T. S. Eliot in our selection of avowed masters of twentieth-century poetry" (Bradley xxviii). Despite—or perhaps because of—the strength of the civil rights movement, the editors avow that "no author was introduced primarily for the purpose of illustrating literary or social history" (Bradley xxix). The 1967 *American Tradition* includes just one writer of color, Amiri Baraka (LeRoi Jones). Social and political movements of the 1960s were well underway, however, posing a challenge to conventional notions of American literary merit.

Along with the civil rights and women's movements, the founding of the American Indian Movement in 1968 spurred changes throughout academia. As Paul Lauter states: "The question of the canon grows directly from the impact of the social movements of the 1960s on the profession. They asked of our courses, our texts, our research, 'Where are the blacks?' 'Where are the women?'" ("Society and the Profession" 7) To those groups I would add Native Americans, who asserted themselves in AIM's social and cultural programs as well as protests against sports teams' Indian mascots long "before recognition of such racism became fashionable in America" (Means 155). In 1969, Russell Means visited his young daughter's school to dispel the lies and stereotypes fed to students about Columbus's "discovery" of America. Eventually, Means says: "We got the Cleveland Public School District to cooperate with us in reviewing and revising its American Indian curriculum" (Means 157). Colleges and universities followed suit. The First Convocation of American Indian Scholars was held in 1970, Dartmouth created a Department of Native American Studies in 1972, anthologies of Native American literature began to proliferate, and Native American novelists achieved critical acclaim, rendering the late 1960s and early 1970s, in Kenneth Lincoln's words, a "Native American Renaissance" (qtd. in Peterson 1).

Mainstream literature anthologies progressed more slowly. In *American Literature: A Study and Research Guide* (1977), editor Lewis Leary declares American literary studies a "rich field, variously cultivated," capable of charting our "cultural heritage" (vii, viii). Meanwhile, his section on major American writers includes Emily Dickinson and twenty-seven white men, curiously referred to in an introductory chapter as "distinctively indigenous" writers of "native literature" (Leary 7, 5). The book's page and a half on "Ethnic Literature" notes increasing interest in African American studies primarily and points readers toward recent anthologies of Mexican American, Native American, and Jewish American writing, among others. Leary mentions Addison Gayle's "radical call for a more racially oriented criticism of black literature," along with the formation of MELUS—the Society for the Study of Multi-Ethnic Literatures of the United States—in 1972 (Leary 22, 23), yet he mentions no ethnic writers by name and eschews substantial discussion of ethnic literary studies. Like many of his predecessors, Leary omits ethnic works from the scope of American writing.

The first edition of the *Norton Anthology of American Literature* (1979) marks a departure from earlier anthologies' dismissal of minority writing. The 1979 *Norton* includes works by numerous African Americans, such as Charles Chesnutt, Jean Toomer, Langston Hughes, Countee Cullen, Richard Wright, Ralph Ellison, James Baldwin, and Gwendolyn Brooks. General editor Ronald Gottesman explains the need to "close the ever-widening gap between the current conception and appraisal of the American literary heritage and the way in which American literature is represented in existing anthologies" (xxiii). He includes long-neglected women and African American authors, yet the preface to "American Literature between the Wars, 1914–1945" mentions the Harlem Renaissance only briefly, allotting greater space to the influx of European artists into New York City at the time. The section on "Contemporary American Prose (1945–)" details three tumultuous decades in American history selectively. Discussing the post-World War II era, the civil rights and women's movements, and other cultural influences upon American letters, the editors do not include or even mention Native American literature. The *Norton* heads in the right direction, however, recognizing previously overlooked works not because of "glamor or contemporaneity, but because they are of high literary merit and because their presence is needed in order to make sense of the literary history of our age" (Gottesman xxiii).

Native American works garnered more recognition in the 1980s, amid "the great canon and curriculum debates" in which "multiculturalism emerged as the new orthodoxy" (Stripes 24). The 1985 *American Tradition in Literature* (sixth edition) contains a small selection of Native American writing. In previous decades, editors selected texts purposefully heedless of America's social and cultural climate. The editors of the 1985 *American Tradition*, on the other hand, state that while "[l]iterary merit remains the most important criterion for selection [. . .] [r]elations between literature and biography or social and intellectual history are discussed in critical introductions to periods and authors" (Perkins ix). Ethnic writers are not specifically mentioned in this context, yet acknowledging the "regional influences, social forces, dominant ideas, historical events, and changing aesthetic values" (Perkins ix) of America leads to a more representative array of all, not just white, American literature.

Nevertheless, Native American tales, oratory, and poetry comprise just ten pages of the anthology's "Nature and Society" section, in a subcategory entitled "The Indian Heritage." The editors betray their ambivalence concerning the value of Native American works with a brief introduction referring repeatedly to white and "red" men. Citing the rich oral traditions of each tribe and the complexities of translating Native American works into English, the editors go on to state: "The same white invasion that was to herald the end of the Indian way of life brought with it not only its own written languages but the tools to devise written records of the various Indian languages and dialects" (Perkins 197). Thus, the white man's arrival appears as a boon to preserving otherwise lost and forgotten Native American works.

The anthology's section on "The Later Twentieth Century: Fiction" contains no Native American writing, despite the 1969 Pulitzer Prize for N. Scott Momaday's *House Made of Dawn* and the 1984 National Book Critics Circle Award for Louise Erdrich's debut, *Love Medicine*. Other early to mid-twentieth-century Native American publications include novels by Mourning Dove, John Milton Oskison, John Joseph Mathews, and D'Arcy McNickle. Native Americans also published drama, poetry, and essays at the time. None appear in the 1985 *American Tradition*, however, and the seventh edition (1990) adds just three more pages to "The Indian Heritage" section and maintains its specious introduction. As A. LaVonne Brown Ruoff notes, Native American work "has too long been allowed to languish unread in research libraries. This significant contribution to American literature must no longer be ignored" (Ruoff, "Old Traditions" 168). Native American and non-Native American scholars continue to struggle for its full incorporation into the curriculum.

The 1989 *Norton Anthology of American Literature* (third edition) begins to redress the omission of Native American writers with selections from Black Elk, Gertrude Simmons Bonnin (Zitkala-Sa), Leslie Marmon Silko, and Louise Erdrich. Such writing, says Ronald Gottesman, elucidates W. E. B. Du Bois' theory of double-consciousness in depicting life in two bordering, conflicting cultures (xxx). Additional African American authors include Booker T. Washington, Zora Neale Hurston, and Alice Walker, among others. Gottesman explains how formatting changes from previous editions, such as moving Whitman and Dickinson to volume I and dividing the twentieth century into three sections, "provide space for more *kinds* of American literature," but not "at the expense of the representation of established [sic] tradition of American writers" (xxix). With works by Native American, Latina/o, Jewish, and African American writers, the 1989 *Norton* was the multiethnic anthology to date.

The Heath Anthology of American Literature, developed in the 1980s, places even greater emphasis on the value of multiethnic writing. In the preface to the first edition (1990), general editor Paul Lauter, a leading figure in literary canon reformation, cites the academy's need to recognize that "blacks and other people of color in American society had developed rich literary cultures" (xxxiii). Throughout the 1970s and early 1980s, scholars nationwide acknowledged the limitations of textbooks and curricula that disregarded feminist and minority scholarship (xxxiv). The *Heath* editors thus recover lost, neglected, and undervalued writing by women and people of color while maintaining the works of traditionally important white male writers, similar to editors at *Norton*. Paul Lauter states: "this *range* of writers offers opportunities for drawing stimulating comparisons between canonical and non-canonical figures, between female and male, between one ethnic writer and another" (xxxv). Previously marginalized works are shown to coexist with and complement more conventional canonical selections.

Volume I of the first edition of the *Heath* begins with "Colonial Period: to 1700," with Native American origin and emergence stories, historical narratives, and trickster tales preceding writing by Christopher Columbus. The volume also includes works by Native American writers William Apess, Elias Boudinot, and John Rollin Ridge along with Native American oral poetry, songs, and ballads. Volume II contains Ghost Dance Songs and writing by John Oskison, Standing Bear, Charles Alexander Eastman, Gertrude Bonnin, Thomas S. Whitecloud, Mourning Dove, N. Scott Momaday, James Welch, Leslie Marmon Silko, Louise Erdrich, Simon Ortiz, and Joy Harjo. With works by 109 women of various races, twenty-five Native Americans, fifty-three African Americans, thirteen Hispanics, and nine Asian Americans, the 1990 *Heath Anthology of American Literature* was the most extensive collection of multiethnic works available (Lauter, *Heath*, 1st ed., xxxvi). Selections throughout the anthology "reconnect literature and its study with the society and culture of which it is fundamentally a part" (Lauter xxxvi), indicating that multiethnic and Euro-American works do not reside in isolation but develop out of their long history of contact.

The idea of a multiethnic canon has met with significant criticism. Hershel Parker, scholar, author, and an editor of the *Norton*, lambastes the *Heath Anthology* for allowing political correctness to eclipse literary merit, for displaying a bias toward leftist or left-leaning writers that neglects other important voices. Parker would revise the canon not by including more ethnic writers but by paying due to what he regards as America's *real* neglected literature: regional writing, sports literature, humorous literature, religious literature, even fundamentalist Protestant writing. Parker does not wish to afford "equal time for political bigots," but advocates listening seriously to the "frightened and angry" conservative writers who affect the attitudes of numerous right-wing Americans (Parker 2). Parker, who is Native American, also bristles when white scholars presume to decide who is a black writer, a Native American writer, and so forth, particularly if the writer in question is, for instance, only a quarter Native American. The *Heath*'s methodology, Parker believes, does little more than assuage white liberal guilt. Such criticism overlooks the preface to the first *Heath*, in which Lauter cites the editorial board's ethnic diversity and polling of thousands of teachers of American Literature on their suggestions for specific texts to include in the anthology.

Parker is not alone in distrusting the *Heath*. Scholar Elizabeth Cook-Lynn, a member of the Crow Creek Sioux tribe, is also wary of the academy's development of Native American studies and views the formation of a multiethnic canon as further abuse of people of color. Like other skeptics of multiethnic literary studies, she believes there is no such thing as disinterested research into another culture, that those who read, teach, or write of a culture other than their own circulate not truths but representations and stereotypes. "Exploitation abounds," states Cook-Lynn. "A few legends here. A myth there. Seattle's famous oration, some poetry and Momaday's 'Man Made of Words' are inserted between the Age of Romanticism and T. S. Eliot just for the purpose of illustrating some kind of cross-cultural interest and fairness" (qtd. in Stripes 27). Richard Ruland similarly doubts the *Heath*'s emphasis on culture and race.

In "Art and a Better America," a lengthy response to the arrival of the *Heath Anthology* on the academic scene, Ruland agrees that all Americans should experience "the multicultural presence in the nation's discourse" (353). Yet he faults many of the *Heath*'s selections and editorial essays for lacking literary sensibility and failing to establish for students the history of traditional canon formation. Lauter privileges "an art of social relevance" over literary merit, Ruland states, "its value based in copies sold and readers motivated to action" (343). Editors of the *Heath* "occasionally make limited literary claims for their choices, but they speak more often of ideological hegemony, power groups, and economic motivations" (Ruland 351). Native American works as represented in the *Heath* are particularly shortchanged, according to Ruland. "As we have the Native American tales, songs, and speeches, they all resonate with much the same translator-ethnographer-anthropologist voice, a kind of movie Indian" (351) that fails to question "just what we are doing when we read a late nineteenth-century rendering of someone's recollection of a Native-American song heard years before and only partially followed at the time" (351–52). Ruland would like to believe the *Heath* has merit, but ultimately reproves the anthology for shaping literary studies around racial, national, and gender differences.

Hans Bak reviews myriad responses to the *Heath* in his article, "The *Heath* is On: Canon or Kaleidoscope?" Many criticize the work, he finds, for suggesting a variety of canons rather than following the standard trajectory of American literature favored by earlier anthologies. Bak explains, however, that while renowned anthologies such as *Norton* and *Harper* expand the canon by adding to their selections of classic writers, the *Heath* "presents American literature as multi-vocal, multi-ethnic and multi-traditional from the start" (Bak 68, 69). Indian creation stories appear before Puritan writings, and Native American oral poetry precedes nineteenth-century white male poets, "thus correcting the traditional idea that [ethnic Americans] worked largely in alienated opposition to American culture [. . .]; rather, they worked from a deep absorption *in* the popular forms of culture around them" (Bak 70). The *Heath's* format unsettles critics, Bak finds, by rejecting images of ethnic Americans as existing only peripherally to the mainstream, demonstrating instead that ethnic groups have always affected American society and literature in meaningful, lasting ways.

The 1994 *Norton Anthology of American Literature* (fourth edition) reflects ensuing multiethnic canon development. Volume I contains a new "Literature to 1620" segment with three sections of oral materials, indicating a dramatic change from previous editions, namely, a stronger emphasis on Native American works. Headnotes for Iroquois and Pima creation stories, for example, explain the "political, cultural, and linguistic complexities of transcription and translation" of Native American works (xxix), corroborating Dennis Tedlock's findings in his study of translating oral narrative: Western translators often alter or omit the repetition, pauses, onomatopoeia, and intonation so vital to Native American orature to conform to Western literary conventions and mollify readers of English-language texts. The *Norton* nevertheless strives to present Native American transcriptions approximating their original forms. Additional Native American works in volume I include the *Memorials of the Cherokees* and works by William Apess, Charles Alexander Eastman, and John Oskison. Volume II contains new sections on "Native American Oratory" and "Native American Chants and Songs."

The 1994 *Norton* also discusses a major figure in contemporary Native American literature, N. Scott Momaday, and includes new excerpts from his *The Way to Rainy Mountain*. A biographical sketch of Momaday cites his achievement in crossing the "boundaries of language, form, and genre, thereby creating [. . .] an American Indian identity in words" (2168). Arnold Krupat, currently an editor at *Norton*, would argue that Momaday interweaves American *and* American Indian identity, since "from 1492 on, neither Euramerican intellectuals nor Native American intellectuals could operate autonomously or uniquely" (Krupat qtd. in Peterson 4). The preface to "American Prose Since 1945" devotes a page to the growing presence of ethnic Americans in literary studies, yet regresses in citing only Faulkner and Hemingway as influencing Native American writer and poet James Welch. In fact Welch adapts Gros Ventre (Northern Plains) oral narratives into his novel *Winter in the Blood*, for instance, and South American surrealism into his poetry (Ruoff, "American Indian Literatures" 307–08). In 1994, *Norton's* editors discuss Native American literature knowledgeably yet do not always fully locate its influences and sites of identity.

In the third edition of the *Heath Anthology* (1998), Paul Lauter views questions of identity as vital to American letters, citing the "cultural, racial, religious, and economic disparities among peoples of the nation" at the end of the nineteenth century due to waves of European immigrants and unresolved issues of citizenship for Indians (825). Consequently, "the 1890s and 1900s [. . .]

saw the emergence of a body of writing, much of it autobiographical, that asked what it meant to be an American in new and challenging ways" (825). The *Heath* reassesses literary history in uncovering what was there all along, overlooked in the texts of white writers and disregarded in the unacknowledged works of ethnic Americans. Lauter enjoins his colleagues to cease imposing upon students "a narrowly construed (white, Western, male, Christian) tradition" for one that might "explore, celebrate, and understand the differing cultures and traditions that shape real life in these United States" ("Society" 16).

Paul Lauter also invokes W. E. B. Du Bois' theory of double-consciousness in his discussion of the marginalized American citizen. "Both belonging and not quite belonging," Lauter writes, "such a person has a double vantage point and often therefore a heightened alertness to what others may unconsciously take for granted" (*Heath*, 3rd ed., 824). Instead of putting a contemporary spin on literature once considered insignificant, as some critics argue, Lauter and his co-editors remedy their predecessors' discrimination against ethnic American writing. The focus of the *Heath* lies not in "legitimating 'new' literatures" but in "exploring the historical origins of differing cultural communities, to designating the differences within such communities, and to exploring the implications of 'minority' cultures for the whole society" (*Heath*, 3rd ed., 2821). The preface to part II, "New Communities, New Identities, New Energies," addresses the Civil Rights, Black Arts, and Women's Movements at length, as well as postwar Jewish writing, Spanish-language literary traditions, and Asian American works, all of which comprise America's literary and cultural landscape. Arnold Krupat concurs, citing the academy's duty not only to recognize the merits of Native American literature, but also to rethink earlier American canonical works. Krupat writes: "To understand better what Native American artists know and think and feel [. . .] may well provoke a rereading, even a reevaluating of other American writers, both older, canonical authors and newer authors on the verge of canonical status" (*Voice* 91).

The main point of contention among critics of the *Heath* is their belief that the anthology contains merely "faddish" texts (Lauter, "Response to Ruland" 330). Reiterating the impact of social movements of the 1960s and 1970s upon American society and academe, however, Lauter situates "social, political, *and* artistic questions" as *"the* questions of our time" ("Response" 330; original emphases). Rather than highlight a person's or group's victimization, the *Heath* helps "students to discover how literary art is created by particularly, but differently, situated human beings who struggle to shape their distinctive narratives and to form, dissolve, reform the borders that categories like race signify" ("Response" 330–31). Critics equating multiethnic canon formation with the reinforcement of stereotype in fact participate in crystallizing a minority-mainstream binary. "I do not think there is any inevitable divide between the 'currently relevant' and what endures," Lauter states, alluding to critics' recurring and disturbing insinuations that writings by people of color are inherently inferior to that of whites.

The most recent *Heath* and *Norton* anthologies refute such prejudice with an array of multiethnic works. The 2002 *Norton*'s Native American selections include numerous trickster tales, creation stories, and an expanded period introduction emphasizing colonial multiethnicity. For the first time in the *Norton*, early Native American works precede writing by Christopher Columbus. Other Native American texts include a new entry by D'Arcy McNickle and works by William Apess, Charles Alexander Eastman, John Oskison, Gertrude Simmons Bonnin, Black Elk, N. Scott Momaday, Gerald Vizenor, Diane Glancy, Simon Ortiz, Joy Harjo, Leslie Marmon Silko, and Louise Erdrich, as well as aforementioned sections on oratory, chants, and songs. Multiethnic additions to the 2002 *Norton* include stories by Rudolfo Anaya, Carlos Bulosan, Sui Sin Far, and Judith Ortiz Cofer, along with Nella Larsen's novel *Quicksand* in its entirety. The 2002 *Norton* contains fewer ethnic American works than the 2002 *Heath*, yet "has longer and more complete selections for those writers who are included," says general editor Nina Baym (Baym e-mail).

Native American selections in the 2002 *Heath* include early-nineteenth-century works by Jane Johnston Schoolcraft, William Apess, John Wannuaucon Quinney, Elias Boudinot, Seattle, George Copway, and John Rollin Ridge; late-nineteenth- and early-twentieth-century writing by John Oskison, Standing Bear, Charles Alexander Eastman, Sarah Winnemucca, E. Pauline Johnson, and Gertrude Bonnin; and mid- to late-twentieth-century literature by Mourning Dove, John Joseph Mathews, Thomas S. Whitecloud, D'Arcy McNickle, N. Scott Momaday, James Welch, Sherman Alexie, Joy Harjo, Louise Erdrich, Wendy Rose, Leslie Marmon Silko, and Simon Ortiz. The extensive index reflects the *Heath*'s commitment to providing students with a comprehensive collection of Native American literature.

With detailed introductions, notes, bibliographies, and timelines for Native American works, the *Heath* and *Norton* should assuage critics' misgivings that anthologizing Native American literature exploits Native American people. Rather, current anthologies illustrate for students the unique, important contributions of Native Americans throughout America's literary history. In a perfect world, or as scholar Jay Fliegelman says, in a "fantasy anthology" (337), teachers could enhance Native American pieces with attention to individual tribal customs, sensibilities, traditions, and religions—the pluralism of Native America. In a survey course with time constraints, however, multiethnic anthologies familiarize students with key facets of America's vast literary heritage.

Scholars continue to question whether, or how, a multiethnic canon improves the lives of contemporary ethnic Americans, as "inclusion does not necessarily or automatically eradicate marginalization" (Schweninger 209). Furthermore, "ethnic empowerment has not reduced racial conflict," writes Berndt Ostendorf, who ruefully notes an increase in racial divides on America's college campuses (210). Kenneth Warren believes "the placement of 'black' and 'ethnic' texts in the hands of 'white' readers" is no "advance on the front of social tolerance and equity" (338). Anthologies only reinscribe tradition, Warren states, rendering irrelevant the particular texts students may be reading. Yet a multiethnic canon rejects America's history of ethnocentrism to encompass a fuller American literary tradition. Surely students familiar with ethnic literature attain a greater understanding and appreciation of the spectrum of American experience. Such knowledge may not translate into immediate political action, but awareness of ethnic diversity, expressed and attained through literature, can only foster better informed readers, writers, and thinkers. As Baym and Lauter point out in their respective *Norton* and *Heath* prefaces, teachers and students today insist upon multiethnic anthologies in their courses.

Lauter, Baym, and Krupat are among many scholars advocating multiethnic literary studies. Native American works are vital to such endeavors, as Native Americans constitute the indigenous population of the United States and profoundly affected colonial American culture, society, and literature. From centuries-old oral narratives to contemporary fiction and poetry, Native American works convey the cultural contributions and unique experiences of people limning the borders of American society. Ultimately, the technique of using multiple narrators in Native American works should be declared legitimate not because William Faulkner uses it, too, but because it incorporates the rich traditions of Native American storytelling (Manley 128). This is but one example not of revising literary history or including "trendy" writers in the canon, but of acknowledging that writings by Euro-Americans exist in tandem with Native American works.

Works Cited

Bak, Hans. "The *Heath* is On: Canon or Kaleidoscope?" *Multiculturalism and the Canon of American Culture*. Ed. Hans Bak. Amsterdam: VU University Press, 1993. 65–80.

Baym, Nina. "Norton Anthology of American Literature." E-mail to author. 4 Dec. 2002.

———, et. al., eds. *The Norton Anthology of American Literature, Sixth ed.* New York: W. W. Norton & Company, Inc., 2002.

Bogan, Louise. *Achievement in American Poetry, 1900–1950*. Chicago: Regnery, 1951.

Bradley, Sculley, ed. "Preface." *The American Tradition in Literature*. New York: W. W. Norton & Company, Inc., 1967.

Chase, Richard, ed. *The American Novel and its Tradition*. New York: Doubleday & Company, Inc., 1957.

Du Bois, W. E. B. *The Souls of Black Folk*. 1903. New York: Penguin, 1989.

Fliegelman, Jay. "Anthologizing the Situation of American Literature." *American Literature* 65:2 (1993): 334–338.

Foerster, Norman, ed. *American Poetry and Prose: A Book of Readings, 1607–1916*. Houghton Mifflin Co., 1925.

Gottesman, Ronald, et. al., eds. *The Norton Anthology of American Literature*. 1st ed. New York: W. W. Norton & Company, Inc., 1979.

———, et. al., eds. *The Norton Anthology of American Literature*. 3rd ed. New York: W. W. Norton & Company, Inc., 1989.
———, et. al., eds. *The Norton Anthology of American Literature*. 4th ed. New York: W. W. Norton & Company, Inc., 1994.
Guillory, John. *Cultural Capital: The Problem of Literary Canon Formation*. Chicago: The University of Chicago Press, 1993.
Hubbell, Jay B., ed. *American Life in Literature*. Vol. 2. New York: Harper & Brothers, 1949.
Kreymborg, Alfred, ed. *Lyric America: An Anthology of American Poetry (1630–1930)*. New York: Coward-McCann, 1930.
Krupat, Arnold. "Multiculturalism, Native Americans, and the 'American Scene.'" *Multiculturalism and the Canon of American Culture*. Ed. Hans Bak. Amsterdam: VU University Press, 1993. 104–114.
———. *The Voice in the Margin: Native American Literature and the Canon*. Berkeley, CA: University of California Press, 1989.
Lauter, Paul. "*The Heath Anthology* and Cultural Boundaries." *English Studies/Culture Studies: Institutionalizing Dissent*. Eds. Isaiah Smithson and Nancy Ruff. Urbana, Chicago: University of Illinois Press, 1994. 180–190.
———, et. al., eds. *The Heath Anthology of American Literature*. 1st ed. Boston: Houghton Mifflin Co., 1990.
———, et. al., eds. *The Heath Anthology of American Literature*. 3rd ed. Boston: Houghton Mifflin Co., 1998.
———, et. al., eds. *The Heath Anthology of American Literature*. 4th ed. Boston: Houghton Mifflin Co., 2002.
———. "On the Implications of the *Heath Anthology*: Response to Ruland." *American Literary History* 4:2 (1992): 329–336.
———. "Race and Gender in the Shaping of the American Literary Canon: A Case Study From the Twenties." *Canons and Contexts*. New York: Oxford University Press, 1991. 22–47.
———. "Society and the Profession." *Canons and Contexts*. New York: Oxford University Press, 1991. 3–21.
Leary, Lewis. *American Literature: A Study and Research Guide*. New York: St. Martin's Press, 1976.
Lee, Charles, ed. *North, East, South, West: A Regional Anthology of American Writing*. New York: Howell, Soskin Publishers, 1945.
Manley, Kathleen E. B. "Decreasing the Distance: Contemporary Native American Texts, Hypertext, and the Concept of Audience." *Southern Folklore* 51:2 (1994): 121–135.
McCovey, Shaunna. "Coyote, It Seems." *Through the Eye of the Deer: An Anthology of Native American Women Writers*. Eds. Carolyn Dunn and Carol Comfort. San Francisco: Aunt Lute Books, 1999. 9.

Means, Russell. *Where White Men Fear to Tread: The Autobiography of Russell Means.* New York: St. Martin's Press, 1995.

Miller, Perry, ed. Preface. *Major Writers of America, Volume I.* New York: Harcourt, Brace & World, 1962.

Morrison, Toni. *Playing in the Dark: Whiteness in the Literary Imagination.* New York: Vintage Books, 1993.

Ostendorf, Berndt. "PC, or Do the Right Thing." *Multiculturalism and the Canon of American Culture.* Ed. Hans Bak. Amsterdam: VU University Press, 1993. 209–227.

Parker, Hershel. "The Price of Diversity: An Ambivalent Minority Report on the American Literary Canon." *College Literature* 18:3 (1991). <http://ehostvgw18.epnet.com/fulltext.asp>.

Perkins, George, et. al., eds. *The American Tradition in Literature.* 6th ed. New York: Random House, 1985.

———, et. al., eds. *The American Tradition in Literature.* 7th ed. New York: Random House, 1990.

Peterson, Nancy J. "Native American Literature—From the Margins to the Mainstream." *Modern Fiction Studies* 45:1 (1999): 1–9.

Preface. *Masterpieces of American Literature.* Cambridge: The Riverside Press, 1891.

Ruland, Richard. "Art and a Better America." *American Literary History* 3:2 (1991): 337–359.

Ruoff, A. LaVonne Brown. "American Indian Literatures: A Guide to Anthologies, Texts, and Research." *Studies in American Indian Literature.* Ed. Paula Gunn Allen. New York: The Modern Language Association of America, 1995. 280–309.

———. "Old Traditions and New Forms." *Studies in American Indian Literature.* Ed. Paula Gunn Allen. New York: The Modern Language Association of America, 1995. 147–168.

Schweninger, Lee. "Racialism and Liberation in Native American Literature." *Post Colonial Literatures: Expanding the Canon.* Ed. Deborah L. Madsen. London and Sterling, VA: Pluto Press, 1999. 206–217.

Spiller, Robert E. *The Cycle of American Literature.* New York: The Macmillan Company, 1957.

Stripes, James. "Beyond the Cameo School: Decolonizing the Academy in a World of Postmodern Multiculturalism." *Wicazo Sa Review* (Spring 1995): 24–32.

Tedlock, Dennis. "On the Translation of Style in Oral Narrative." *Smoothing the Ground: Essays on Native American Oral Literature.* Ed. Brian Swann. Berkeley, University of California Press, 1983. 57–77.

Tyler, Moses Coit. *A History of American Literature, 1607–1783.* Chicago: The University of Chicago Press, 1967.

Warren, Kenneth. "The Problem of Anthologies, or Making the Dead Wince." *American Literature* 65:2 (1993): 338–342.

Warrior, Robert Allen. "Literature and Students in the Emergence of Native American Studies." *Studying Native America: Problems and Prospects*. Ed. Russell Thornton. Madison, WI: The University of Wisconsin Press, 1998. 111–129.

PART II

TEXTUAL READINGS

Chapter 4

'But is it Great?'

The Question of the Canon for Italian American Women Writers

Mary Jo Bona

> ... [T]he revision of the literary canon has ... been necessary because in the 1920s processes were set in motion that virtually eliminated black, white female, and all working-class writers from the canon.... The literary canon is, in short, a means by which culture validates social power.
>
> —Paul Lauter, *Canons and Contexts*

> For when the record is not recognized, it is in effect denied. This was the case for Italian American women writers.... Yes, the Italian American woman writer exists, and her experience is registered in an honorable literary record.
>
> —Helen Barolini, *Chiaroscuro: Essays of Identity*

I. Defining the Canon and the Creation of Italian American Literature

Classroom anecdotes often illustrate how easily persuaded students are by the status quo. Students are traditionally not encouraged to question the reasoning behind a professor's literary choices. In general American literature classes and special topic courses, such as a class on Italian American literature, students are used to completing the reading assignments with little discussion about the aesthetic virtues of a work. As a case in point, during a discussion of the 1896 American novel *The Country of the*

Pointed Firs by Sarah Orne Jewett, I required English majors at my former university provide the class with their judgment of Jewett's work. When the class initially fell silent, I wondered if the modernist structure of Jewett's novel unmoored the students, throwing them into confusion about how to read itself. Once their tongues loosened, however, several students spoke of the novel in convincing ways. They spoke of Jewett's devotion to storytelling; they saw that transmitting stories orally from one generation to the next helped unite the author's fictionalized community and made living in a post-Civil War environment emotionally viable. They recognized how incorporating the Western tradition of the quest allowed Jewett to revise this narrative to explore the needs of a female community largely bereft of men, and how the quest for Jewett's community of women in Maine is just as much about adventure as it is about coming home.[1] A couple of the usually spirited students, however, remained unusually silent.

In an effort to engage them, I wrote on the board a value judgment made by Willa Cather, who was mentored by Jewett. Cather placed Jewett's *The Country of the Pointed Firs* alongside Hawthorne's *The Scarlet Letter* and Twain's *The Adventures of Huckleberry Finn*—in effect granting Jewett's lesser-known novel equal status with established American texts. Hawthorne and Twain already were deemed foremost literary talents during their lives; students in high school and college have been exposed to their most famous works for well over a half-century. However, Cather's gesture of canonization on behalf of Sarah Orne Jewett was an effort to grant an American *woman's* work permanent recognition, akin to Hawthorne's and Twain's work achieved decades earlier:

> I can think of no others that confront time and change so serenely, . . . I like to think with what pleasure, with what a sense of rich discovery, the young student of American literature in far distant years to come will take up this book and say, "A masterpiece!" (qtd. in Pryse v)

Nodding their heads in agreement, many of my students found the comparison between Jewett and her male compatriots apt. They also recognized their own participation in rendering a judgment of Jewett's work. However, when I asked one of the silent students to contribute her thoughts on the merit of Jewett's novel, she answered that she did not think *The Country of the Pointed Firs* should be judged alongside a novel like *The Scarlet Letter*, which she considered truly great. I asked her to explain what it was about Hawthorne's work that gave it such literary merit. She replied that she had not read *The Scarlet Letter*—yet—but she already knew that it was great. Clearly certain American works, Hawthorne's among them, have become, as Lillian Robinson explains, "institutionalized as canonical literature," and therefore putatively immune from further assessment (118).

Such a classroom anecdote is not meant to deride a young student; rather, it reveals an omission that is regularly evident within syllabi and general curricula. Before a semester begins, professors already have made decisions about the content of students' reading, based on the two closely intertwined phenomena of text availability and judgments about worth. In my effort to introduce students to lesser-known literary texts, I explain that people create canons and that they have not descended, as the stone tablets did for Moses, directly from God. I further elaborate by saying that professors (along with reviewers, editors, critics, and publishers) decide what is worthy, publishable, and therefore available to students in the classroom.

Wendell Harris explains that citing a biblical parallel in discussions of literary canons is inappropriate despite the word's core meaning of "rule" or "measure,"

> and by extrapolation, "correct" or "authoritative," ... the process of biblical canonizing was toward closure, whereas literary canons have always implicitly allowed for at least the possibility of adding new or revalued works. (110, 111)

Feminist literary criticism has been in the vanguard of countering the dominant canon not only by offering an alternative list of writers, a "female counter-canon," but also by "radically redefining literary quality itself" (Robinson 122, 124). Given the vituperative responses in the 1980s and early 1990s to the dismantling of the traditionally male-dominated literary canon, it is not surprising to hear Paul Lauter and others call the question of the canon a "cultural battle" (ix).[2]

Lauter's description of the canon is instrumental in understanding the difficulty in achieving recognition for both male and female Italian American writers:

> By "canon" I mean the set of literary works, the grouping of significant philosophical, political, and religious texts, the particular accounts of history generally accorded cultural weight within a society. How one defines a cultural canon obviously shapes collegiate curricula and research priorities, but it also helps determine precisely whose experiences and ideas become central to academic study. (ix)

Without publishers and reviewers to make writers visible, without critics to assess the value of specific books, without professors in classrooms teaching such works, and without marketing strategies to keep books in print, writers of significant strength find themselves locked outside the American literary canon.

Defining the canon of *American* literature helps illuminate the struggle of Italian American women writers whose existence as an aesthetically resonant cultural group has only recently come to light. The American literary canon refers to "that set of authors and works generally included in basic American literature college courses and textbooks, and those ordinarily discussed in standard volumes of literary history, bibliography, or criticism" (Lauter 23). In his seminal article on canonicity (rpt. in *Canons and Contexts*)—"Race and Gender in the Shaping of the American Literary Canon: *A Case Study from the Twenties*"—Lauter offers a detailed analysis of the institutional, theoretical, and historiographic reasons for the exclusion of female, black, and all working-class writers from the canon. This description, of course, includes all Italian American writers. Lauter, in *Canons and Contexts*, cites three important factors that account for the progressive elimination of such writers from the American literary canon:

> The professionalization of the teaching of literature, the development of an aesthetic theory that privileged certain

texts, and the historiographic organization of the body of literature into conventional "periods" and "themes." (27)

In 1919, Fred Lewis Pattee published his anthology, *Century Readings for a Course in American Literature*. In it, he included works by Harriet Beecher Stowe, Mary Wilkins Freeman, Sarah Orne Jewett, Helen Hunt Jackson, Rose Terry Cooke and more. Less than twenty years later, Howard Mumford Jones and Ernest E. Leisy published *Major American Writers*, which included no women at all. By 1948, when the National Council of Teachers of English (NCTE) reviewed American literature in the college curriculum, Lauter reported in *Canons and Contexts* that "only three women appeared in the ninety syllabi of survey courses studied" (25–26).

What happened? Many factors contributed to the exclusion of women and minorities from anthologies and syllabi, not the least of which was the way the teaching of literature was organized according to a historiographic model, which focused on periods and themes, such as world wars and male experiences abroad. What remains clear to Lauter and to me is a cold fact that constricted the canon until the inception of movements for social change in the 1960s and 1970s: "The arbiters of taste, scholars and critics alike were . . . drawn from a narrow stratum of American society" (36). For sixty years, the dominant literati did not consider the literary works of women and other minority groups worthy of examination.

Professors and pedagogical agendas have changed in recent years. Thus, female, black, and working-class writers increasingly appear in American literature anthologies and on syllabi. However, coming late to the conversation about canon formation, most Italian American writers have not yet achieved a cultural standing that exerts influence on American readers' choices. Nonetheless, I would not go so far to suggest that Italian American writers would be permanently denied entrance to the hallowed halls of canonicity. To do so would be to overlook the malleable nature of canons themselves and the institutional context out of which they emerge. As John Guillory explains, an institutional context is "a setting in which it is possible to insure the *reproduction* of the work, its continual reintroduction to generations of readers" (237). Certainly, such institutional viability is in its infancy within Italian American letters. In fact, we have increased the recognition of and reproduction of works by Italian American writers.[3] The view that Italian Americans are nonreaders harnessed by a heritage of *omertà* has diminished considerably in the past fifteen years. I do, however, concur with Dana Gioia, who reluctantly supports Gay Talese's statement that "there is no *widely recognized* body of work in American literature" that portrays Italian American immigration experiences (Talese 23; italics mine).[4]

Recognizing that stereotypes about a culture are dismantled when "someone has first had the courage to enunciate [them] in all [their] unlovely specificity," Robert Viscusi moves beyond the predictable lament of Italian Americans who bemoan the preoccupation of editors and the general public with grotesque themes regarding Italian American behavior and values. Constructing an Italian American literary canon occurs, Viscusi affirms, when

> a people begins to possess its own charter myth—when a people begins, that is, to inquire into the sources of its own historical identity—then the books its writers produce have something to say to the general reader that it will be very much in the general reader's interest to follow and understand. (267–272)

Inquiries into the historical life of Italian Americans have flowed not only from traditional academic disciplines such as anthropology, history, sociology, and English, but also from interdisciplinary fields such as women's studies, American studies, and ethnic/cultural studies. Benefiting from a dual heritage, Italian Americans must explore the creative dimensions of their cultural hybridism, crossing borders "geo-intellectually" and defining the cultural specificity of Italian American identities (Tamburri 129). Describing Robert Viscusi and Helen Barolini as the elder statespersons of an Italian American critical generation, Anthony Tamburri suggests that these two scholars have "paved the way for the rest of us to work in . . . with a . . . vast[er] critical arsenal" (125).[5] Helen Barolini's groundbreaking 1985 publication of *The Dream Book* stakes a serious claim by opening up new vistas of literary writing, redressing long-neglected women writers of Italian American extraction. In doing so, Barolini began establishing the importance of these writers to the development of an Italian American literary canon.

II. Blazing a Trail for Italian American Women Writers: Barolini's Manifesto

Perhaps no other critic of Italian American women's culture has offered more insight into this ethnic group's *literary* cohesion than has Helen Barolini. According to Alice Walker's back cover commendation, *The Dream Book* was a "heroic recovery and affirmation." Placing Italian American women writers on the map for the first time in American literary history, Barolini explodes the silence of these writers by exploring the historical and social underpinnings of Italian cultural life and the literary hegemonies and oversights of the American publishing world. Describing her anthology of fifty-six Italian American women writers as her "literary manifesto," Barolini intended to establish "once and for all, that we exist, we are writers, we are part of the national literature" (qtd. in Ahearn 47). Establishing a list of writers, Barolini initiated the process of Italian American canonization.

A year after the appearance of *The Dream Book*, Barolini published an autobiographical essay called "Becoming a Literary Person Out of Context," explaining her elusive identity as a writer was "completely out of context with my Italian American background": "An Italian American woman becomes a writer out of the void. She has to be self-birthed, without models, without inner validation" (263). Similarly, when writing her first novel, *Umbertina* (1979), Barolini was moved by "the burden of history, the need to tell the story in order to understand myself" (qtd. in Ahearn 47). Aware of the fact that Anglo-American literature dominated the literary landscape when she was growing up in the 1940s and 1950s and did not fully speak to her southern Italian background, Barolini took up the pen herself: "If books did not tell me who I was, I would write those that did" ("Becoming a Literary Person" 265).

For Barolini, becoming a literary person required that she simultaneously also become a critic, a literary archeologist digging up the voices of the past and the voices of those presently unheard. Since the emergence of her auspicious anthology, Barolini has managed to see each of her books back in print, including a 2000 reprint of *The Dream Book*. Her reintroduction to *The Dream Book* also appears in her revised book of essays, *Chiaroscuro*, which offers an update on the literary situation for Italian American women writers. Since the inception of *The Dream Book*, writers represented in it who once thought of themselves as unique, without literary models from their individual ethnic group, "became aware of each other, held joint readings, formed groups, began to appear in collections, were asked to talk at colleges and at women's history events" (*Chiaroscuro* 172). This anthology triggered responses of deep emotion from the writers themselves, who had previously perceived, as Barolini did herself, that they were writing out of a void, without models and without inner validation.

In 1987, when actor and writer Emelise Aleandri staged "The Dream Book Revue" at the CUNY Graduate Center in New York, Italian American writers featured in *The Dream Book* "were visibly brought together for the first time as a collective presence and voice" (*Chiaroscuro* 172). Italian American women finally became visible to each other. Providing mentorship and continuity with each other, perhaps for the first time in their literary history, Italian American women writers were no longer without models from their ethnic background.

Barolini's update of *The Dream Book* also records the literary achievements of Italian American women writers throughout the decade of the 1990s. Although in 1985 Barolini was correct in lamenting the paucity of literary critics to probe the background of Italian American women and "unlock the reasons for silence" (*The Dream Book* 32), her 1999 assessment of scholars in the field of Italian American studies is remarkably reticent and dated. In fact, Italian American critics have been at the forefront of the workaday tasks of making such books as Barolini's available in paperback and accessible to students and a general reading public. Most notable is Fred Gardaphé's landmark study, *Italian*

Signs, American Streets: The Evolution of Italian American Narrative, for its application of Giambattista Vico's notion of *corso* and *recorso* to "illuminate the recent rise in power of minority American literature" (13). According to Gardaphé, Italian American literature has been abandoned by its Italian and American cultures, and "relegated to the *vicoli*, or 'side streets' of literary discourse" (8). Tracing the development of an "indigenous critical voice," Gardaphé deciphers the codes specific to Italian American culture, compiling an inventory of "Italian signs" from the early immigrant works to contemporary modernist writings (8, 11).

Using Vico's evolutionary paradigm of cultural history, Gardaphé applies this philosopher's ideas of a culture's three ages to a reading of the movement from an orally based Italian immigrant culture to an Italian American one based on literary tradition (15). Utilizing a culture-specific approach to analyze the works of male and female writers, Gardaphé fulfills Barolini's requirements of the function of the critic: "the critic . . . takes the long view and decides what becomes part of the canon" (*Chiaroscuro* 191). In an effort to design an approach to reading Italian American literature, Gardaphé also turned to the critical works on other minority literatures, most particularly those of Henry Louis Gates. Gates's following comment in "Criticism in the Jungle," provided Gardaphé with a strategic imperative—to provide readers with the long view:

> W. E. B. Du Bois argued that evidence of critical activity is a sign of a tradition's sophistication, since criticism implies an awareness of the process of art itself and is a second-order reflection upon those primary texts that define a tradition and its canon. . . . All great writers demand great critics. (qtd. in *Italian Signs, American Streets* 3)

Other scholars like Gardaphé recognize the necessity of establishing indigenous critical theories to analyze works that might present contrasting ideologies to those represented by the traditional literary canon. Barolini, Viscusi, Tamburri, and Gardaphé, have been engaged in enlarging the discursive power of Italian Americans as a literary group.[6]

III. Italian American Women's Writing: *Rosa*, An Uncanonical Classic

Recurring themes in Italian American women's literature transcend the topics of migration history, family culture, and gender identity, but those very topics help define Italian American literary traditions and efforts to authenticate them through reprints, classroom teaching, and scholarly essays. Like their male compatriots, Italian American women writers have been drawn to tell ancestral narratives of Italian family life in the homeland and the New World. A fidelity to the story of immigration and resettlement shapes the constructions of many narratives, from Rosa Cassettari's late-nineteenth- and early-twentieth-century experience in Italy and America in Marie Hall Ets' *Rosa: The Life of an Italian Immigrant*, to Renée Manfredi's late-twentieth-century depiction of Pittsburgh's Little Italy in her first short story collection, *Where Loves Leaves Us*.

Keeping in mind Wendell Harris's assertion that literary canons always implicitly allow for the possibility of adding new or revalued works, the recent reprinting of *Rosa: The Life of an Italian Immigrant* might initiate an "ongoing critical colloquy" with other autobiographies (111). Both Marie Hall Ets, who transcribed and edited the unlettered Rosa's story, and historian Rudolph Vecoli, who initially sponsored the book by writing the foreword to *Rosa*, knew a good story when they heard one. *Rosa: The Life of an Italian Immigrant* is an as told to autobiography written down by Marie Hall Ets, a social worker at the Chicago Commons, a settlement house like its model, Hull House, that helped "Italian women in the assimilation process . . . [and] used education as a method of social reform" (Batinich 165). Ets befriended Rosa in 1918 and transcribed her stories, many of which remain unpublished and stored at the Immigration History Research Center at The University of Minnesota.

As late as 1970, Vecoli bemoaned the fact that the historian who "aspires to write the history of this inarticulate or silent majority is hindered by the paucity of sources" (Foreword vi). By 1979, however, he was able to note that research into ordinary lives were rectifying the situation. As Winifred Farrant Bevilacqua points out, oral histories were becoming central areas of immigration research:

> Immigrant letters and diaries, organizational records, church archives, and other similar materials were becoming more readily accessible in the nation's libraries and research centers. . . . [S]cholars had started creating new documents by gathering oral reminiscences of members of ethnic communities. (546)

Vecoli's initial sponsorship of this oral autobiography helped place an unschooled Italian immigrant woman at the center of the historical stage. Conferring upon *Rosa* literary as well as historical value, Vecoli enlarged the work's discursive power by suggesting that it bore more resemblance to fictional accounts of immigrant life than to immigrant autobiographies. By placing Rosa's story alongside Willa Cather's Antonia or O. E. Rölvaag's Beret, Vecoli in effect offered a hermeneutical approach to a generically indeterminate work (Foreword vi). As a "bicultural document," Rosa's story comes to readers "through the filter of an American recorder and editor," thus making this work generically complex (Gardaphé 31).

Reprinted in 1999 in the Wisconsin Studies in Autobiography series, *Rosa* has achieved a life-support system that includes not only Rudolph J. Vecoli's scholarly foreword, but also an introductory note by Helen Barolini, who earlier excerpted *Rosa* in *The Dream Book*. Apropos of such collaboration, Wendell V. Harris's description of "academic recirculation" as it relates to canon preservation reinforces the intersection between text availability and scholarly sponsorship: "What is easily available in print tends to be what is being taught and written about; what is written about tends to be what one is teaching or others are writing about" (114). Not yet canonized, Rosa's nontraditional narrative of triumph—she never achieves upward social mobility and remains a cleaning woman all her life, but feels triumphant as an American—is a rare bicultural document bridging two centuries and two nations.

Told from the perspective of a working-class person, Rosa's story demonstrates how one woman overcomes the fears and superstitions of her peasant culture of Lombardy without jettisoning her lifelong commitment to the Madonna. A staple feature of Italian Catholicism, the cult of the Blessed Virgin is not only, as Marina Warner explains, "the refuge of a poverty-stricken peasantry" (xxii). On the contrary, Rosa's dependence on the Madonna as an intercessor helps sustain her in several ways. Throughout the entire autobiography, Rosa relies on the Virgin Mary to support her emotionally, provide her with a strong sense of female identity, and give her courage during dire situations.

Rosa Cassettari's story charts her life from childhood in 1870s northern Italy to old age in Chicago, where she died in 1943. An expert teller of tales, Rosa learned the art of spinning in nineteenth-century Lombardy from the men in the stables, the central domicile of storytelling in communities with scarce resources. The warmest place of domesticity, the stable was also the area most accessible to family and people outside the household, and the place where most of the important community exchanges took place, including the telling of old stories. As folklorist Roger Abrahams explains, the stables were the places where "stories were spun and woven: the trope is not a conceit, for it is the traditional way in which storytelling is described in most of the world in which weaving is done" (xi).

That Rosa in childhood simultaneously became a skilled silk-maker in the local mills and a storyteller should come as no surprise, for she was sent to work by her adoptive mother at the age of seven and used stories to entertain the girls in the factories. Rosa was abandoned at birth, withstood agonizingly long hours at the silk mills, and was kept ignorant and fearful by Italy's rigid economic and class system. In early adulthood, Rosa was forced by her adoptive mother to marry a much older man, whom she loathed. Despite the harrowing fact that Rosa only learned the connection between sexual activity and parturition when self-delivering her second child, she never lost hope in her future in America, or her faith in the Madonna's worldly intercession on her behalf. As Gardaphé explains, Rosa's immigrant experience "strengthens her Italian-created religious convictions" (35). However, Rosa ultimately maintains her individual sense of self through storytelling. Winifred F. Bevilacqua observes how Rosa refuses to retreat into "an attitude of victimization," adopting instead the major strategy of cultivating

> the art of telling stories, which earns her the attention of others, gives her an identity that is related to her community and expressive of her individuality, and is an outlet for the richness of her inner world, so in contrast to her external poverty. (548–49)

Despite her limiting circumstances both in northern Italy and later in America (to which she immigrated in 1884), Rosa continued to assert herself through the art of storytelling, an activity nearly denied her by an abusive husband from whom she managed to escape by going to Chicago. Anyone who has read Rosa's story knows its breathtaking quality, which makes it comparable not only to other narratives of immigrant life (such as Mary Antin's *The Promised Land*), but also to the slave narrative in its emphasis on escape and transcendence. Having achieved canonical status in the past decade or so, Harriet Jacobs's *Incidents in the Life of a Slave Girl* (the quintessential female slave narrative) might be usefully taught alongside *Rosa: The Life of an Italian Immigrant*. For both women, the painful acquisition of a personal voice is related to the act of creating a public, historical self. Rosa learned to speak in her adopted tongue, which provided her the means to tell her stories to various audiences in Chicago. According to Marie Hall Ets, Rosa's storytelling was known throughout all the settlement houses in Chicago, as well as several women's clubs and universities ("Introduction" 5). Although Rosa remained unlettered in her native and adopted tongues, her verbal artistry stemmed from oral traditions, which she mastered as a child.

For both women, the decision to refer to themselves pseudonymously and the editorial supervision they received deeply influenced what they said and how they said it. Pervading both documents are silences, especially regarding matters of a sexual nature. Both prematurely sexualized, Harriet A. Jacobs and Rosa Cassettari are compelled to reexamine nineteenth-century sexual mores. Jacobs's status as a female slave denies her the capacity to fulfill the ideology of the cult of true womanhood.[7] The Italian cultural beliefs in *fare bella figura* (creating a beautiful public figure)[8] and *omertà* have particular resonance for Italian women. When these beliefs conflict with her unwavering faith, Rosa does not always maintain them. In fact, after she migrates to America, Rosa divorces her cruel husband, managing to win a sense of freedom from her Old World *destino*. Finally, both narratives are fundamentally about the quest to find a home, a safe place where Jacobs and Cassettari could be secure from the male prerogative of dominance, insult, and violence. Rescuing themselves from abominably treacherous living conditions, each woman manages to find reasonably safe living quarters.

Placing *Incidents* and *Rosa* side by side reveals important commonalities. In discussing curricular issues in the reconstruction of American literature, Lauter examines the transformation in perception that occurs when a traditional category is shattered by adding different works: "Familiar works change when we read them alongside others, less familiar, . . . that grew from the same historical soil" (111). Although Jacobs and Cassettari may have come initially from different countries, their eventual escape to a free land and their nineteenth-century attitudes about faith, womanhood, and domesticity unite them vis-à-vis the literary study of American women searching for community.[9]

IV. Italian American Women's Writing: Some Themes, Forms and Influences

Oral storytelling, autobiography, memoir, poetry, fiction, and creative nonfiction comprise the various genres to which Italian American women recently have gravitated to relate their ancestral narratives of Italian family life in America. Although a fidelity to the story of immigration and resettlement often shapes the construction of Italian American narratives, the familial experience simultaneously governs the movement of many of the stories. Moreover, many works are set in ethnic neighborhoods, which undergo gradual but inevitable dismantling due to changing demography and class mobility. The destruction of the Little Italies of the early twentieth century has produced elegiac narratives, perhaps the most poignant of which is Tina De Rosa's *Paper*

Fish. De Rosa beautifully renders the wounds suffered by the West Side colony of Chicago's Italians, whose neighborhood was razed. Bearing witness to the dispersed Italian community of her childhood, De Rosa's epilogue functions as snapshots of people who are taking their leave: "The city said the Italian ghetto should go, and before the people could drop their forks next to their plates and say pardon me?, the streets were cleared" (120). De Rosa's description supports Rudolph Vecoli's assertion that the death of such a neighborhood marks "the end of the first chapter of the history of Italians in America" ("Are Italian Americans Just White Folks?" 4).

The Feminist Press's republication of De Rosa's novel serves as an important milestone in Italian American women's literature. The first in a series of Italian American women's narratives to be republished by this press, *Paper Fish* is De Rosa's virtuoso performance as a modernist writer. Louise DeSalvo's front-cover commendation of De Rosa's novel is no exaggeration: "The best Italian-American novel by a woman of this century." Such high praise is indeed a gesture of canonization, paralleling Willa Cather's description of Sarah Orne Jewett's novel as a "masterpiece!" De Rosa's story of Little Italy in Chicago and her enormously evocative writing style distinguish her as an important voice of Italian America and a singularly compelling stylist.[10]

Other writers of Italian American background commemorate places long gone and, in doing so, recover and make historical an essential part of their ancestors' complicated development in the adopted land. In her novel *Like Lesser Gods*, Mari Tomasi's story of the quarrying industry in Barre, Vermont, richly details the lives and untimely deaths of northern Italian artisans in the first decades of the twentieth century. Dorothy Bryant's *Miss Giardino* portrays the effects of subsequent migrations after the transatlantic crossing when Italian male mine workers moved from the East to the West Coast and often suffered from debilitating illnesses. Josephine Gattuso Hendin's *The Right Thing to Do* explores the conflict between generations as the rebellious daughter strives to break away from her parents' ethnic neighborhood in Astoria, Queens. Rita Ciresi's collection of stories, *Sometimes I Dream in Italian*, traces the childhood and adulthood of two sisters who struggle to negotiate their ethnic and gender identities in an economically depressed New Haven, Connecticut. Dissatisfied with their life choices in adulthood, these sisters long for a connection to their Italian background that has been lost in their parents' generation. Although the Italian American identities of Ciresi's characters are not as submerged as they are in Agnes Rossi's collection of stories, *The Quick*, Ciresi's stories, like Rossi's, examine with compassion the emotional costs of loving a harsh parent and losing the language of the ancestors.

Perhaps a principal feature of Italian American culture and of several of its literary texts is the appearance of sibling solidarity in the midst of family crisis. De Rosa's *Paper Fish*, Rossi's *The Quick*, Ciresi's *Sometimes I Dream in Italian*, Rachel Guido deVries's *Tender Warriors*, Carole Maso's *Ghost Dance*, and Louisa Ermelino's *The Sisters Mallone* are just a few of the narratives that incorporate siblings not only to reflect the duality of ethnic identity, but also to deflect some of the family's suffering. Although not overtly using Italian American characters, Mary (Bucci) Bush's collection of stories, *A Place of Light*, depicts the lives of rural working-class families in upstate, New York. Siblings covertly inscribe their ethnicity through rituals of healing as Great Aunt Maria tries to heal the sick mother in "Cure" with a poultice and Josie in "Bread" uses a staple of Italian American culinary life—a fresh loaf of bakery bread—to give herself permission to heal from an operation *and* a difficult family.

Accompanying the narrative topics of immigration, geographical provenance, social class, and commemoration of the history and development of the Italian family in America, other features of *italianità* give Italian American writing its distinct ethnic flavor. A few examples follow. An emphasis on the strength and inspiration of grandmothers and mothers, who are sometimes compared to the Madonna, the preeminent figure in Italian Catholicism, informs the narratives of several writers, including the traditionalist Mari Tomasi and the modernist Carole Maso. In *Like Lesser Gods* and *Ghost Dance*, the mothers are associated with the Madonna: Maria Dalli of Tomasi's novel is compared by the town's maestro to Leonardo's *Madonna of the Rocks*; Christine Wing of Maso's novel is linked with flight and the Assumption, the Christian feast celebrating Mary's ascension to heaven.

Italian American women's writing also integrates spirituality and *festa* in which celebration of faith reveals the intense love Italians hold for the Virgin Mary and their favorite patron saints. Consider Susan Caperna Lloyd's spiritual memoir, *No Pictures in My Grave*, and Mary Caponegro's postmodern story "Materia Prima" in *The Star Café and Other Stories* for varying but nonetheless intensive renderings of Italian American spiritual beliefs. Closely related to *festa* is the respect and devotion to food and the pride taken in its preparation and in the garden, which, like the kitchen, is a sacramental place for Italian Americans. Sprinkled liberally throughout the writings of so many Italian American women, culinary references inform the narrative movements of such works as Helen Barolini's *Festa*, Lynn Vannucci's "An Accidental Murder," Louisa Ermelino's *The Black Madonna*, and the poetry of Maria Gillan, Sandra Gilbert, Rose Romano and Maria Fama. Rose Romano unites the fundamental necessities of eating and composing a life for Italian American writers in her lines: "Everybody must know / that we eat. Until we have / a right to this place" (26).[11]

Some Italian American women have chosen the topic of Italy itself and have traveled there in order to renew ancestral ties with relatives. In doing so, recent writers have reversed earlier portrayals of Italy by nineteenth-century American writers, who often depicted contemporary Italian culture as corrupt.[12] For Italian American writers who return to the homeland, Italy is not the malevolent force that strips Americans of their innocence; rather, writers such as Anna Monardo (*The Courtyard of Dreams*), Anne Calcagno (*Pray for Yourself and Other Stories*), and Theresa Maggio (*Mattanza*), recognize the homeland as a source of nutrition, feeding them literally and imaginatively.

The spirit of feminism and its placement of women at the center of the literary stage are reflected in each of the works discussed in this essay. Italian American writers also have inherited the aims of modernism by using unconventional modes of ordering their works and radically subverting their portrayals of character, replacing outward depiction of behavior with inward states of consciousness. Like many twentieth-century women writers, Italian American women unite the creative strategies of modernism with the political aims of feminism, recognizing a complex identity based on the intersecting topics of ethnicity, class, and sexuality. Diane di Prima's *Memoirs of a Beatnik* (1969) preceded second-wave feminism in her transgressive memoir about sexuality and the complication of female identity within a world devoted to male pleasure. Di Prima's depiction of lesbian sex appears quotidian when juxtaposed to the horrifying realization that Diane's female lover is trapped emotionally and sexually inside her home by a rapist father and brother, anticipating by nearly thirty years the novels of English writer, Jeanette Winterson (especially *Art and Lies*).

Alongside their undertaking to create new artistic forms and styles, modernist writers also introduce silenced and often *verboten* subject matters. The sheer bluntness of Louise DeSalvo's memoir, *Vertigo* (1996) makes it one of the first to reveal the unhappiness she felt inside the traditionally venerated Italian American home. Unwilling to tolerate a reality that would divorce her from the complexity of her life as a second-generation Italian American from a poor family, DeSalvo writes about the effects of suppressed rage, financial struggle, and family conflict. Breaking away from the familiar Italian American story of family continuity and cultural cohesion, DeSalvo pursues a deeper understanding of her mother's life of constant housework, thwarted literary aspirations, and fear of the outside world. The inspirational engagements in culinary traditions, spiritual celebrations, and extended family gatherings are markedly absent in *Vertigo*. For Italian Americans, a forbidden subject matter might well be the unfortunate fact that a mother cannot provide her family with delicious meals. Louise dutifully revises her memories of unappetizing meals by becoming the mother she did not have as a child. Happily, DeSalvo succeeds in rewriting her mother's life by becoming a writer *and* a good cook, two intimately related phenomena.

An important indicator of an ongoing tradition of Italian American women writers is literary influence. Since the publication of several anthologies of Italian American writing, reprints of novels, and recent publications by writers such as Carole Maso, Mary Caponegro, Beverly Donofrio, and Louisa Ermelino, writers have been actively engaged in reading one another's work. It is a testimonial to the emergence of a visible presence of

Italian American women writers that makes the existence of influence so thrilling. For example, Mary Cappello's *Night Bloom* echoes the concerns of DeSalvo's *Vertigo*. In her emphasis on her mother's agoraphobia and her father's rage, Cappello, like DeSalvo before her, explodes the silences traditionally informing Italian American family life. DeSalvo's back-cover blurb of Cappello's debut memoir exclaims that she was "knocked out by [Cappello's] original voice." Similarly, Carole Maso's back-cover commendation of Chris Mazza's *Your Name Here:——* describes the book as a "complicated, . . . unflinching portrait of violence" and Rita Ciresi's flap-cover blurb praises Louisa Ermelino's *The Black Madonna* as worthy as a *"festa."* Italian American women are reading and supporting their sisters, reinforcing their visible presence, and providing viable models for present and future writers.

When assembling her critical anthology of antebellum American women's writing, Judith Fetterley juxtaposed images of hunger and satiation to describe the process of introducing unknown women writers. In contrast to "their well-fed brothers," Fetterley writes, American women were "thin, starving, and on their own" (*Provisions* 34). Pursuing with difficulty her anthology project, Fetterley first recognized that male American classics were

> surrounded by placentas . . . each firmly centered in a rich nutrient mass of critical books and articles, scholarly biographies, exhaustive bibliographies, special and regular MLA sessions, hundreds of discussions in hundreds of classrooms, cheap and accessible paperback editions, richly elegant coffee-table editions, government-funded standard text editions. (34)

Such evidence, Fetterley explains, testifies to the presumed worthiness of such texts to be fed. In stark contrast, women writers of the American literary tradition were like the fictional children of many nineteenth-century writers—motherless and starving. In an effort to "begin the task of feeding," Fetterley, like Barolini, began the arduous task of discovering, retrieving, and getting the literature of women back in print (34).

In 1985, Barolini's *The Dream Book: An Anthology of Writings by Italian American Women* and Fetterley's *Provisions: A Reader from 19th-Century American Women* were published, each with impressive introductions. With almost no body of scholarly material in existence to aid either critic, each had no other choice but to blaze a trail individually. As Barolini says, "paths are made by walking. Books are made by questioning" (*The Dream Book* ix). In 1985, Fetterley anthologized an excerpt from Harriet Jacobs's *Incidents in the Life of a Slave Girl* and the entire text of Rebecca Harding Davis's *Life in the Iron Mills*, which earlier benefited from publication by The Feminist Press and from Tillie Olsen's biographical introduction. Since then, both works have achieved canonical status; their representation in *The Norton Anthology of American Literature* epitomizes their revalued status. In contrast, Barolini in 1985 anthologized excerpts in *The Dream Book* from the works of such writers as Louise DeSalvo, Rosa Cassettari, Gioia Timpanelli, and Diana Cavallo, all of whose works are presently available or back in print, though none are represented in any major American anthology.[13]

Italian American literature does not yet have the placenta that can give it a rich nutrient mass of support. Nonetheless, this field of literary study does have its growing core of critics. With an increase in scholarly interest in Italian American women's writing, we are in the process of defining this body of literature, exploring its greatness, and insuring the reproduction of this work. Like Willa Cather before us, we will be able to exclaim with complete clarity that a work like Tina De Rosa's *Paper Fish* or Diana Cavallo's *A Bridge of Leaves* is a "masterpiece!" and should be read by the young student of American literature.

Notes

1. See Sandra A. Zagarell's essay "Narrative of Community: The Identification of a Genre" for an analysis of works of nineteenth-century literature, including Jewett's *The Country of the Pointed Firs*, that take as their primary subject the life of the community and portray a communitarian aesthetic that "deliberately refuses linearity in order to achieve an inclusive circularity" (521–22). Several twentieth-century novels by Italian American writers, including Mari Tomasi's *Like Lesser*

Gods and Pietro di Donato's *Christ in Concrete*, also portray the ordinary processes of the community constructed around from what Zagarell describes as the "continuous small-scale negotiations and daily procedures through which communities sustain themselves" (503).

2. Two 1987 works that became best sellers and advocated a return to conservative educational values and a narrow understanding of the literary canon are Allan Bloom's *The Closing of the American Mind* and E. D. Hirsch's *Cultural Literacy*. For a spirited and well-reasoned response to such views, see Gerald Graff's *Beyond the Culture Wars: How Teaching the Conflicts Can Revitalize American Education*.

3. Several publishing houses have been instrumental in increasing the recognition of Italian American women's writing. The Feminist Press has republished Tina De Rosa's *Paper Fish*, Helen Barolini's *Umbertina*, Dorothy Bryant's *Miss Giardino*, Josephine Gattuso Hendin's *The Right Thing to Do*, and Louise DeSalvo's *Vertigo*; Guernica Editions, Diana Cavallo's *A Bridge of Leaves*; Syracuse University Press, Helen Barolini's *The Dream Book*; the University of Wisconsin Press, Marie Hall Ets's *Rosa: The Life of an Italian Immigrant*, and the New England Press, Mari Tomasi's *Like Lesser Gods*.

4. Talese's lead article in the book review of *The New York Times* is called "Where Are the Italian American Novelists?" *Italian Americana* (a cultural and historical review journal) devoted two of its issues to a candid exchange on Talese's essay, including Dana Gioia's response, "Low Visibility: Thoughts on Italian American Writers" (7–12).

5. Without institutional support and a network of scholars in the field of Italian American studies, earlier critics of Italian America such as Giovanni Schiavo, Jerre Mangione, Olga Peragallo, Leonard Covello, Rose Basile Green, Rudolph Vecoli, and Betty Boyd Caroli nonetheless produced important work. For an appreciation of their contributions, including the formation of the American Italian Historical Association in 1966, see Frank Cavaioli's "The Rise of Italian American Studies and The American Italian Historical Association" (1–22).

6. Other critics include but are not limited to the following: William Boelhower, Theresa Carilli, Pellegrino D'Acierno, Edvige Giunta, Josephine Gattuso Hendin, Blossom Kirschenbaum, Mary Ann Mannino, Mary Frances Pipino, Roseanne Quinn, and John Paul Russo.

7. For an overview of the cardinal virtues comprising the cult of true womanhood for nineteenth-century American women, see Barbara Welter's *Dimity Convictions: The American Woman in the Nineteenth Century*, chapter two.

8. See Gloria Nardini's *Che Bella Figura!* for an ethnographic analysis of the meanings and contexts of this cultural phenomenon.

9. Rosa's narrative also might be usefully read alongside Gioia Timpanelli's *Sometimes the Soul* and Adria Bernardi's *In the Gathering Woods*. Each writer incorporates storytelling techniques in her narrative, resuming the traditional role of the *cantastoria*, a singer/teller of old tales.

10. For close literary analyses of the aesthetic merits of De Rosa's virtuoso novel, see individual chapters of Gardaphé's *Italian Signs, American Streets* and Bona's *Claiming a Tradition*. Article-length analyses include Giunta's afterword to *Paper Fish*, Bona's "Broken Images, Broken Lives: Carmolina's Journey in Tina De Rosa's *Paper Fish*," and DeSalvo's "*Paper Fish* by Tina De Rosa: An Appreciation."

11. The Feminist Press published an anthology of poetry and short works around the topic of food called *The Milk of Almonds: Italian American Women Writers on Food and Culture*, edited by Louise DeSalvo and Edvige Giunta.

12. In *American Novelists in Italy*, Nathalia Wright explains that nineteenth-century American writers such as Hawthorne and James often depicted Italian civilization as corrupt, but the Italian past as edenic. Several twentieth-century Italian American writers, on the contrary, often regard the Italy of their ancestors and of the present as the place of health. Illness and suffering are equated with America. See my *Claiming a Tradition: Italian American Women Writers*, especially chapter one.

13. *The Norton Book of American Autobiography*, edited by Jay Parini, includes excerpts from Pascal D'Angelo's *Son of Italy*, Gay Talese's *Unto the Sons*, and Alane Salierno Mason's "Respect." For a more generous selection of Italian American women's memoirs, see *Beyond the Godfather: Italian American Writers on the Real Italian American Experience*, edited by A. Kenneth Ciongoli and Jay Parini.

Works Cited

Abrahams, Roger D. "Foreword." *Italian Folktales in America: The Verbal Art of an Immigrant Woman*. Eds. Elizabeth Mathias and Richard Raspa. Detroit: Wayne State University Press, 1988. ix–xv.

Ahearn, Carol Bonomo. "Interview: Helen Barolini." *Fra Noi* (September 1986): 47.

Antin, Mary. *The Promised Land*. 1940. New Jersey: Princeton University Press, 1969.

Barolini, Helen. "Becoming a Literary Person Out of Context." *Massachusetts Review* 27.2 (1986): 262–74.

———. *Chiaroscuro: Essays of Identity.* 1997. Rev. ed. Madison: University of Wisconsin Press, 1999.
———. ed. *The Dream Book: An Anthology of Writings by Italian American Women.* 1985. Syracuse, NY: Syracuse University Press, 2000.
———. *Festa: Recipes and Recollections of Italian Holidays.* New York: Harcourt, 1988.
———. *Umbertina.* 1979. New York: Feminist Press, 1999.
Batinich, Mary Ellen Mancina. "The Interaction Between Italian Immigrant Women and the Chicago Commons Settlement House, 1909–1944." *The Italian Immigrant Woman in North America.* Eds. Betty Boyd Caroli, Robert F. Harney, and Lydio F. Tomasi. Proc. of the Tenth Annual Conference of the American Italian Historical Association. Toronto: Multicultural History Society, 1978. 154–167.
Bernardi, Adria. *In the Gathering Woods.* Pittsburgh, PA: University of Pittsburgh Press, 2000.
Bevilacqua, Winifred Farrant. "Rosa: The Life of an Italian Immigrant—The Oral History Memoir of a Working-Class Woman." *Italy and Italians in America. Rivista di studi anglo-americani* 3.4–5 (1984–85): 545-55.
Bloom, Allan. *The Closing of the American Mind: How Higher Education Has Failed Democracy and Impoverished the Souls of Today's Students.* New York: Simon and Schuster, 1987.
Bona, Mary Jo. "Broken Images, Broken Lives: Carmolina's Journey in Tina De Rosa's *Paper Fish.*" *MELUS* 14. 3–4 (1987): 87–106.
———. *Claiming a Tradition: Italian American Women Writers.* Carbondale: Southern Illinois University Press, 1999.
Bryant, Dorothy. *Miss Giardino* 1978. New York: Feminist Press, 1997.
Bush, Mary. *A Place of Light.* New York: William Morrow, 1990.
Calcagno, Anne. *Pray for Yourself and Other Stories.* Evanston, IL: Northwestern University Press, 1993.
Caponegro, Mary. *The Star Café and Other Stories.* New York: Macmillan, 1990.
Cappello, Mary. *Night Bloom.* Boston: Beacon Press, 1998.
Cavaioli, Frank. "The Rise of Italian American Studies and the American Italian Historical Association." *The Italian American Review* 5.1 (1996): 1–22.
Cavallo, Diana. *A Bridge of Leaves.* 1961. Toronto: Guernica, 1997.
Ciongoli, A. Kenneth and Jay Parini, eds. *Beyond the Godfather: Italian American Writers on the Real Italian American Experience.* Fairfield, CT: University Press of New England, 1997.

Ciresi, Rita. *Sometimes I Dream in Italian*. New York: Delacorte Press, 2000.
Davis, Rebecca Harding. *Life in the Iron Mills*. New York: Feminist Press, 1972.
De Rosa, Tina. *Paper Fish*. 1980. New York: Feminist Press, 1996.
DeSalvo, Louise. *Vertigo: A Memoir*. New York: Dutton, 1996.
——— and Edvige Giunta, eds. *The Milk of Almonds: Italian American Women Writers on Food and Culture*. New York: Feminist Press, 2002.
———. "*Paper Fish* by Tina De Rosa: An Appreciation." *Voices in Italian Americana* 7.2 (1996): 249–255.
deVries, Rachel Guido. *Tender Warriors*. Ithaca: Firebrand, 1986.
Di Donato, Pietro. *Christ in Concrete*. 1937. New York: Signet, 1993.
di Prima, Diane. *Memoirs of a Beatnik*. 1969. New York: Viking, 1998.
Ermelino, Louisa. *The Black Madonna*. New York: Simon & Schuster, 2001.
———. *The Sisters Mallone: Una Storia di Famiglia*. New York: Simon & Schuster, 2002.
Ets, Marie Hall. *Rosa: The Life of an Italian Immigrant*. 1970. Madison: University of Wisconsin Press, 1999.
Fama, Maria. *Identification*. Philadelphia: Allora Press, 1996.
Fetterley, Judith. ed. *Provisions: A Reader from 19th-Century American Women*. Bloomington, IN: Indiana University Press, 1985.
Gardaphé, Fred L. *Italian Signs, American Streets: The Evolution of Italian American Narrative*. Durham, NC: Duke University Press, 1996.
Gates, Henry Louis. "Criticism in the Jungle." *Black Literature and Literary Theory*. Ed. Henry Louis Gates. New York: Methuen, 1984. 1–24.
Gilbert, Sandra M. *Blood Pressure*. New York: W. W. Norton and Company, Inc., 1988.
Gillan, Maria. *Where I Come From: Selected and New Poems*. Toronto: Guernica Editions, 1995.
Gioia, Dana. "Low Visibility: Thoughts On Italian American Writers." *Italian Americana* (Fall/Winter, 1993): 7–12.
Giunta, Edvige. Afterword. "A Song from the Ghetto." *Paper Fish* by Tina De Rosa. New York: Feminist Press, 1996. 123–157.
Graff, Gerald. *Beyond the Culture Wars: How Teaching the Conflicts Can Revitalize American Education*. New York: W. W. Norton and Company, Inc., 1992.
Guillory, John. "Canon." *Critical Terms for Literary Study*. Eds. Frank Lentricchia and Thomas McLaughlin. Chicago: University of Chicago Press, 1990. 233–249.
Harris, Wendell V. "Canonicity." *PMLA* 106 (1991): 110–121.

Hendin, Josephine Gattuso. *The Right Thing to Do.* 1988. New York: Feminist Press, 1999.
Hirsch, E. D. *Cultural Literacy: What Every American Needs to Know.* New York: Vintage Press, 1988.
Jacobs, Harriet A. *Incidents in the Life of a Slave Girl.* Ed. Jean Fagan Yellin. Cambridge: Harvard University Press, 1987.
Jewett, Sarah Orne. *The Country of the Pointed Firs and Other Stories.* New York: W. W. Norton and Company, Inc., 1988.
Lauter, *Canons and Contexts.* New York: Oxford University Press, 1991.
Lloyd, Susan Caperna. *No Pictures in My Grave: A Spiritual Journey in Sicily.* San Francisco: Mercury, 1992.
Maggio, Theresa. *Mattanza: The Ancient Sicilian Ritual of Bluefin Tuna Fishing.* New York: Penguin, 2000.
Manfredi, Renée. *Where Love Leaves Us.* Iowa City: University of Iowa Press, 1994.
Maso, Carole. *Ghost Dance.* Hopewell, NJ: Ecco, 1990.
Mazza, Chris. *Your Name Here:———.* Minneapolis, MN: Coffee House Press, 1995.
Monardo, Anna. *The Courtyard of Dreams.* New York: Doubleday, 1993.
Nardini, Gloria. *Che Bella Figura! The Power of Performance in an Italian Ladies' Club.* New York: State University of New York Press, 1999.
Parini, Jay, ed. *The Norton Book of American Autobiography.* New York: W. W. Norton and Company, Inc., 1999.
Pattee, Fred Lewis. *Century Readings for a Course in American Literature.* New York: Century Co., 1919.
Pipino, Mary Frances. *'I Have Found My Voice': The Italian-American Woman Writer.* New York: Peter Lang, 2000.
Pryse, Marjorie. "Introduction." *The Country of the Pointed Firs* by Sarah Orne Jewett. New York: W. W. Norton and Company, Inc., 1981. v–xx.
Robinson, Lillian S. "Treason Our Text: Feminist Challenges to the Literary Canon." *The New Feminist Criticism: Essays on Women, Literature, and Theory.* Ed. Elaine Showalter. New York: Pantheon, 1985. 118–134.
Romano, Rose. *Vendetta.* San Francisco: Malafemmina Press, 1990.
Rossi, Agnes. *The Quick: A Novella and Stories.* New York: W. W. Norton and Company, Inc., 1992.
Talese, Gay. "Where Are the Italian-American Novelists?" *New York Times Book Review* 14 March 1993: 1+.
Tamburri, Anthony Julian. *A Semiotic of Ethnicity: In (Re) cognition of the Italian/American Writer.* Albany: State University of New York Press, 1998.

Timpanelli, Gioia. *Sometimes The Soul: Two Novellas of Sicily*. New York: Vintage, 1998.

Tomasi, Mari. *Like Lesser Gods*. 1949. Shelburne, VT: New England Press, 1988.

Vannucci, Lynn. "An Accidental Murder." *The Voices We Carry: Recent Italian American Women's Fiction*. Ed. Mary Jo Bona. Montreal: Guernica Editions, 1994. 371–76.

Vecoli, Rudolph J. "Are Italian Americans Just White Folks?" *Italian and Italian American Images in the Media*. Eds. Mary Jo Bona and Anthony J. Tamburri. Proc. of the 27th Annual Conference of the American Italian Historical Association. Staten Island: American Italian Historical Association, 1996. 3–17. Rpt. in *Beyond the Godfather: Italian American Writers on the Real Italian American Experience*. Eds. A. Kenneth Ciongoli and Jay Parini. Hanover: University Press of New England, 1997. 311–322.

———. "Foreword." *Rosa: The Life of an Italian Immigrant*. By Marie Hall Ets. Madison: University of Wisconsin Press, 1999. v–xv.

Viscusi, Robert. "Where to Find Italian American Literature." *Italian Americana* 12.2 (Summer 1994): 267–272.

Warner, Marina. *Alone of All Her Sex: The Myth and Cult of the Virgin Mary*. New York: Vintage, 1976.

Welter, Barbara. *Dimity Convictions: The American Woman in the Nineteenth Century*. Athens, OH: Ohio University Press, 1976.

Winterson, Jeanette. *Art and Lies*. New York: Vintage Press, 1994.

Wright, Nathalia. *American Novelists in Italy: The Discoverers Allston to James*. Philadelphia: University of Pennsylvania Press, 1965.

Zagarell, Sandra A. "Narrative of Community: The Identification of a Genre." *Signs* 13.3 (1988): 498–527.

Chapter 5

Racial Politics and the Literary Reception of Zora Neale Hurston's *Their Eyes Were Watching God*

Stephen Spencer

By the time *Their Eyes Were Watching God* was published in 1937 Zora Neale Hurston had already made a name for herself, especially among intellectuals associated with the Harlem Renaissance, through the publication of folklore, stories, and articles and the recognition she had received through several awards. However, of her contemporaries, only Richard Wright and Langston Hughes seemed able to make a living from their writing. At the end of the Great Depression Wright's *Native Son*, chosen by the Book-of-the-Month Club, had sold more than three hundred thousand copies, compared to less than five thousand of *Their Eyes Were Watching God*. Although the novel was out of print by the end of the 1930s, critics from that decade into the 1970s commented occasionally on Hurston's work, especially *Their Eyes Were Watching God*, keeping alive a certain degree of awareness. However, a space in the academy for Hurston's work did not exist until feminist criticism, black aesthetics, and cultural studies emerged as important interpretive strategies. After decades of obscurity, Alice Walker "rediscovered" Hurston in the 1970s and paid homage by marking her grave in Florida and writing about her work. Robert Hemenway's *Zora Neale Hurston: A Literary Biography* followed Walker's lead in the early 1980s, and Mary Lyons's *Sorrow's Kitchen: The Life and Folklore of Zora Neale Hurston* carried Hurston's influence into the 1990s. Henry Louis Gates and K. Anthony Appiah now place Hurston as central to the canons of African American and women's literatures.

Stanley Corkin and Phyllis Frus characterize Hurston as "one of only three or four 20th-century writers who have achieved a canonical status" along with Wright, Ellison, and perhaps Morrison (193). A cursory glance at the archives of T-Amlit, electronic resources to support the *Heath Anthology of American Literature*, reveals dozens of syllabi across the United States that list *Their Eyes Were Watching God* as required reading for courses in American literature at all levels.

Hurston's position as an educated African American woman, the content of her work, and her often controversial political positions have brought the issue of Hurston's racial politics to the forefront of discussions of her work and its place in the canon of American literature. The initial reception of *Their Eyes Were Watching God* established the lines of debate that continue to characterize the responses to Hurston's work. On the one hand, critics, beginning with Richard Wright's scathing critiques in the 1930s, have condemned Hurston's work for representing racial stereotypes and ignoring the harmful effects of racism. On the other hand, critics, beginning with positive reviews in the 1930s, have praised Hurston's work for accurately reflecting folkways and promoting black self-esteem. An examination of the racial politics reflected in *Their Eyes Were Watching God* reveals a more complex understanding of race and the processes of its construction than the bifurcated responses to her work suggest and has particular implications for discussions of canonicity.

Soon after the initial publication of *Their Eyes Were Watching God* some critics and reviewers praised the novel for its realistic representation of black life. As Sterling Brown remarked in *The Nation* in 1937, Hurston's characters are "not naïve primitives" (409). They live in all-black towns, Brown argues, to escape the worst pressures of a racist society. "There," Brown writes, "is little harshness; there is enough money and work to go around" (410). In the *New Republic*, Otis Ferguson writes that *Their Eyes Were Watching God* "is absolutely free of Uncle Toms, absolutely unlimbered of the clumsy formality, defiance and apology of a Minority Cause" (276). Franz Boas, in his preface to *Mules and Men* says that Hurston effectively captures the "true inner life" of blacks for the white observer (xiii).

Many of Hurston's contemporaries involved in the Harlem Renaissance, however, including W. E. B. Du Bois, Alain Locke, Ralph Ellison, and Richard Wright, criticized her work for stereotyping and oversimplifying black life. In his review of *Their Eyes Were Watching God*, Locke makes clear his vision for black literature: "Progressive southern fiction has already banished the legend of these entertaining pseudo-primitives whom the reading public still loves to laugh with, weap [sic] over and envy" (18). Locke in his review asks when the black artist will "come to grips with motive fiction and social document fiction," and accuses Hurston of condescension and oversimplification (18). In his review, Richard Wright, Hurston's harshest critic, places *Their Eyes Were Watching God* in the tradition of minstrelsy and describes its characters as caught "in that safe and narrow orbit in which America likes to see the Negro life: between laughter and tears" (17). Hurston, Wright claims, "exploits the phase of Negro life which is 'quaint,' the phase which evokes a piteous smile on the lips of the 'superior' race" (17). Many black intellectuals in the 1930s saw the primary responsibility of the black artist to create social protest fiction that explored America's historical mistreatment of blacks, exposed racism, and changed racist attitudes in the process. Other intellectuals in the Harlem Renaissance, however, praised the folk heritage as pure, transcendent, high art, capturing the primitive essences of black culture and consecrating them for a cultured audience that included both blacks and whites. Herein lies a central contradiction in the attitudes of many black intellectuals in the 1930s to folk forms. Black intellectuals were not interested in folk forms within their natural cultural contexts, but instead were interested in placing folk forms within the safe contexts of a cosmopolitan intellectual setting. For example, spirituals were typically performed by artists such as Paul Robeson with black tie and tails, on a concert stage with only a piano and singer, to wealthy audiences, a practice which Hurston openly criticized. The Harlem literati expressed the need for a conscious art that would capture the unconscious artistry of folk art. Therefore, folklore was acceptable as art, only if removed from its folk context and examined as an aesthetic object in the ways in which other forms of high art were studied.

Hurston was caught between the exoticism of the Harlem Renaissance, represented by Langston Hughes and Claude McKay on one side, and the social protest tradition, represented by Richard Wright and Ralph Ellison, on the other. By the end of the Depression, Wright's brand of social protest had gained widespread acceptance and would come to characterize the literary history of the 1930s.

Echoing Hurston's contemporaries, who criticized Hurston for glossing over race relations, Stanley Corkin and Phyllis Frus have more recently argued that Hurston's current appeal is in part a result of her denial of the "reality of the effects of segregation . . . on most black Americans" (194). Corkin and Frus assert that Hurston, for assimilationists, "evokes a nostalgic, utopian past that does not represent a threat to the status quo" (195). Hazel Carby, in her significant essay on Hurston, refers to "Hurston's discursive displacement of contemporary social crises in her writing" (32). Hurston, Carby argues, substitutes the "social contradictions and disruption of her contemporary moment" with a utopian vision of her childhood experiences (32). Carby argues that such a nostalgic construction of the rural community essentializes negroness (32). Hurston's vision of black life, according to Carby, was a result of the "romantic" and "colonial imagination" of anthropological practices in the 1920s and 1930s (34). At the end of her essay, Carby asks if the current popularity of *Their Eyes Were Watching God* assures us that "the black folk are happy and healthy" (41). One of Carby's implicit assumptions is that any individual writer does, somehow, represent or essentialize an entire group of people. Indeed, Carby contradicts her own assumption when she writes, "Hurston's anthropological work concentrated upon the cultural 'other' that existed within the racist order of North America" (35). Hurston, Carby writes, was "concerned with the relationships between the lives and cultures that she reconstructed, and with her own search for a construction of the self" (35). Hurston, as Carby herself admits, was aware of her own cultural position and knew that the people about which she wrote did not represent all African Americans. Hurston, according to Carby's admission, was also aware that she was constructing an individual self through the character of Janie.

Indeed, Hurston's positions on race, which have often stirred controversy, add to the contradictory nature of many of the responses to her work. Despite Hurston's involvement with other black artists during the Harlem Renaissance, her position on race relations, like many of her literary and political positions, was counter to the moderate view of the NAACP and black intellectuals during the 1920s. James Weldon Johnson, in his "Negro Americans, What Now?", argued that the struggle for equality through integration, not segregation or nationalism, is the most certain path to racial justice. Many black intellectuals of the Harlem Renaissance wanted a literature that reflected bourgeois aspirations to overcome racist obstacles. Alain Locke believed that the young black writers would speak for the as yet inarticulate masses, interpreting their race for the world. The hope was that this "talented tenth" would become the intellectual and political leaders for black culture.

Hurston often criticized affirmative action programs and efforts to desegregate American life. She supported the presidential bid of Robert Taft in 1952 and criticized the Supreme Court's decision on *Brown v. Board of Education*. Concerning the Court decision, Hurston said: "The whole matter revolves around the self-respect of my people. How much satisfaction can I get from a court order for somebody to associate with me who does not wish me near them? . . . I regard the ruling of the United States Supreme Court as insulting rather than honoring my race" (Wright et al. 58). Hurston knew that the black folk represented in her work did not need the sanction of white culture to affirm their worth. However, the reality of life during the Harlem Renaissance placed black artists in a double bind: white patrons and audiences provided a paying audience for their work, but at the same time accepted a particular view of black life. This dilemma was a central conflict for black artists during the 1920s. To the literati of the Harlem Renaissance, culture meant high culture. Their expressed aim was to uplift the race by exposing blacks, and whites as well, to great black art that would prove to be as good, as aesthetically demanding, as white art. Attempts by artists of the Harlem Renaissance, including those of Hurston, to affirm African origins, folklore, and slave histories were often met with charges of regression, nostalgia, or primitivism. Despite the resistance to turn to African origins and a slave past for themes, during the Harlem Renaissance much literature was nonetheless explicitly about race, more specifically the construction of blackness as a racial identity. Alain Locke's *The New Negro* sought to consciously define and affirm a black identity. Race was an important concern for writers such as Wallace Thurman in *The Blacker the Berry*, Jessie Fauset in *Plum Bun* and *The Chinaberry Tree*, and Nella Larsen in *Quicksand* and *Passing*. The essential conflict of African American intellectuals of the Harlem Renaissance, as Michael Awkward has noted, is the conflict over whether to emphasize likeness or difference, Americanness or blackness.

Although critics have characterized *Their Eyes Were Watching God* as representing either side of this conflict, a closer examination of the novel suggests a more complex understanding of race and the processes of its construction. For the first years of her life, Janie is raised in a white home and she herself is racially mixed. Later in the novel direct confrontation comes when Janie and Tea Cake are denied space on the bridge and when Tea Cake and other men are forced to divide and bury victims of the hurricane according to the victims' race. Even though many of the bodies are so badly decomposing that determining race is difficult, the authorities insist that the victims still be divided by race. The storm dissolves one boundary after another, male/female, young/old, rich/poor, natural/man-made, human/animal, living/dead, forcing diverse groups into contact with one another. In the midst of the storm, however, whites attempt to maintain the boundary between black and white by seizing the safety of the bridge at Six Mile Bend and after the storm insisting on separating the corpses of victims by race. During her trial for killing Tea Cake, Janie faces an all white jury and the black community sits in the balconies observing, and, at times, disturbing the court proceedings. These incidents, which some critics have viewed as isolated examples of racial injustice, are part of a complex pattern that was being established all along in the novel.

Throughout the novel Janie's contact with white culture reveals Hurston's sophisticated understanding of racial construction in American culture. From the beginning of *Their Eyes Were*

Watching God, blacks and whites are defined in opposition to each other. Janie had been raised by her grandmother who lived with "quality white folks," with whose children she played. When a man sells the family a photograph of all the children, including Janie, she does not see herself, but only "a real dark little girl with long hair" (Hurston 9). "'Ah'm colored!'" she exclaims, realizing for the first time at six years old that she is not white. At that moment, Janie becomes "colored," or raced, while whiteness remains colorless or non-raced. Later in the novel Mrs. Turner takes this sense of difference to its extreme. Her pointed nose, thin lips, and other physical features "to her way of thinking . . . set her aside from negroes" (134). When she comes to visit Janie she says, "Ah ain't useter 'ssociatin' wid black folks," and "Ah jus' couldn't see mahself married to no black man. It's too many black folks already. We oughta lighten up de race" (134–35). "Ah can't stand black niggers," Mrs. Turner continues, "Ah don't blame de white folks from hatin' 'em 'cause Ah can't stand 'em mahself. 'Nother thing, Ah hates tuh see folks lak me and you mixed up wid 'em. Us oughta class off" (135). Mrs. Turner stereotypes blacks as always laughing, singing, and "'cuttin' de monkey for white folks'" (135). She thinks the black folks are holding people like her back and creating the race problem themselves. However, in her mind the race problem is not a result of racism, oppression, or poverty, but simply of "de color and de features" (135). In contrast to other blacks in her community, Mrs. Turner says she has "white folks' features" and should not be classed with all the other black folks (136). "Mrs Turner," the narrator says, "built an altar to the unattainable—Caucasian characteristics for all," an altar she defended with fanaticism (139). Janie sees that in Mrs. Turner's mind, anyone who looks more white than she is justified in mistreating her, just as she is justified in mistreating anyone less white than she.

In their interactions with people "more white" than Mrs. Turner, Tea Cake and Janie suffer the real consequences of a system based on race. After the hurricane Tea Cake is forced at gunpoint to gather bodies and bury them in segregated cemeteries. The white men with rifles order the workers to carefully check the bodies to determine if they are black or white. Whites get coffins while blacks get dumped indiscriminately in mass graves.

When the men cannot identify the decomposing bodies as black or white, the overseers of the operation tell them to check their hair when they cannot tell any other way. "And don't lemme ketch none uh y'all dumpin' white folks," the men say, "and don't be wastin' no boxes on colored" (163). Clearly Tea Cake has experienced this kind of treatment before, telling Janie that "'each and every white man think he know all de GOOD darkies already'" (164). Janie learns these same lessons when she faces the white judge and jury for killing Tea Cake. Janie notices the men on the jury are well-fed and well-dressed, not "poor white folks" (176). When blacks in the back of the courtroom raise their voices, the prosecutor says, "'We are handling this case. Another word out of *you*, out of any of you niggers back there, and I'll bind you over to the big court'" (178). The white women in the courtroom applaud the prosecutor's words and later cry and stand around Janie "like a protecting wall" between her and the other blacks (179). Black men at the boarding house where Janie is staying say that no white men are going to convict a woman that looks like her and that as long as she doesn't commit a crime against a white man, "'she kin kill jus' as many niggers as she please'" (179). Janie's light skin prompts the white women to protect her, while Tea Cake's blackness justifies the verdict. Janie provides a protected zone between whites and blacks. Tea Cake's attention to Janie diverts, symbolically, his attention from white women, and in killing Tea Cake, Janie has protected the white women from their worst fear: rape by an animalistic black man.

Priscilla Wald has recognized Du Bois's idea of "double-consciousness" in *Their Eyes Were Watching God*, but Hurston, Wald argues, unlike Du Bois, fails to recognize its subversive potential as a political strategy. Defining "blackness" in terms of "whiteness," according to Wald, authorizes dominant discourse. For Wald, Hurston's discourse assigns African Americans to the margins but explores the indeterminate nature of racial identities. Hurston, Wald asserts, uses an African American language that redefines the representation of identity itself, upsetting the "dualisms of the dominant discourse" (87). Rather than essential, blackness for Hurston becomes experiential, and she "redesignates 'color' as performance in a process that draws her readers into the dynamics of 'coloration'" (Wald 87). Hemenway agrees when he says the tension between Hurston's educational experience, Eatonville, and Harlem is complicated by gender, race, and nationality, "that whole complex of ambiguous identifications American culture imposes on its members" ("Zora Neale Hurston and the Eatonville Anthropology" 199). *Their Eyes Were Watching God*, like *Mules and Men*, is in many ways a trickster tale, full of linguistic play, like the folktales upon which Hurston draws. The novel's complexity accurately reflects the multilayered and contradictory nature of racial construction in American culture.

Unlike writers like Wright, Hurston's social protest is more subtle. Hurston does not simply resist the dualistic construction of racial identities, nor does she reify an individual or group identity, but re-constructs identity through the complexity of experience. Janie in the end concludes, "You got tuh *go* there tuh *know* there." Robert Hemenway agrees when he identifies the single theme of her work as immediate experience taking "precedence over analysis, emotion over reason, the self over society, the personal over the theoretical" ("Zora Neale Hurston and the Eatonville Anthropology" 208). Read in this way, Hurston's choice to portray Janie as a Mulatto, one who is both "black" and "white," is fitting. Janie's movement, then, can be seen as a movement from binarism to plurality, from essentialism to relativism. In the beginning of the novel, her identity is defined in opposition to whiteness, when she acknowledges, "Ah'm colored!" Later both Joe Starks and Mrs. Turner see Janie's lightness as a mark of status, setting her apart from other blacks. However, in the end Janie has moved to a subject position, able to define her identity through her experience, not through the eyes of others. In the end, Janie defies simple categorization: she is both dark and light, woman (in references to her hair and beauty) and man (her dirty overalls, her handling of a gun), rich (she owns property and has money in the bank), and poor (she has worked on the muck and lived in migrant shacks). Finally, she is able to tell her own story to Phoeby; Phoeby, the community, and the readers, can do what they want with it. Janie becomes the ultimate cultural relativist, resisting easy categorization. This view of Janie reflects Hurston's expressed view of racial categorization. "'I found,'" Hurston stated, "'that I had no need of either class or race prejudice, those scourges of humanity. The solace of easy generalization was taken from me, but I received the richer gift of individualism. . . . So Race Pride and Race Consciousness seem to me to be not only fallacious, but a thing to be abhorred'" (qtd. in Wright et al. 64).

Rather than essential, blackness for Hurston becomes experiential, and she, according to Priscilla Wald, "redesignates 'color' as performance in a process that draws her readers into the dynamics of 'coloration'" (87). Hemenway agrees when he says the tension between Hurston's educational experience, Eatonville, and Harlem is complicated by gender, race, and nationality, "that whole complex of ambiguous identifications American culture imposes on its members" ("Zora Neale Hurston" 199).

In response to her contemporaries, Hurston redefines blackness through African American folk culture, not in the romanticism of popular fiction or the realism of social protest. Hurston, in Hemenway's analysis, spent her career focussing on the blacks at the bottom who found racial liberation, not in the terms of white domination, but in the beauty and wisdom of their own culture. Black people became free, not by acting white like Joe Starks, but by developing and affirming their own cultural institutions. Alice Walker, in her introduction to Hemenway's *A Literary Biography*, says the most characteristic quality of Hurston's works is "racial health—a sense of black people as complete, complex, *undiminished* human beings" (xii). As Hurston was rediscovered in the 1970s many critics, like Annette Trefzer, recognized *Their Eyes Were Watching God* as an affirmation of black identity. June Jordan praised Hurston's work as representing a world of "a total black reality" in which blacks represent "their own, particular selves in a Family/Community setting . . . that fosters the natural, person-postures of courting, jealousy, ambition, dream, sex, work, partying, sorrow, bitterness, celebration, and fellowship" (6). Jordan goes on to call *Their Eyes Were Watching God* an "exemplary novel of Blacklove" (7). Hurston's attempts to distinguish black culture from white forecast sociological and critical efforts to do so later, efforts to define a black aesthetic and to delineate cultural traits that are distinctly African American, what

Hemenway calls "Afro-American cultural domains" (*A Literary Biography* 331). She decenters visions of the black, the national, and the southern community as totalizing concepts. The central theme of Hurston's work is that "material poverty is not tantamount to spiritual poverty or experiential deprivation" (Wall, *Women* 140). In response to a culture that defines whiteness as an asset and blessing and blackness as a liability and a curse, Hurston's Janie simply asserts her own definition of self. Hurston calls attention to the fact that identity is an act of continual production. Janie's identity, like all selves, must be wed to contexts of history and community.

Although critics in the 1950s, 1960s, and 1970s commented occasionally on Hurston's work, especially *Their Eyes Were Watching God*, not until feminist and cultural criticism emerged as important interpretive strategies in the academy, did a space exist for the study of Hurston's work. Like feminist critics and writers, scholars established black studies programs in colleges and universities. Just as feminism in the 1960s and 1970s gained ground in the worlds of academe and literary criticism, so black critics and writers worked to change the canon in other ways. The critics Houston A. Baker, Jr., Henry Louis Gates, Jr., and Addison Gayle, Jr., would articulate a new Black Aesthetic that placed the sources of contemporary black literature and culture in the communal music and oral folk tradition. Baker's *Blues, Ideology, and Afro-American Literature: A Vernacular Theory*, for example, explored the ways tales, songs, oratory, sermons, blues, and jazz made black culture in America distinctive. Thus, texts like Zora Neale Hurston's *Mules and Men* exploring the folk culture of rural Florida would become important. At the same time the critics Barbara Christian, Gloria Hull, Barbara Smith, and Mary Helen Washington and the writers Toni Cade Bambara, Audre Lorde, and Alice Walker would shape a distinctive black feminism, making a place for writers like Zora Neale Hurston, whose rediscovery was initiated by Alice Walker. The efforts to establish such programs paved the way for similar ethnic studies programs and the revision of the canon.

Now that *Their Eyes Were Watching God* has assured Hurston's status in the canon, how can scholars interrogate the novel in the context of the canonicity it has achieved? What does its canonicity reveal about current assumptions about multiethnic literature in general and race, gender, and power in particular? What does the status of *Their Eyes Were Watching God* reveal about the directions that discussions of canonicity and multiethnic literature are taking?

The canonical success of *Their Eyes Were Watching God* suggests that Hurston's work anticipated the direction canonicity and multiethnic literature have taken. Hurston's work moved beyond prevailing theories of identity construction in the twentieth century into what Mikhail Bakhtin and Robert Young call "hybridity," what postcolonial theorist Homi Bhabha calls "the third space," what gender studies calls "the space-in-between," and what Chicano/a scholars and writers Virgilio Elizondo and Gloria Anzaldúa call "mestizo/a" and "borderlands." Such attempts to mix, blur, and cross are certainly not a recent phenomenon. In his thorough history and analysis of the origin and development of the concept of hybridity, Robert Young argues that many English writers of the present and past have written "almost obsessively about the uncertain crossing and invasion of identities," whether of class, gender, culture, or race, to such an extent that we might say such crossing is "the dominant *motif* of much English fiction" (2–3). This obsession, Young claims, has always existed because attempts to identify the essentialness of Englishness have never been successful. Young's analysis applies equally to definitions of Americanness, which were rooted in Anglophile conceptions of identity as the idea of America as a nation formed. Attempts to essentialize an American identity have never been successful, because it was never really possible. Ethnically mixed writers and writers excluded from the mainstream definitions of Americanness have always known this.

Some critics argue that attempts at hybridity, border crossing, and cultural relativism inevitably run the risk of reinforcing the very lines they seek to blur or redefine. Gerry Smyth argues that "hybridity is hegemonically recuperable, easily absorbed by those with an interest in denying the validity of a coherent discourse of resistance"(43). Smyth argues that hybridity, despite its claims for resistance and redefinition of border, could instead reinforce the stereotypical assumptions which created the very borders it seeks to blur. The danger, for Smyth, is that hybridity may be "re-absorbed into disabling neo-colonialist narratives" (52). Hybridity, for Smyth, denies the ability of the other to rationalize his or her position, and thus undermines resistance. He concludes his argument by suggesting that a politics organized around border crossing denies the most powerful form of resistance: silence. Postcolonial criticism, according to Young, has also reinforced the very categories it seeks to resist by constructing two antithetical groups, with the second group depending for its existence on the first group, which was an artificial construction in the first place. Multiculturalism, Young argues, has done the same thing by encouraging different groups to "reify their individual and different identities at their most different" (5).

Hurston does not really seem to care if her discourse will be "re-absorbed into disabling neo-colonialist narratives" or reify difference. But she certainly cares about speaking. Institutionally organized power does all it can to silence; therefore, Hurston is actively resisting. Silence could also be interpreted as concession rather than resistance. Isn't silence what the oppressor wants? It is certainly what Joe Starks demands, and it is what the white court commands at the end of *Their Eyes Were Watching God*. Janie's rendition of her own story is then a significant act of resistance *and* redefinition. It resists essentialism and dismantles race as inherent and self-evident, revealing it as a construct and means of oppression. It redefines the borders of race and gender through Janie's self-definition. Hurston replaces essentializing categories of difference with a new model that reflects the current, and I would argue the next, moment in multiethnic theory. Hurston expresses hybridity, a third space, a borderland through both sex (Janie as literal racial hybrid) and language (the blending of male/female language, standard English/dialect, formal prose/folklore). Thus, Zora Neale Hurston is a writer who reflects the current moment of literary history. Hurston, a black woman drawing consciously on a folk tradition in her work, presents a vision of American life that can be read with and against evolving notions of race, gender, and power in American culture.

Works Cited

Anzaldúa, Gloria. *Borderlands/La Frontera: The New Mestiza*. San Francisco: Aunt Lute Books, 1987.

Awkward, Michael, ed. *New Essays on Their Eyes Were Watching God*. New York: Cambridge, 1990.

Baker, Houston. *Blues, Ideology, and Afro-American Literature: A Vernacular Theory*. Chicago: University of Chicago, 1984.

Bakhtin, Mikhail. *The Dialogic Imagination: Four Essays by M. M. Bakhtin*. Trans. Caryl Emerson and Michael Holquist. Austin, TX: University of Texas Press, 1994.

Benesch, Klaus. "Oral Narrative and Literary Text: Afro-American Folklore in *Their Eyes Were Watching God*." *Callaloo* 11 (1988): 627–635.

Bhabha, Homi K. *The Location of Culture*. London: Lawrence and Winhart, 1990.

Boas, Franz. "Introduction." *Mules and Men*. By Zora Neale Hurston. New York: Trubner, 1936.

Brown, Sterling A. "Luck Is a Fortune." *The Nation* 145 (1937): 409–410.

Carby, Hazel. "The Politics of Fiction, Anthropology, and the Folk: Zora Neale Hurston." *History and Memory in African-American Culture*. Eds. Genevieve Fabre and Robert O'Meally. New York: Oxford University Press, 1994. 28–44.

Corkin, Stanley, and Phyllis Frus. "An Ex-centric Approach to American Cultural Studies: The Interesting Case of Zora Neale Hurston as a Noncanonical Writer." *Prospects Volume 21: An Annual of American Cultural Studies*. Ed. Jack Salzman. New York: Cambridge University Press, 1996. 193–228.

Elizondo, Virgilio. *The Future is Mestizo: Life Where Cultures Meet*. Boulder, CO: University Press of Colorado, 2000.

Fauset, Jessie. *Plum Bun*. New York: Frederick A. Stokes, 1929.

———. *The Chinaberry Tree*. London: Mathews and Marrott, 1932.

Ferguson, Otis. "You Can't Hear Their Voices." *Critical Essays on Zora Neale Hurston*. Ed. Gloria L. Cronin. New York: G. K. Hall, 1998. 77–79.

Gates, Henry Louis, Jr., and K. A. Appiah, eds. *Zora Neale Hurston: Critical Perspectives Past and Present*. New York: Amistad, 1993.

Gates, Henry Louis, Jr. "Zora Neale Hurston: 'A Negro Way of Saying.'" *Mules and Men*. New York: Harper, 1990. 287–297.

Harrison, Beth. "Zora Neale Hurston and Mary Austin: A Case Study in Ethnography, Literary Modernism, and Contemporary Ethnic Fiction." *MELUS* 21.2 (Summer 1996): 89–106.

Hemenway, Robert E. "Zora Neale Hurston and the Eatonville Anthropology." *The Harlem Renaissance Remembered*. Eds. Langston Hughes and Arna Bontemps. New York: Dodd Mead, 1972. 190–214.

———. *Zora Neale Hurston: A Literary Biography*. Chicago: University of Illinois Press, 1977.

Hurst, Fannie. "Introduction." *Jonah's Gourd Vine*. By Zora Neale Hurston. New York: Lippincott, 1934.

Hurston, Zora Neale. *Mules and Men*. 1935. New York: Perennial Classics, 1990.

———. *Their Eyes Were Watching God*. 1937. New York: Perennial Classics, 1998.

Johnson, James Weldon. *Negro Americans, What Now?* New York: Viking, 1934.

Jordan, June. *Black World*. New York: Johnson Publishing, 1974.

Larsen, Nella. *Quicksand* and *Passing*. New Brunswick, NJ: Rutgers University Press, 1986.

Locke, Alain. "Their Eyes Were Watching God." *Zora Neale Hurston: Critical Perspectives Past and Present*. Eds. Henry Louis Gates Jr. and K. A. Appiah. New York: Amistad, 1993.

———. *The New Negro*. New York: A. and C. Boni, 1925.

Lyons, Mary E. *Sorrow's Kitchen: The Life and Folklore of Zora Neale Hurston*. New York: Scribner's, 1990.

Smyth, Gerry. "The Politics of Hybridity: Some Problems with Crossing the Border." *Comparing Postcolonial Literatures: Dislocations*. Eds. Ashok Bery and Patricia Murray. New York: St. Martin's, 2000. 43–55.

Thurman, Wallace. *The Blacker the Berry*. New York: Macaulay Company, 1929.

Trefzer, Annette. "'Let us all be Kissing-Friends?': Zora Neale Hurston and Race Politics in Dixie." *Journal of American Studies* 31(1997): 69–78.

Wald, Priscilla. "Becoming 'Colored': The Self-Authorized Language of Difference in Zora Neale Hurston." *American Literary History* 2 (1990): 79–100.

Walker, Alice. *In Search of Our Mother's Gardens*. New York: Harcourt, 1983.

Wall, Cheryl. "Zora Neale Hurston: Changing Her Own Words." *American Novelists Revisited: Essays in Feminist Criticism*. Ed. Fritz Fleischmann. New York: Hall, 1982. 371–393.

———. *Women of the Harlem Renaissance*. Bloomington, IN: Indiana University Press, 1995.

Wright, Richard. "Their Eyes Were Watching God." *Zora Neale Hurston: Critical Perspectives Past and Present*. Eds. Henry Louis Gates Jr. and K. A. Appiah. New York: Amistad, 1993. 16–17.
Young, Robert J. C. *Colonial Desire: Hybridity in Theory, Culture and Race*. London: Routledge, 1995.

Chapter 6

De-Centering the Canon

Understanding *The Great Gatsby* as an Ethnic Novel

Joe Kraus

I

Few books are as central to the American literary canon as *The Great Gatsby*. It is one of a handful of novels that students still read in wide numbers while they are in high school, and it remains a work that receives widespread critical attention in scholarly journals and in graduate studies. The idea that it might stand as an ethnic novel, as a work that reflects the tensions that racial, national, or ethnic minorities feel as they contemplate their place in a larger American context, might therefore surprise many. That is because, as critics of ethnic literature can attest, the term "ethnic novel" often carries the connotation that a text is peripheral to the literary mainstream and, generally, that it is a minor work as well. I argue that *Gatsby* is very much concerned with questions of ethnicity, however, and that fact matters for two reasons. First, putting the novel in such a light brings into relief its representations of immigrant crime and jingoism and puts it into conversation with a range of other literature, much of it ethnic. Second, proposing *Gatsby* as ethnic reemphasizes the idea that much of canonical American literature—however we define the canon—is centrally concerned with categories of social difference. As a result, such an approach to *Gatsby* can become a template for a larger approach to American literature. The questions it raises about how characters move from outside a variously defined

America to inside it go beyond the fiction we call ethnic and into the heart of many versions of American literary history.

When I read and teach *Gatsby*, I am always haunted by the figure of Meyer Wolfshiem. He is, for the narrator Nick Carraway, an emblematic ethnic, someone who is so foreign that he cannot be a part of America as Nick understands it. As Nick describes his first impression: "A small flat-nosed Jew raised his large head and regarded me with two fine growths of hair which luxuriated in either nostril. After a moment I discovered his tiny eyes in the half darkness" (Fitzgerald 73–74). It's a dehumanizing description; Wolfshiem—as the first syllable of his name asserts—seems as much an animal as he is a man, someone who is unfit for the "civilized" world that Nick knows from his midwestern boyhood and that he expects to find in New York. Above all, though, the description jumps out for me because of the blatant way it labels Wolfshiem a "Jew." Whatever else Nick sees, he understands Wolfshiem as outside society because he is other, not just culturally but racially. Such a Jew, as Nick believes early in the novel, cannot be a part of the real America. He lacks even the provisional whiteness—in Matthew Frye Jacobson's terminology—that Nick and others descended from the "free white" people of America's Founding Fathers extend to many European ethnics. He is outside the bounds of assimilability, and he is therefore someone whom Nick feels he can ignore.

As the novel unfolds, Nick more or less sticks to his insistence that Wolfshiem is entirely outside the world of his concern—keep in mind that Nick is a notoriously unreliable narrator—but the force of circumstance makes it increasingly clear that this Jew is one of the key powers in the novel's vision of modern America. Wolfshiem is a gangster, and he has discovered a variety of ways to prey on society's institutions and social contracts. He makes money from bootlegging, from the sale of stolen bonds, and through various forms of gambling. He has, most notoriously, perpetrated one of the stunning crimes of the young century: fixing the 1919 World Series. In addition, he has accumulated a vast series of "gonnegtions" that insulate him from police investigation and prosecution. He is, in fact, one of the most powerful men in New York, a kingpin in an underworld economy that services many of the political and business leaders of the country. Nick, reluctant to move beyond his initial essentialized understanding of the man, never allows himself to acknowledge that Wolfshiem is more central to the economy of the Eastern elite than he himself can ever hope to be. Nick still wants to believe that the World Series scandal "merely *happened*," that it was "the end of some inevitable chain" (78); he cannot accept that a man like Wolfshiem would have the power to pull strings that can move America itself.

The most immediate truth about Wolfshiem that Nick tries to ignore, however, is that Gatsby owes his wealth—and therefore his ability to reinvent himself—to the gangster's assorted enterprises. Nick wants to see Gatsby as a creature of the ether—he refers to him at one point as someone who "sprang from his Platonic conception of himself" (104)—and so he pays little attention (or simply denies) the material circumstances of Gatsby's self-reinvention. As we learn later, Gatsby was a starving and friendless World War I veteran when he first met Wolfshiem at a pool hall. Wolfshiem recognized immediately that Gatsby, a "fine appearing gentlemanly young man" (179), would be a perfect agent for operations that required moving in social circles closed to him as a Jew. As he boasts, one of the first things he does is to get Gatsby to join the American Legion, at the time a notoriously anti-immigrant organization.[1] Caught up in the glamour of Gatsby's dream, Nick never permits himself to see the degree to which Wolfshiem's "gonnegtions" make Gatsby's rise possible. He refuses to open his eyes to what becomes clear from the snatches of conversation and phone messages that he overhears: Gatsby is effective as a criminal operative because he presents a white face and an unaccented voice for a gang of inner-city immigrant ethnics.

Gatsby's role as an emissary from Wolfshiem to the 'respectable' America that is closed to Jews is particularly ironic given that he eventually calls on Nick to be his own representative to a world he himself cannot enter. That world, the old-money enclave of Daisy and Tom Buchanan, is built even more fundamentally than the American Legion on the principle of exclusion. Because Nick is of that world himself—he is Daisy's cousin, and he attended Yale with Tom—he can help Gatsby get a foothold in it, giving Gatsby the chance to win back Daisy's love. In gratitude,

Gatsby invites him to come to work for him, presumably handling the sale of stolen securities. "You wouldn't have to do any business with Wolfshiem" (88), he promises Nick, implying that he's aware it would be a comedown for someone of Nick's background to be associated with a character so outside legitimate society. Nick bristles at the offer—although he acknowledges it might have tempted him if it had come under less crass circumstances—but he again overlooks the way in which his implicit sense of social order has turned on its head. Where he once felt that he could ignore Wolfshiem altogether, he finds himself tempted by the wealth the man could make possible for him. He may not like it, but he knows that he is connected to the Jew through the very market forces that he unenthusiastically pursues in his erstwhile job as a stockbroker.

In that light, Nick and Gatsby have this in common: they are men in-between. Each has uprooted himself from the Midwest and entered an East Coast context where identity is comparatively fluid. In changing his name from Gatz to Gatsby, Gatsby has effectively erased his German or Slavic ethnicity in favor of something he regards as more American. At the same time, he has risen dramatically in class, using his youth and white skin as capital in his dealings with Dan Cody and then with Wolfshiem. Nick's change in identity is far less dramatic, but he does present it as a speculative risk. By leaving his midwestern city, he severs his connection to the Scots-Irish forebears who built the family fortune, and he takes a step downward in class—only temporarily, he trusts—in hopes of making his own original fortune. He does so with a sense that he is echoing the pioneering spirit of westward expansion. However, he has gone East to establish himself on his own terms, feeling himself nonetheless a "pathfinder, an original settler" (8). That is, he sees himself as James Fenimore Cooper's Hawkeye even though he is heading into the city rather than the wilderness. There is clearly a measure of irony in that self-identification, but the fact remains that he sees himself as a pioneer in some light.

Nick uses such parallel reinventions—Nick at least tries to see himself as parallel to Gatsby—to imply the illusion of an American platform on which anyone with talent and the sufficiently proper background can be successful. Nick the writer, a man reflecting on his experiences out East as the narrator of the novel, recognizes that platform as an illusion. Nick the character, however, a young man who has gone East because he believes in that fiction, finds himself swept up in it. That younger Nick believes that he could become a competent stockbroker if he cared enough to try, and he believes that he can establish an identity for himself independent of what his family has done. He celebrates Gatsby for having done so already and, while he finds the parties excessive and in poor taste, he keeps returning to them, drawn, it seems, by their carnivalesque promise that anyone can be anything he or she chooses so long as the music is playing. He sees himself and Gatsby as examples of individuals out to make something of themselves in the face of settled and established privilege. As he declares at one point, he felt a "scornful solidarity between Gatsby and me against them all" (173).

Even the young Nick understands that there are boundaries to such self-reinvention, however. As he and Gatsby drive to Manhattan together, they encounter a succession of characters who may aspire to the same wealth and standing as they do, but each is clearly denied that opportunity by virtue of a race written as plainly on them as on Wolfshiem. The two first speed by an Italian funeral, and Nick notes, condescendingly, "the tragic eyes and short upper lips of south-eastern Europe" (73), and he is glad that his and Gatsby's passing gives an element of splendor to their sad occasion. Immediately thereafter, they pass a limousine chauffeured by a white driver and bearing, "three modish Negroes, two bucks and a girl" (73). Nick laughs out loud at what he sees as the "haughty rivalry" of the other riders. He knows that their black skin and cartoonishly large eyes mark them as people who can have no real hope of assuming the power and standing that he and Gatsby want. Such people can play at reinventing themselves all they like, Nick seems to declare, but there is no way they can hope to overcome the circumstances of their birth and race. Put in racial terms, Italians and African Americans do not count; there is no reason to pay any attention to them.[2]

In one of the novel's many subtle ironies, however, they pass by that succession of alien faces as they make their way to the 42nd Street Cellar where Nick meets Wolfshiem for the first time.[3] Wolfshiem then strikes Nick as yet another such face, yet someone else whose outsider-ness is written into his ethnicity. Nick is so unprepared for Wolfshiem's power and his role in Gatsby's career that he takes him for a dentist rather than recognizing him as Gatsby's superior. It is only from his perspective as narrator, and even then he refuses fully to acknowledge the fact, that Nick recognizes the extent of Wolfshiem's power and influence. Without Wolfshiem, there would be no Gatsby. Without that racially other Jew, Gatsby would be a struggling young man rather than the embodiment of American potential and fulfillment.

In that light, Wolfshiem is—to paraphrase Wilson Neate—an "unwelcome remainder" reminding Nick that Gatsby's unsavory route to self-reinvention required dealing with elements foreign to the America Nick claims to seek. Nick very much wants to see Gatsby as "a son of God" (104), and Wolfshiem's shadow makes that illusion difficult to hold. Wolfshiem is a constant in a world that promises change. His racial otherness is too profound to imagine that it could melt away or become irrelevant, as do Gatsby and Nick's class status. In his own person, Wolfshiem challenges Nick's fundamental notion of America. Success is not necessarily the product of great personal powers; instead, it is rooted in the connections that a person can establish and exploit. Wolfshiem does not need to enter into the America that is closed to him; he can remain outside it and, through Gatsby, manipulate it as he sees fit.

In another parallel, Nick's own most influential connection, Tom Buchanan, is also unassimilable. With his obsession over the purity of the "Nordic race," Tom refuses to have any part in the speculative world that makes Gatsby possible and that so fires Nick's imagination. He is fueled by his reading of Goddard, a clear fictional stand-in for Lathrop Stoddard, a sociologist/historian of the 1920s who popularized the notion that widespread immigration and disparate birth rates threatened the supremacy of "the white race" (17). Where Wolfshiem stood below the social order as someone denied admission to a world that might have drawn him, Tom stands above it. He could join the American Legion if he chose; he could take part in almost any business or social venture that interested him. He chooses to segregate himself, however. He understands that he is part of an exclusive set, and believing his privilege under siege from "the Coloured Empires," he withdraws from the hubbub that Nick desperately wants to see as the true America of the pioneers. He throws his own parties—both with Myrtle and in a stiff drawing room—but he does so on his own terms. Where Wolfshiem is barred from participating in the latter-day pioneering experience of self-reinvention, Tom refuses to do so.

Both men, then, are constants. Together, Tom and Wolfshiem represent the extremes of the spectrum of American identity, a spectrum that Nick and Gatsby have thrown themselves into the middle of so vigorously. Tom and Wolfshiem recognize the carnival that makes a Gatsby possible, but neither participates, and each milks his power and connections to continue making the sorts of fortunes that will always elude Nick. Each stands outside the middle ground of the novel—one by his own choice and one as the result of discrimination—and each uses powerful connections to do more than any lone pioneer could ever accomplish for himself.

II

As such, Tom and Wolfshiem are more than just parallel figures. They are, as the novel makes clear, representative of the hard fact of social categories against which Gatsby's dream and Nick's aspirations shatter. I call *The Great Gatsby* an "ethnic novel" because it so emphatically asks the question of who can claim status as an American. It asks that question, for the most part, from the perspective of the ensconced who are exploring the boundaries of their privilege rather than from the outsider-immigrant perspective of most of what we term "ethnic literature," but it remains the same fundamental question despite the shift in perspective. While the young Nick has an ambitious sense of what America makes possible in terms of self-reinvention, the Nick who narrates the novel recognizes his own naïveté. He sees what has become of Gatsby's resolve after Tom uses Gatsby's association with Wolfshiem to taint him permanently in Daisy's eyes. He recognizes that the idea of his own playing at being a pioneer is little more than a fantasy. No one is a "son of God"; everyone's opportunities are circumscribed by the circumstances of his or her birth and culture. The time of the pioneer is over. The major events of America do not "merely *happen*"; men like Tom and Wolfshiem make them happen through the machinery of connections and established wealth.

The connection between those two powerful men is clearer since Nick paints each as so extreme in his identification with a specific social group. As Thomas H. Pauly argues, Wolfshiem is all the more apparently a deliberate ethnic caricature in the context of his contrast with Arnold Rothstein, a clear historical basis for his character. Rothstein was recognized at the time of the novel's publication as the man who had fixed the World Series, and most readers would likely have made that association.[4] If that connection weren't strong enough, Fitzgerald wrote in a 1937 letter that he had actually once met Rothstein and taken the encounter as part of his inspiration for writing *Gatsby*. As he put it: "In *Gatsby* I selected the stuff to fit a given mood or 'hauntedness' or whatever you might call it, rejecting in advance in *Gatsby*, for instance, all of the ordinary material for Long Island, big crooks, adultery theme and always starting from the *small* focal point that interested me—my meeting with Arnold Rothstein for instance" (*Letters* 551). In other words, he found in his encounter with Rothstein a face for the sort of things the naïve Nick thought of as merely happening without any apparent author.

While there is no other record of Fitzgerald's meeting Rothstein, it's likely that the bulk of what he knew of the man came through the media rather than through anything he learned first hand. As he puts it in the letter, what he seems to have gathered from that encounter was an idea of "focus," an idea that it would be dramatically effective to have a single character serve as the face for criminal and economic forces large enough to shape America. He cannot have discussed criminal operations with Rothstein; what sort of criminal would reveal anything of his operations to a stranger, particularly to a stranger who is a well-known writer? Instead, he seems to have taken from the encounter only a sense of what it was like to be with someone so powerfully connected that he could single-handedly "play with the faith of fifty million people" (78). Meeting Rothstein inspired him because it brought him face-to-face with a man who, alone in his person, could represent an entire powerful subcommunity.

Despite so clearly leaning on Rothstein as a historical model, though, Fitzgerald gives Wolfshiem none of the gangster's personal graces. By all accounts, Rothstein was dapper and debonair. To someone with the careful social distinctions of Fitzgerald, he may well have appeared as a mere upper-class poseur, but to most observers he was an epitome of style. His father was a well-to-do figure in the tailoring industry, and Rothstein grew up in comfort and relative luxury. He had little to no accent, and he was almost as far removed as possible from the extreme racial/ethnic Jew of Wolfshiem. In other words, Fitzgerald made a clear decision to make his version of the gangster mastermind a much more ethnically charged figure than was true historically. As Thomas H. Pauly puts it, "Rothstein's skills at engineering social mobility so far surpassed those of Gatsby that he would have had no need for him" (230). That is, Rothstein is a model for both Gatsby and Wolfshiem. Gatsby is the socially mobile half of the duo, approximating the Rothstein whom Fitzgerald met. Wolfshiem is the darker half, a strongly exaggerated reminder that it was ethnic, even racial, others who controlled organized crime in America.

At the same time as Wolfshiem is thereby racialized in Fitzgerald's caricature, Tom achieves, as it were, gangsterdom. At the end of the novel, through his manipulation of Wilson, Tom literally gets away with murder. In addition, Daisy kills Myrtle, and Tom makes certain that knowledge remains secret. Tom is, of course, the reason that Myrtle is in the path of the speeding car, and he is the man against whom Wilson should seek revenge. Instead, through a sleight of hand that Nick can only speculate about, Tom, in conversation with Wilson, redirects that revenge onto Gatsby. In that way, Tom is the mastermind behind the murder of Gatsby, the most spectacular and gangster-like action in the course of Nick's year out East. Moreover, Tom avoids legal trouble as if he is an old hand at it. On the night before Gatsby's murder, he has a long conversation with Daisy, spelling out to her the nature of the story they will tell. As Nick describes the scene from his shared vantage with Gatsby outside the window, "anybody would have said that they were conspiring together" (153). Later, Nick reflects that Tom and Daisy are careless, that they hurt others and smash things before retreating to their wealth and privilege to ". . . let other people clean up the mess they had made" (188). Such an air of conspiracy and such clear reliance on one's connections to cover up crimes reflects Wolfshiem's gangster method.[5] Tom's manipulation of Wilson is at least as heartless and practical as Wolfshiem's advice to support friends while they are alive but to forget them in death. Tom has taken what he has wanted from whomever he liked, and he has thrived while doing it. He has enough power to make certain that others pay for his crimes and, by the novel's end, he has chosen to head back to the Midwest for the further comfort it promises. Like Wolfshiem, who has fixed the World Series and suffered no repercussions, Tom is someone the authorities cannot "get."

As a gangster, even in so attenuated a fashion, Tom strikes Nick as all the more associated with ethnic characteristics. The first time he meets Tom in the novel—the occasion on which Tom holds forth on his "Nordic" status—Nick observes that "Two shining, arrogant eyes had established dominance over his face" (11). Such a detail in its own right is hardly a sign of ethnicity, but the sentence so explicitly foreshadows the one describing Wolfshiem—"After a moment I discovered his tiny eyes in the half darkness"—that the two descriptions echo one another. Both are men whom Nick understands in physical terms before he can come to grips with their social position.[6] More tellingly, in the minutes after Tom triumphantly unmasks Gatsby as a gangster and confidently sees Gatsby and Daisy off on the drive that ends in Myrtle's death, Nick finds himself alienated from the self-described "Nordic." As he puts it, "his voice was as remote from Jordan and me as the foreign clamor on the sidewalk" (143). That is, Nick experiences Tom's difference from himself exactly as if Tom were a part of the immigrant throng of New York City. He feels as disconnected from Tom's utterances as he would if Tom were snarling in Italian or Yiddish.

The parallels between Tom and Wolfshiem go even deeper than Nick's general sense that each is ethnic in contrast to his sense of himself and Gatsby as legitimately American. They balance Gatsby in social terms—one is "above" him and the other "below"—and they function together to personify the power closed to self-imagined pioneers. Nick sees them occupying a shared relationship to power, and he uses the penultimate scene of the novel to assert a literal "link" between them. As he walks down the street, he accidentally encounters Tom and wants nothing to do with him. After an unpleasant exchange in which he realizes that none of the experiences with Gatsby have touched the man in any meaningful way, he watches him head into a jewelry store. At that, Nick imagines, "Then he went into the jewelry store to buy a pearl necklace—or perhaps only a pair of cuff buttons" (188). In a novel as carefully written as *Gatsby*, it's hard not to see that detail as significant. The only other reference to a pair of cuff links in the novel is Wolfshiem's, the ones made of human teeth that serve as his gruesome totem. Tom will no doubt have better taste than to display the molars so threateningly, but such taste will not obscure what the parallel reinforces. Both men will use whatever violence and whatever ensconced power they need to retain the privilege that they exercise, and both personify the idea that true power lies in a corporate structure of connections rather than in any individual's virtues. Together they demonstrate that categories of social difference—of race, religion, class, and national origin—are irreducible when it comes to defining the extremes of American power and identity.

III

Fitzgerald's own career at first stands as a retort to the claim that categories of social difference are insurmountable since he himself managed to become an elite figure in American literature despite being born into a Catholic Irish American family. That background is not entirely invisible, however, and there is a tradition of reading him through his ethnic status. As Malcolm Cowley declared in 1954, Fitzgerald's "Irishness was a little disguised, but it remained an undertone in all his stories; it gave him a sense of standing apart that sharpened his observation of social differences" (153). Cowley made his claim in the context of an early study about the ways that "racial provenience" (152) of American authors has shaped the literature, and he was conscious of himself as making only the first furrows in a field that others would need to cultivate a great deal more carefully. All the same, his observation is provocative in light of a reading of *Gatsby* that foregrounds its concern with ethnic and group constructions of identity. It suggests a direct and simple way to recoup *Gatsby* as ethnic fiction in its own right. If we simply recall that there is a case for describing Fitzgerald as an ethnic-American writer, then it follows that we might read his fiction as ethnic in its own right.

And yet, such an idea closes many more ways of reading Fitzgerald than it opens. Fitzgerald was certainly conscious of his Irish ancestry, but he was far more conscious of exploring how he could take advantage of his talent, fame, and youth in the jazzy years after World War I. As Werner Sollors points out in reaction to Cowley's observation, weighing him as an Irish American writer imagines him as part of a literary conversation with Finley Peter Dunne, "with whom, of course, he has otherwise little in common" (14). That sort of reading displaces him from the contemporary Modernists such as Ernest Hemingway and Gertrude Stein whom he generally understood as his own circle, and it puts him in an ill-fitting frame. It is clear that Fitzgerald was concerned with "social differences," but that no more marks him an Irish American writer than it does an American one. As Sollors argues in *Beyond Ethnicity*, we should recognize Fitzgerald as an American writer concerned at least in part with the consuming question of what it is that each of us consents to when we acknowledge ourselves as American.[7] That is, it hardly matters whether his descent influenced him. What is relevant and central to understanding Fitzgerald is to see him as someone trying to understand the role of the individual in the vast collective experience of America.

Critics of ethnic-American literature have more work to do to insure that the texts we value become a part of the canon that serves the broader curriculum of college literary studies. We need, above all, to continue challenging the latent assumption that minority literature is minor literature. There is a still-prevalent sense, measured most accurately by looking at syllabi in introductory literature classes, that ethnic literature is something "extra," something that can be sufficiently covered when it's shoehorned in at the end of a semester or represented through a single story by a writer of color. Many of our colleagues seem to understand course offerings and reading lists as zero-sum quantities; when we urge them to introduce stories by Bharati Mukherjee, Sherman Alexie, or Maxine Hong Kingston, they see us as calling for them to drop something they value, perhaps even Fitzgerald. If we allow others to define our multiethnic agenda as one that calls for pitting the new and multicultural against the established and conventionally American, then we will find ourselves in an immediately defensive position.

Putting the conflict in such a light creates a false dichotomy, however. There may be no room for new classes in the standard English department curriculum—and there may be limited room for defining new areas of research that administrations will support—but there is plenty of room for redefining the way we teach literature itself, in particular American literature. Rather than fighting for new space with and against other 'hyphenated' multicultural literatures, we can turn our energy toward the legitimate and ongoing debates over how to shape curricula for American literature surveys and how to tell the history of American literature at large. Rather than understanding postcolonial literature as our competition, we can wish our colleagues in the field good luck in their parallel challenge of helping to redefine the story of British literature. There is room for both of us provided we can demonstrate to the majority of our colleagues that we belong at the center of literary study rather than the periphery.

I argue that recognizing *The Great Gatsby* as, among other things, an ethnic novel is ultimately part of that effort. Calling *Gatsby* ethnic does not need to mean accepting Cowley's limited argument on the basis of Fitzgerald's own ethnicity. Instead, it means broadening the notion of "ethnic" to re-emphasize its fundamental sense of the concern over how difference functions in the larger American context.[8] It means accepting the widespread sense that American literary history is, in many respects, a history of individuals who feel outside the collective experience of America imagining how that collective functions and exploring the extent to which they might more fully participate in it. As Sacvan Bercovitch argues, American identity is the product of a negotiation between those who understand themselves as outsiders and the American rhetorical tradition that invites the individual to tell the story of America through his or her own experience. In place of a stable definition of what it means to be an American, he proposes a succession of "auto-American-biographies," many by self-understood outsiders, transforming the definition of America as they explore a world that they see but feel they cannot enter. In other words, one consistent element of American identity is to stand outside America and imagine entering it, an experience central to much of the ethnic American literature that we champion.

Looked at in such a way, *Gatsby* is, in part, a novel about the way immigrants and ethnics attempt to enter into a variously defined mainstream America. Nick's famous closing meditation about the "fresh green breast of the New World" drawing the original Dutch settlers shows him reflecting on the original way in which foreigners transformed themselves and their descendents into Americans. It's a dark and a degrading process, however. In his view, even America's founders did little more than rape the New World. Their descendents—and the descendents of settlers only a generation or two behind them—found one resource after another to exploit, drain, and turn into the kind of elusive money that haunts both Nick and Gatsby. Nick can never quite bring himself to admit it, but when he sees Wolfshiem, he sees the future of America. He refuses to acknowledge Wolfshiem's role in shaping Gatsby. He refuses to recognize that the dashing figure he wants to see as above history is, in fact, very much the creation of a Jewish gangster occupying a sordid little office in the midst of an ethnic enclave. But a future governed by Wolfshiem is likely no worse than a past overseen by the Tom Buchanans of the world. One murders and steals today; the other's ancestors murdered and stole just as boldly in generations past.

The American Dream that Nick ascribes to Gatsby isn't so much noble as it is blinkered. It takes an enormous act of not-seeing for Nick to regard Gatsby as heir to a mythic past where it took only individual effort to rise to wealth and prominence. In declaring that Gatsby "sprang from his Platonic conception of himself," he offers his own wish that Gatsby might somehow be separate from any group identity. He sustains the fantasy that Gatsby is beyond any real and human tradition and that Gatsby is therefore central to the world that excludes Wolfshiem and that Tom feels he is above. Examining the evidence that Nick ignores, recognizing that Gatsby is very much implicated in the social, economic, and criminal networks through which he moves, lets us see that Gatsby is a representative American for the very opposite reasons Nick wants to be true.

That is, Gatsby is no self-creation; he is instead Wolfshiem's creation. As a consequence, Gatsby is part of a four-century game of moving from the outside in. He is someone who wrestles with creating a new identity, one that will give him access to an America that he believes is closed to him in his original identity, and he is someone who ultimately turns out to live at the intersection of both of his identities. Gatsby may not be ethnic in the sense that Wolfshiem is, nor even in the self-declared and self-limiting way of Tom, but he is nonetheless someone caught up in the same forces confronting anyone trying to find his or her way into what he imagines as America. In telling Gatsby's story, Nick assumes the right to speak for America; however he wrestles with some of the same questions of difference that lie at the heart of literature narrated by those who feel themselves even more explicitly outside it.

Notes

1. The original constitution of the American Legion, adopted May 10, 1919, pledged, "to foster and perpetuate a one hundred percent Americanism" and offered a separate resolution calling for the deportation of "alien slackers," immigrants who had applied for, but not received, citizenship before the war and used such a loophole to avoid military service (Wheat 193, 204–05). In their 1921 convention, the Legion further resolved "to make a thorough study of the immigration question with a view of suggesting to the Government means by which immigrants who subscribe to American ideals may be properly assimilated, and those who do not desire to so subscribe, deported" (James 80). At the same time, it called for the specific end to Japanese immigration. All of this took place, of course, in the midst of the larger political debate that resulted in the series of federal immigration reform legislation culminating in the 1924 Immigration Restriction Act.

2. As Matthew Frye Jacobson makes clear, the indeterminacy of race meant that there were occasions in which Italians were seen as black. As he interprets the case of *Rollins v. Alabama* from 1922, an African American man was found innocent on charges of miscegenation on the grounds that the Italian American woman with whom he had had relations could not conclusively be shown to be "white." As Jacobson puts it: "Edith

Labue *may* have been white . . . [but] she was not the sort of white woman whose purity was to be 'protected' by that bulwark of white supremacism, the miscegenation statute" (4). *Gatsby* reflects that sensibility further in the detail of a "grey, scrawny Italian child" (30) as the only one at all acknowledging that the Fourth of July is coming. The scene, in the valley of ashes under the gaze of Doctor T. J. Eckleburg, presents a spectacle of waste and abandonment; the boy's small celebration is a reminder of America as a great social experiment, but his efforts are irrelevant and nobody seems to regard him.

3. The location of their meeting would have been significant to most readers at the time. The blocks along Broadway in Manhattan running from 39th Street to the lower 50s were notorious as the playground of New York's leading underworld figures. Several major gangsters owned—or had unofficial control over—nightclubs along the strip, and it was a location colorful enough to be a popular locale for the well-to-do who enjoyed 'slumming' and to be the source of much of the reporting that Broadway columnists offered their readers. In that spirit, Damon Runyon titled the first of his published Broadway stories, "Romance in the Roaring Forties."

4. Whether Rothstein really did fix the World Series is a complicated question. He was clearly involved, but the plot may have originated with some of his associates who used his name to make their scheme appear solid to their fellow conspirators. (See *Eight Men Out* by Eliot Asinof and *Rothstein* by David Pietrusza for the most thorough studies of Rothstein's role in the scandal.) In any case, even though Rothstein was never convicted of any involvement with the fix, he was widely associated with it in newspaper accounts of the criminal trial that found the eight accused players innocent and in the subsequent controversy over the commissioner of baseball's banning those eight for life.

5. For many observers of the 1920s, specific gangster crimes were less shocking than was the inability of law enforcement to do anything about the gangsters who were clearly benefiting from such crimes. When Gatsby declares of Wolfshiem "They can't get him, old sport. He's a smart man" (78), he reflects a widespread sense of gangsters as 'untouchables.' As Donald Henderson Clarke put it in the first book-length biography of Rothstein, published in 1929 only months after his murder: "This book will make plain how the law worked in the case of Arnold Rothstein—to mention only the chief character—who openly violated our legal code every day of his adult life in the City of New York" (xi). Until prosecutors of organized crime cases began to apply Racketeer Influenced and Corrupt Organizations (RICO) statutes in the 1970s, there was little anybody could do to convict gangsters for reap-

ing the rewards of their associates' crimes. In one brazen example from the 1920s, Al Capone established his alibi for the 1929 St. Valentine's Day Massacre by visiting the office of a Miami area district attorney at the very minute the massacre took place. While Capone clearly stood to benefit from the murder of seven associates of the rival Bugs Moran gang, he accomplished the murders through connections that nobody could entirely determine, and neither he nor any of his associates was ever convicted of the decade's most notorious crime.

6. In contrast to the well-defined eyes of each of the men at the extremes of identity, the other best known eyes in the book belong to figures in the middle and, as such, demonstrate their own failed experiments with self-reinvention. "Owl Eyes" is a character named for his glasses, rather than his actual eyes and, when he removes them at Gatsby's funeral, it is as if he has doffed the identity he assumed for himself at the party. More famously, Dr. T. J. Eckleberg has vanished, leaving behind only the massive, empty-eyed billboard that he had intended to use as the basis for his optical practice.

7. Throughout his book, Werner Sollors argues that we should move "beyond ethnicity" as a stable category of difference. As he sees it, the shared understanding of an American identity to which we consent is more determinative of actual identity than is the principle of descent.

8. I refer in particular to Georges Devereux's influential argument about the nature of ethnicity in which he maintains that ethnicity is the product of the desire to categorize difference in a given society. His central claim is that recognition of the other logically precedes a recognition of the self. That is, without a sense of what one is not, it is difficult even to comprehend the necessity for describing what one is. Werner Sollors takes up that fundamental theoretical position and makes it central to *Beyond Ethnicity* and much of his other work.

Works Cited

Asinof, Eliot. *Eight Men Out: The Black Sox and the 1919 World Series.* New York: Holt, Rinehart and Winston, 1963.

Bercovitch, Sacvan. *The Puritan Origins of the American Self.* New Haven, CT: Yale University Press, 1975.

Clarke, Donald Henderson. *In the Reign of Rothstein.* New York: Grosset & Dunlap, 1929.

Cowley, Malcolm. *The Literary Situation.* New York: Viking, 1954.

Devereux, George. "Ethnic Identity: Its Logical Foundations and Its Dysfunctions." 1970. *Ethnopsychoanalysis: Psychoanalysis and An-*

thropology as Complementary Frames of Reference. Berkeley, CA: University of California Press, 1978: 136–76.

Fitzgerald, F. Scott. *The Great Gatsby: The Authorized Text.* 1925. Ed. Matthew J. Bruccoli. New York: Collier, 1992.

———. *The Letters of F. Scott Fitzgerald.* Ed. Andrew Turnbull. New York: Charles Scribner's Sons, 1963.

Jacobson, Matthew Frye. *Whiteness of a Different Color: European Immigrants and the Alchemy of Race.* Cambridge, MA: Harvard University Press, 1998.

James, Marquis. *A History of the American Legion.* New York: W. Green, 1923.

Neate, Wilson. "Unwelcome Remainders, Welcome Reminders." *MELUS* 19.2 (Summer, 1994): 17–35.

Pauly, Thomas H. "Gatsby as Gangster." *Studies in American Fiction* 21.2 (Autumn, 1993): 225–36.

Pietrusza, David. *Rothstein: The Life, Times, and Murder of the Criminal Genius who Fixed the 1919 World Series.* New York: Carroll & Graf, 2003.

Runyon, Damon. "Romance in the Roaring Forties." *Guys and Dolls.* New York: Blue Ribbon Books, 1931. 121–42.

Sollors, Werner. *Beyond Ethnicity: Consent and Descent in American Culture.* New York: Oxford University Press, 1986.

Wheat, George Seay. *The Story of the American Legion.* New York: G. P. Putnam's Sons, 1919.

Chapter 7

An Exile's Will to Canon and Its Tension with Ethnicity

Li-Young Lee

Wenying Xu

Readers of Li-Young Lee's elegant poetry find pleasure and solace in his sensual portrayal of a mind's meanderings from the diurnal to the divine that take them by surprise. That his poetry takes such a spiritual journey may be attributed to his condition of exile—being an ethnic Chinese without the birthright to an ancestral culture, without a grounding knowledge of the Chinese language, and without the community of a Chinatown or a suburban Asian American community—an exile who converts homelessness into metaphysics. As a result, his ontological condition as an exile produces a poetics that argues for transcendence at the exclusion of the cultural and material. In his transcendentalism, the poet's true self becomes the "universe mind" unfettered by cultural/ethnic allegiances (Marshall 134). As such, the poet has no dialogue, as Lee claims, with his sociocultural composition (132).

His disavowals of ethnic identification, however, place him squarely within a cultural location—the American transcendentalist poetry whose canonicity is beyond question. (One may add that its canonicity is precisely due to its transcendentalism.) Contrary to his wishes, Lee's own transcendentalism does not produce a culturally naked self; rather it engenders a *will to canon* that is tied to the dominant sociocultural practice of exclusion in the name of universalism and aesthetics. Furthermore, his rejection of ethnicity in order to be regarded as a transcendentalist poet among canonical poets creates a dynamic tension with his frequent usage of ethnic signifiers in his poetry.

This essay takes three steps: first it explicates how Lee's exilic condition determines his self-representation and how his Asian diasporic sensibility resists his transcendentalism; second, it demonstrates his will to canon via transcendentalism; and third, it argues, through a close reading of his long poem, "The Cleaving," that his will to canon is exercised precisely through ethnic signifiers, particularly through Asian cuisine.

Exilic Intellectual as Winged Seed

Lee's lyrical memoir, *The Winged Seed*, sets in motion a kaleidoscopic journey into his family history of wanderings.[1] Primarily centering on his father and himself, the memoir represents both as exilic intellectuals. Edward Said offers a model of the exilic intellectual who is blessed with a double perspective, dis-allegiance, and ironic distance. He describes this figure as "a shipwrecked person who learns how to live in a certain sense *with* the land, not *on* it" (*Reader* 378). To live *with* the land is to be open to strangeness, which one does not attempt to dominate and domesticate. To live *with* the land is also to carry one's home in memory, to not lose hope, the sense of wonder, or critical acuity. This exilic intellectual does not hopelessly seek belonging, either in the impossible return to the "true" home or by giving into the assimilatory impulse of the new locale. Rather he/she experiences "the fate [of exile] not as a deprivation and as something to be bewailed, but as a sort of freedom, a process of discovery [. . .]" (*Reader* 380). Lee is such an exilic intellectual, for what fuels his poetic engine is not a nostalgic despairing for an origin as a ground for self-definition. Rather, it is his recurrent conceit of "the winged seed" that serves as a self-representation.

Interestingly, "diaspora" is composed of "dia" (through, throughout) and "spora" (spore), a notion with a strong affinity to Lee's "winged seed" (Peter 23). Deeply rooted in the *Song of Songs*, Lee takes the trope from his father's Thanksgiving sermon.

> East of you or me [. . .] lived a sentient perfume, an inbreathing and uttering seed, our original agent. [. . .] it

> is the mother of spices; the song of songs [. . .] both the late wine and our original milk, it is a fecund nard. And there go forth from this vital seed figures distilled a day, or a year, or a century [. . .] An ark, all fragrance, is our trove, the Seed [. . .] "We are embalmed in a shabby human closet," he [father] said. "Get out! Get to the garden of nutmeg." (*Seed* 90)

Contrary to its connotation of ungroundedness or Lee's aspiration to the transcendent, however, the seed trope turns out to be deeply rooted in Asian history. In the West spices became vital to medicine, cosmetics, cuisine, and the religious ceremonial ever since the conquest of Alexander forced the East into contact with the Hellenic world. Not until the 1500s, however, did spices become one of the most coveted commodities in Europe, so coveted that they were compared to gold.

The history of the spice trade is a portal into the violent history of colonialism. Lee's seed trope carries with it the memory of that history. His father's sermon does not only point to the complex beginning of the Old Testament, but also to the colonial destruction of the spice gardens in the Orient. In the early 1500s the Spice Islands became irresistible to the Occidental.[2] One can say that the voyages to the Spice Islands were the precursor to the Western colonization of Asia. Giles Milton writes: "Nutmeg [. . .] was the most coveted luxury in seventeenth-century Europe, a spice held to have such powerful medicinal properties that men would risk their lives to acquire it" (3). At the beginning of its trade, "ten pounds of nutmeg cost less than one English penny. In London, it was sold at a markup of staggering 60,000 percent" (Milton 6).[3] In the context of British history, it is the spice trade that necessitated the formation of the East India Company that played a vital role in the opium trade and in subjugating Asia, particularly South Asia.[4] In the seed conceit Lee represents his father's as well as his own wandering in the postcolonial world—the seed is "born flying," "to begin its longest journey to find its birthplace, that place of eternal unrest. From unrest to unrest it [is] moving. And without so much as a map to guide it, and without so much as a light" (*Seed* 92). Having been transported to unknown places, the only destination the seed knows is journey itself.

Lee's seed trope, bearing the memory of the colonial beginnings fraught with grand dreams, plunder, and violence, sets out to be a political trope that points to both the politics that necessitates exile and the politics that operates the exile's positioning in a new place. While meditating about his father, Lee imagines the seed to have come from violence. "Did he say seed is told, kept cold, scored with a pocketknife, and then left out to die, in order to come into further seed, speaking the father seed, leading to seed [. . .] a road we sow ahead of our arrival?" (*Seed* 46–47). Despite its violent beginning, the seed multiplies itself and sows a path into the future. In this lyrical imagining of the seed, he discloses the exile's violent partition from home and kinsmen, promises memory and father's legacy, and offers a Utopian impulse. For in the seed "may be growing the flower that will overthrow all governments of crows or senators. [. . .] This seed revises all existing boundaries to proclaim the dimensions of an ungrasped hour. This seed carries news of a new continent and our first citizenship [. . .]" (*Seed* 36). Here Lee's notion of citizenship challenges the ordinary meaning of a national, political identity and envisions the "first citizenship" of a Utopian world that has revised "all existing boundaries." Such "a new continent" would cease to practice categories like exiles, insiders, outsiders, nationals, refugees, immigrants, or illegal immigrants. Impelled by this Utopian *telos*, his seed/exile can never wallow in what Edward Said calls "an uncritical gregariousness" ("The Mind in Winter" 54). Although an American citizen, Lee has never stopped feeling like an outsider, often examining this country critically. In "The City in Which I Love You," he presents a picture of the American street as chaotic and dangerous as that of Jakarta from which his family escaped. "Past the guarded schoolyards, the boarded-up churches, swastikaed / synagogues, defended houses of worship, past / newspapered windows of tenements, among the violated, / the prosecuted citizenry, throughout this / storied, buttressed, scavenged, policed / city I call home, in which I am a guest. . . ." (*City* 51). Compact in this sharp imagery are stories of crime, racism, poverty, and inhumanity that are commonplace in urban America.

Lee's portrayal of himself as an exile manifests conflicting impulses. On the one hand the trope of winged seed denotes his transcendentalist compulsion, and on the other, he as the winged seed must settle in fertile soil, the material world, in order to regenerate. This material world that nourishes the seed is the memory about China through his parents' stories and cooking. The re-vision of home for the Chinese Diaspora (or for any other ethnic group) heavily relies on the discursive pleasure of storytelling and the nondiscursive pleasure of food. This truth is amply evident in Asian American literature and film. Removed from their homelands, the overseas Chinese vest their homesickness in the maintenance of rituals and festivals, both of which depend on storytelling and food practices. "Our way of life," described by Slavoj Žižek, is the "disconnected fragments of the way our community organizes its feasts, its rituals of mating, its initiation ceremonies, in short, all the details by which is made visible the unique way a community *organizes* its *enjoyment*" (201). In some cases, such as Lee's, those in exile don't have access to a community; the closest to it is the extended or nuclear family. Foodways nevertheless continue to be the bloodline that keeps alive ethnic identity and the bittersweet longing for home. Despite his rejection of ethnicity in favor of transcendentalism, Lee's writings are rich with ethnic food reference.

For the exile his/her culture's particular foodways must function as a cushion from displacement and homelessness, comfort food that momentarily transports the exile to the ever elusive home. Lee evokes the pathos of the exiled with the single sharp image of "the black cooking pot" that his family "carried through seven countries" during their wanderings (*Seed*, 88). This image, suggesting a snail which carries its home on its back, vividly captures the state of being of the exile—home is on the road, as protean as it is imaginary. In turn home cooking carries its heavy burden for those it feeds—that of belonging and togetherness. Alternatively, those who are eager to assimilate into the mainstream culture feel ashamed of the enjoyment of their ethnic foodways. Lee recounts his childhood fascination with a beautiful Chinese girl who "spurned" her "own kind." He captures the girl's shame of her heritage by two significant details—"She pretended to not be able to speak Chinese. She pretended to not know how to eat black eggs with sugar and sesame seeds sprinkled on top" (*Seed* 131).

In an alien environment, the aroma of home cooking arouses a deeply entangled feeling of nostalgia and belonging. In his imagination, Lee takes flights of stairs in search of memory and finds food for thought. "On the fifth I smell fried salted fish [...] I jump to the sixth, where my grandmother is stirring a soup of ginger, young hen, lemon grass, and tom yum [...] crying, *Memory is salt. Don't forget me*" (*Seed* 136). This lemony, salty, and spicy soup unique to South East Asia not only reminds Lee of the comfort of home, but also conveys the injunction for memory for those in exile. The double meaning of salt unites the themes of food and home, food and love, and food and the survival of the exiled. "Memory is salt," Lee's grandmother instructs. Without it elements of food don't come together to make a savory dish. Without it family or community cannot stay whole under the stress of transplantation. Exiles are haunted by the urge to look back, as Salman Rushdie puts it, "even at the risk of being mutated into pillars of salt" (10).

Salt, with its connotations of sorrow and flavor, is a long-standing mythological trope expressive of the intertwining pangs of homelessness and the relish of remembrance. The biblical tale of Lot's wife turning into a pillar of salt for looking back, other than failing to heed the command to obey God, may also suggest the arrested state of the exile when one turns one's gaze only upon the past—looking at it as a factual past, as though that past were unmediated by memory, narrative, fantasy, and myth filtered and constructed by the present. Speaking of Indian writers in exile, Rushdie writes, "our physical alienation from India almost inevitably means that we will not be capable of reclaiming precisely the thing that was lost; that we will, in short, create fictions [...] imaginary homelands, Indias of the mind" (10). In theorizing identity as an endless production, Stuart Hall resonates with Rushdie and writes that "our relationship to it [the past], like the child's relationship to the mother, is always-already 'after the break'" (395). We can never return to our past as if we had never left. The cultural identity of an exile is a constellation of narrative acts enunciating the past as well as the present.

If salt is memory, as Lee has his grandmother say, then his prizing of salt can be interpreted as his valorization of memory in the invention of home and community. To him neither is stable or fixed. One must imagine it, create it, and sustain it with memory. As salt makes cuisine possible, so does memory make possible a past cathected with love and longing. To demonstrate this point he singles out the cook as one who understands best the function of salt/memory—"Only the baker knows that bread is a form of our deepest human wish, a shape of love [. . .]. [. . .] Know how bread is knit by salt. For tears alone are active seed, leavening perishing forms, apparent at an imperishable wheel of hunger" (*Seed* 137). If bread is love and salt memory, it is memory that creates and sustains love. As bread is knit by salt to bring out its sweetness, sugar/salt or love/sorrow are agents for mutual fulfillment. In other words, sugar cannot bring forth gratifying sweetness without the complement of salt. The sweetness of home is made possible through feelings of sadness and displacement, and the plenitude of home made imaginable through feelings of lack and loss.

Will to Canon via Transcendentalism

Most critics classify Lee as an Asian American poet and choose to focus on his experience as an émigré and his double identity as a Chinese in exile and an American in citizenship. For example, Judith Kitchen in *The Georgia Review* attributes Lee's poetry to his unique subject position as "a Chinese American trying to make sense of both his heritage and his inheritance" (160). Yibing Huang in *Amerasia Journal* assesses Lee's book of prose poetry, *The Winged Seed*, to be "a typical fable of Asian American experience, of how tradition and the parents' generation are always, in consciousness or the unconscious, linked with pain and burden" (190). Lee himself, however, strongly objects to this classification. In an interview with Tod Marshall, he remarks,

> I have no dialogue with cultural existence. Culture made that up—Asian American, African American, whatever. I have no interest in that. I have an interest in spiritual lineage to poetry—through Eliot, Donne, Lorca, Tu Fu, Neruda, David the Psalmist. [. . .] Somehow an artist has to discover a dialogue that is so essential to his being, to his self, that it is no longer cultural or canonical, but a dialogue with his truest self. His most naked spirit. (132)

Lee believes that poetry in dialogue with the cultural is a "lower form of art" (131). True poetry, he claims, sheds the poet's false/cultural identity. Despite his polemical dismissal of the canon, he, nevertheless, places himself in a canonical lineage with the masters, and the language of "high" and "low," "true" and "false" in evaluating literature is part and parcel of the discourse of canon.

What compels him to reject the identity as an Asian American poet, however, is more than his will to canon, for such rejection does not manifest a willing surrender to the ideology of assimilation. His response to his exile in the form of transcendence aims to counter the stereotypes of Asians in the U.S. popular culture. In a conversation with James Kyun-Jin Lee, he explains:

> The culture we live in offers or imposes versions of "somebodyhoods" that are really shallow and false. [. . .] If I can attain a state of "nobodyhood," which is the same thing as the state of "everybodyhood," that's much richer and more full of potential than some false, made up, Hollywood magazine, university, or cultural version of "somebodyhood." (275–76)

The seeming paradox of nobody being everybody is central to his transcendentalism, which strives to achieve the state of the naked self in relationship to God, or, in the discourse of the canon, the disembodied self-propounding universal truth.

Diaspora or exile, for Lee, is not a uniquely ethnic condition; rather it is a human condition, a view derived from *Genesis* in which human history begins in dual exile from the Garden of Eden and the presence of God. "It is arrogant of the dominant culture," he comments, "to think it's not part of a diaspora" (Lee 279). He regards himself exilic in this sense—"The difficulty is that the earth is not my home" (Lee 279). Consequently, his affinity with the universalistic concept of humankind overrides his affinity with that of the Asian. Xiaojing Zhou argues against the tendency of some critics to interpret Lee's poetry by emphasizing his Chinese ethnicity. By reducing his art to expressions of his ethnicity, Zhou points out, Lee's critics minimize "the rich cross-cultural sources of influence on Lee's work and of the creative experiment in his poetry" (114). In his excellent essay on Lee's "Persimmons," Steven G. Yao points out that many of Lee's critics (including Zhou) "have relied on an overly simplistic model for cross-cultural literary production" (3). Through a close reading of Lee's most anthologized poem, Yao makes the case that "Lee achieves only a superficial integration, or 'hybridization,' of Chinese and American culture" and "'grafting' offers a more exact term than hybridity for understanding Lee's accomplishment in "Persimmons" (19–20). Both Zhou and Yao's efforts to free Lee from interpretive limitations, however, only partially meet his own self-portrait as a poet on a quest for the Absolute. To be Asian, American, or Asian American occupies little space in his self-representation. His elaborate metaphysical schema aims to rid him of such labels—"My true self is universe or God. I assume that my true nature is God. I assume that I am God in my true nature" (Marshall 134).

Subscribing to the discourse of canon, Lee evokes the distinction between the universal and the local, the soul and the self, echoing Helen Vendler who clarifies, "Selves come with a history: souls are independent of time and space" (*Soul Says* 3). What Lee claims to be true of himself he attributes to all true poets. "When I read poetry, I feel I'm in the presence of universe mind; that is, a mind I would describe as a 360 degree seeing; it is manifold in consciousness" (Marshall 130). In other words, "true" poets are superhumans free from sociocultural contingencies. Vendler speaks in the same vein, "the traditional [meaning "canonical"] lyric desires a stripping-away of the details associated with a socially specified self in order to reach its desired all-purpose abstraction" (*Soul Says* 3). Harold Bloom, demarcating the social and the aesthetic, asserts likewise, "One breaks into the canon only by aesthetic strength," and the Western canon offers "the proper use of one's own solitude, that solitude whose final form is one's confrontation with one's own mortality" (*The Western Canon* 29, 30). Participating in this discourse, Lee's polemics on transcendentalism can hardly be disguised as anything but a *will to canon*.

Lee's polemics bear a strong resemblance to Emerson's, whose famous declaration in "Nature" goes, "[. . .] all mean egotism vanishes, I become a transparent eyeball; I am nothing; I see all" (39). Lee's "360 degree seeing," a faithful version of Emerson's "transparent eyeball," offers a political liberal license to all "true" poets to be free from all the forces that condition other human beings. In his statement, "I am born into the great, the universal mind. I, the imperfect, adore my own Perfect" (224), Emerson anticipates Lee's self-anointment as God, a god that is twin to Emerson's "Oversoul, within which every man's particular being is contained and made one with all others" (206). The concept of "self" in both men's articulations of the transcendent, therefore, is seated in essentialism. Bloom in his usual abstruse eloquence describes Emersonianism as the American Religion, "*Self*-reliance, in Emerson [. . .] is the religion that celebrates and reveres what in the self is before the Creation, a whatness which from the perspective of religious orthodoxy can only be the primal Abyss" (*Agon* 146).

As an American transcendentalist, Lee is situated within the American poetic tradition of the sublime. His appeal to that which is *other* of the social is an appeal to what Helen Vendler calls "the grand, the sublime, and the unnamable" (*Part of Nature* 2). Departing from European Romanticism, the object of the sublime in American poetry is much more than nature itself; it is nation, technology, and power that have been elevated to sublimity.[5] Many of the major interpreters of American poetry regard the American sublime as a sensibility that defines the national poetic canon as much as the national spirit. Nativist in sentiment, their assessment of American poetry would probably annoy Lee, if not affront him, who refuses to be a grateful guest in this country by critiquing it and by considering it "a country / wholly unfound to himself" (*Book of My Nights* 6).

Rob Wilson, interrogating the nationalist implication in the American sublime, puts forth his thesis that "[a]s a poetic genre, the American sublime helped to produce the subject and site of American subjection as sublime" (3). Or in my blunt paraphrase, the American poetic expression of the sublime is a performance of a distinctively American subject substantiated through the subjugation of land and its first peoples. Centering on "the material sublime" in American poetry, Wilson points out that the will to American sublimity finds its representation in a "landscape of immensity and wildness" that serves as the "Americanized self's inalienable ground" (3–4). Although Lee does not participate in the representation of such an American material sublime, he is nevertheless part of this American poetic tradition in which wild immensity, be it nature, force, or rhetoric, predictably accompanies self-deification and hyperbolic imagination. In "Degrees of Blue," he evokes the sublime through grand language of power—"How is he going to explain / the moon taken hostage, the sea / risen to fill up all the mirrors? / How is he going to explain the branches / beginning to grow from his ribs and throat, / the cries and trills starting in his own mouth? / And now that ancient sorrow between his hips, / his body's ripe listening / the planet / knowing itself at last" (*Book of My Nights* 31). In this vast field of vision traversing the private, the historical, and the planetary, Lee centers himself as the knower and seer. His rhetorical will to power and his self-deification place him squarely within what Wilson calls the American "collective will-to-sublimity" (6). Lee's disavowal of all that is cultural cannot hide his will to canon even when his disavowal is sublimated into a metaphysical form of mysticism.

Tension between Transcendentalism and Ethnicity

Lee's will to canon via metaphysics is fraught with ambivalence. On the one hand, to identify with canonical figures in poetry he must denounce his ethnic identification, with the discourse of canon valorizing universal/transcendent values. On the other, he must speak from a cultural and material place in order to reach the transcendent, and this place is predominantly ethnic in his poetry. Let us look at one of his best long works, "The Cleaving," in *The City in Which I Love You*, in which ethnic cuisine is central to its themes and aesthetics.[6] Only after the indulgence in the carnal does he arrive at a meditation on the transcendent. Only after a montage of ethnic markers—Chinese cuisine and physical features—is he able to empty out ethnicity in the attempt to transcend it. "The Cleaving," set in a Chinatown, begins by the speaker's identification with the man working in "the Hon Kee Grocery" (*City* 77). "He gossips like my grandmother, this man / with my face" (77). Emanating from the first few lines is a sense of belonging: "[. . .] I could stand / amused all afternoon / in the Hon Kee Grocery" (77). What amuses the speaker is not the exotic that attracts tourists into Chinatown; it is rather the familiar sights, smells, and tastes associative with home. The following lines present an aromatic and alimentary image of meats hung inside the grocery. "[. . .] roast pork cut / from a hog hung / by nose and shoulders, / her entire skin burnt / crisp, flesh I know / to be sweet, / her shining / face grinning / up at ducks / dangling single file, / each pierced by black / hooks through breast, bill, / and steaming from a hole / stitched shut at the ass" (*City* 77). Lee depicts this scene with such ease that the seeming violence is muted by humor and appetite. Such a scene takes the risk of disgusting some mainstream readers and being perceived as barbaric. The loving details about roast pork and ducks serving as markers of his ethnic subjectivity—"flesh I know / to be sweet"—seem to appeal to the sensory, the bodily. Significantly, the line break occurs at "know," not "flesh," to underscore that the speaker's ethnicity is based on intellectual as well as visceral knowledge.

Such union of the mind and the body when constructing the speaker's ethnic self enjoys a high moment in the fourth stanza describing roast ducks. "The head, flung from the body, / opens down the middle where the butcher / cleanly halved it between / the eyes, and I / see, foetal-crouched / inside the skull, the homunculus, / gray brain grainy / to eat. [. . .] / The butcher sees me eye this delicacy. / With a finger, he picks it / out of the skull-cradle / and offers it to me. / I take it gingerly between my fingers / and suck it down. / I eat my man" (79–80). On the surface this moment describes the fellowship between two Chinese men expressed in their mutual enjoyment of duck brains. The particular association of duck brains with "man" and "foetal-crouched [. . .] homunculus," however, has far reaching meanings in ethnicizing the speaker. Lee alludes to the Chinese legend of Yue Fei, a general during the Song Dynasty, who defeated the foreign invaders but was unjustly punished by the emperor under the advice of a corrupt courtier. Afterwards, everywhere the courtier went, people spat and threw stones at him. Hated and chased by people, he couldn't find any better refuge than inside a chicken's skull. Since then the Chinese eat fowls' brains with glee.[7] His allusion to this legend serves to wed the mind (that is familiar with the Chinese cultural tradition) with the body (that relishes hardcore Chinese cuisine) in order to give an impression[8] of the speaker's ethnic authenticity. Lee has expressed a sense of helpless regret that he has lost the Chinese language, such as in "Persimmons," and the reference to the legend of Yue Fei provides a measure of redemption in establishing himself as a cultural insider.

His evocation of this legend through duck brains not only defines the speaker's ethnicity, but also initiates the unifying trope of eating in this poem, which weaves together several strands of otherwise disparate motifs in this poem. From duck brains, he moves on to eating nonfood matters such as people, their actions, their manners, and their history. The trope of eating figures for appropriation, incorporation, and assimilation, all that we take in through our senses and becomes us.

> What is it in me will not let
> the world be, would eat
> not just this fish,
> but the one who killed it,
> the butcher who cleaned it.
> I would eat the way he
> reaches into the plastic tubs
> and pulls out a fish, clubs it, takes it
> to the sink, guts it, drops it on the weighing pan.
> I would eat that thrash
> and plunge of the watery body
> in the water, that liquid violence
> between the man's hands,
> I would eat
> the gutless twitching on the scales,
> three pounds of dumb
> nerve and pulse, I would eat it all
> to utter it. (82–83)

The prominence of orality here connotes the poet's voracious desire to understand the world, as he appropriately explains, "my reading a kind of eating, my eating / a kind of reading" (82), for eating is a kind of assimilation that translates the foreign into the familiar or converts the threatening into the nourishing. Only through introducing the outside into the inside can one understand the concerned matter. As a poet Lee believes that he must "eat it all / to utter it." This understanding of one's relationship to others and their worlds resonates with Hans-Georg Gadamer, whose hermeneutics promotes understanding through genuine dialogues. In a dialogic encounter with a text, a culture, or even with an individual, one risks the stability of one's own prejudgment by opening oneself up to a different "prejudice," incorporating what is foreign into one's mental landscape. Such risks, Gadamer promises us, often result in desirable change, which he calls "a fusion of horizons" (358). Lee's eating trope certainly suggests the kind of risks involved in introducing into the self what is *other*. This act of seeming assimilation, however, does not produce homogeny by effacing differences as some of Gadamer's critics charge.[9]

"The Cleaving" is by far the strongest Asian American poem in Lee's oeuvre. Walter A. Hesford goes as far as asserting that "[i]n the central 'City' the poet denies his Asian past and identity to cleave to his American beloved; in the concluding 'Cleaving' he cleaves to his Asian past and Chinese-American identity" (53). The celebratory embrace of his ethnicity takes the form of gleeful indulgence in Chinese cuisine and appetite—the appetite that establishes him to be a big eater of not only food but also his race: "I would devour this race to sing it" (83). Eating his race to sing it entails the incorporation of Asian American history, which is fraught with injustice and sacrifice. Deploying "death" as a metonymy for this history, he sings, "[. . .] I would eat, / [. . .] the standing deaths / at the counters, in the aisles, / the walking deaths in the streets, / the death-far-from-home, the death- / in-a-strange-land, these Chinatown / deaths, these American deaths" (83). His eating and singing of this history serves as an elegy for all the Asian Americans who died after eating much bitterness. By eating their misery and deaths, he endeavors to understand and place himself within Asian American history.

The trope of eating takes two diametrically opposed actions. On the one hand, it stands for the poet's eager and loving absorption of all that is around him in order to turn daily life into poetry. On the other, it figures for the poet's negation of his adversary, in this case racial hostility. In psychoanalytical theory, orality is associated with both pleasure and aggression. Although orality is mostly discussed vis-à-vis infants, Sigmund Freud and Jacques Lacan never disassociate infant modality from adults. Indeed when Lacan theorizes the Real that is constantly threatening the stability of the Symbolic, he makes it clear that the primordial underlies as well as frustrates the social. Lee's imagery of orality integrates into the self what is pleasant as well as vanquishes what is hostile. In response to Emerson's offensive remark about the Chinese, Lee interpositions both implications of the eating trope. "I would devour this race to sing it, / this race that according to Emerson / *managed to preserve to a hair / for three or four thousand years / the ugliest features in the world* / I would eat these features, eat / the last three or four thousand years, every hair. / And I would eat Emerson, his transparent soul, his / soporific transcendence" (83).

The racial othering by Emerson is particularly alienating.[10] Although Lee has never acknowledged Emerson's influence, the two men's transcendentalisms, as I have discussed, bear a strong resemblance. Thus, it may strike one as curious that Lee belittles Emerson's philosophy as a "soporific transcendence" in order to cut down the virility of the master's (father's) influence, reducing it to an old man's ramble—an oedipal antagonism Lee displays via aggressive orality. The young poet, therefore, avenges himself and the Chinese by subjecting Emerson and his racist remark to the trope of eating, and with the same trope he simultaneously embraces his people and their four thousand years of history. "Eating" (*che*) in Mandarin has the connotation of defeating or overcoming, such as in chess where one eats the opponent's pieces. In *The Woman Warrior*, Maxine Hong Kingston tells the story of her mother, who overcomes the sitting ghost by catching it, cooking it, and eating it (78–88). Lee situates himself in the Chinese semantic tradition of eating oppositions and joins the battle against racial injustice. Or borrowing Sau-Ling Cynthia Wong's words, Lee belongs to "[. . .] the company of fabulous Chinese heroes who overcome ghosts, monsters, and assorted evils by devouring them" (25). In this poem, the eating trope creates a cross-cultural site in which Lee performs his Chinese American self.

As soon as the ethnic self is constructed, he proceeds to empty it out by moving his motif of eating to that of death and by meditating on the nothingness of this material world in order to "witness the spirit, the invisible, the law" (Marshall 141). The poem's metaphysical moment, therefore, is made possible only through the extravagant display of ethnicity. Mutating the trope of eating to metaphysics , he writes,

> Bodies eating bodies, heads eating heads,
> we are nothing eating nothing,
> and though we feast,
> are filled, overfilled,
> we go famished.
> We gang the doors of death.
> That is, our deaths are fed
> that we may continue our daily dying,
> Out bodies going
> down, while the plates-soon-empty
> are passed around, that true
> direction of our true prayers, [. . .]
> As we eat we're eaten. (85)

The references of eating, being eaten, and dying configure to voice his transcendentalism. Materials fade away and only the pure consciousness of the universe mind endures. Only after he establishes the trope of eating is he able to cancel out materiality and cultural/ethnic identification in favor of metaphysics.

In the poem's conclusion Lee returns to the theme of ethnicity. Only this time it has become expanded by his metaphysical meditation to include a diverse cluster of ethnic markers which may or may not be described as Asian, only to be rid of them all. Urged on by his reflection on death and change, he releases the rein on his Utopian impulse to de-ethnicize, de-gender the Chinese butcher by exploding his ethnicity to such an extent that its overflowing labels come to mean nothing; what remains after such explosion of signifiers is the singularity of his face. "[. . .] the sorrow of his Shang / dynasty face, / African face with slit eyes. He is / my sister, this / beautiful Bedouin, this Shulamite, / keeper of Sabbaths, diviner / of holy texts, this dark / dancer, this

Jew, this Asian, this one / with the Cambodian face, Vietnamese face, this Chinese / I daily face, / this immigrant, / this man with my own face" (86–87). The butcher after passing through conventional ethnic/cultural markers like Shang dynasty, slit eyes, dark dancer, Jew, Vietnamese, immigrant, and so forth, in the last line simply becomes "this man with my own face," embodying all, therefore emptied out of all ethnicities. Simultaneously, Lee also purges the butcher's gender by referring to him as "my sister" and "this dark dancer." The Chinese butcher becomes the transcendent self embodying all ethnicities and genders and being tied down by none.

In settling for the final identification of the butcher as "this man with my own face," Lee also postulates that the specificity of an individual cannot be reduced to his/her socially constituted identities. The I-Thou encounter (which Gadamer regards to be the necessary presupposition of all discourse) must transcend socially constructed categories. This ethics finds a theoretical articulation in Emmanuel Levinas who argues that interpersonal relationships have priority over each individual's social identity. We are different because of a singularity that, in such encounters, calls for a responsibility to the other which cannot be passed off to anyone else (116–125). The poem's last word "face" captures this ethical relationship best. It is the face-to-face encounter that is central to our relationship with others, and in such an encounter resemblance overwhelms difference.

Lee's interpersonal ethics originates from his transcendentalist impulse that aspires to render cultural differentiation meaningless, and much of that impulse comes from his exilic condition. Yet, it is precisely his cultural and diasporic difference that makes him a fascinating poet. His disavowal of his ethnic identification in order to be regarded as a transcendentalist poet among canonical poets creates a dynamic tension in his poetry. On the one hand, Lee's poetry works its way exactly through Asian diasporic signifiers, and on the other, his wish to be stripped of all cultural identifications and politics ironically places him within American transcendentalist and sublimic tradition, a culture irrevocably tied to the U.S. history of imperialism, as Rob Wilson explicates convincingly. Lee's poetic journey toward the transcendent turns out to be a cornucopia of cultural particularities such as Asian food. His wonderful poetry reveals profoundly his strong affiliations with both Asian and American cultures, neither of which is free from political implications. It is his poetry that best argues against his own polemical position and demonstrates that his will to canon must be exercised through ethnicity.

Notes

1. From hereon *The Winged Seed* will be abbreviated to *Seed*.
2. The ancient trade routes "stretched from China to the Atlantic, whose terminals were the Chinese and Roman Empires" (Miller 119). Before the European merchants began to travel to the East Indies, spices, silk, and other commodities reached Europe via Byzantium and Venus. For the history of the ancient spice trade, see J. Innés Miller's *The Spice Trade of the Roman Empire*.
3. The ruthless competition among the European traders escalated the price of spices and resulted in rampant violence against each other as well as the islanders. Writing about the Dutch ship *Mauritius* that set sail in the spring of 1595 for the Spice Islands, Giles Milton accounted for the happening upon its landing. "Angered by the escalating price of spices," the crew of the ship went loose. "What followed was an orgy of destruction that was to set the pattern for the Dutch presence in the East Indies. The town was bombarded with cannon fire and prisoners were sentenced to death" (61).
4. For an account of the relationship between the East India Company and the opium trade, and its consequent wars between China and Europe, see Wenying Xu, "The Opium Trade and *Little Dorrit*: A Case of Reading Silences," 53–66.
5. See Rob Wilson's *American Sublime* for a Foucauldian interpretation of the American poetic tradition that offers an excellent examination of the ideological underpinnings of the American sublime.
6. From hereon *The City in Which I Love You* will be abbreviated to *City*.
7. Centered on this legend, there is an interesting intertextuality between two other Chinese American writers. In Maxine Hong Kingston, the words of revenge that Yue Fei's mother tattooed on his back become transferred to the back of the female protagonist in "The White Tiger" of *The Woman Warrior*. Chin faults Kingston for feminizing the legendary figure ("Come All Ye Asian American Writers of the Real and the Fake!" 3).
8. I use "impression" to indicate that Lee is fundamentally opposed to such notions of ethnic authenticity. This will be made apparent near the end of my discussion.

9. Such as T. K. Seung, *Semiotics and Thematics in Hermeneutics* (New York: Columbia University Press, 1982, 189) and Terry Eagleton, *Literary Theory* (Minneapolis: University of Minnesota Press, 1983), 72, who interpret Gadamer's notion of fusion of horizons as expounding the impossible homogenization of incommensurate worlds of differences. David Hoy, however, points out that the background of a text or a reader is not a substance which can be fully fused together. See David Couzens Hoy and Thomas McCarthy (Cambridge: Blackwell, 1994), 188–200.

10. About Emerson's racism, see Cornell West, *The American Evasion of Philosophy* (Madison, WI: University of Wisconsin, 1989), 29–35.

Works Cited

Bloom, Harold. *Agon*. New York: Oxford University Press, 1982.

———. *The Western Canon*. New York: Harcourt Brace, 1994.

Chin, Frank. "Come All Ye Asian American Writers of the Real and the Fake!" *The Big Aiiieeeee! An Anthology of Chinese American and Japanese American Literature*. Eds. Jeffrey Paul Chan, Frank Chin, Lawson Fusao Inada, and Shawn Hsu Wong. New York: Meridian, 1991. 1–92.

Emerson, Ralph Waldo. *Ralph Waldo Emerson: Selected Essays*. Ed. Larzer Ziff. New York: Penguin, 1982.

Gadamer, Hans-George. *Truth and Method*. New York: The Continuum, 1975.

Hall, Stuart. "Cultural Identity and Diaspora." *Colonial Discourse and Post-Colonial Theory: A Reader*. Eds. Patrick Williams and Laura Chrisman. New York: Columbia University Press, 1994. 392–403.

Hesford, Walter A. "*The City in Which I Love You*: Li-Young Lee's Excellent Song." *Christianity Literature* 46.1 (Autumn 1996): 37–60.

Hoy, David Couzens and Thomas McCarthy. *Critical Theory*. Cambridge: Blackwell, 1994.

Huang, Yibing. "Li-Young Lee: *Winged Seed*." *Amerasia Journal* 24.2 (1998): 189–191.

Kingston, Maxine Hong. *The Woman Warrior: Memoirs of a Girlhood among Ghosts*. New York: Vintage Books, 1977.

Kitchen, Judith. "Li-Young Lee's *The City in Which I Love You*." *The Georgia Review* 45 (Spring 1991): 160.

Lee, James Kyung-Jin. "Li-Young Lee." *Words Matter: Conversations with Asian American Writers*. Ed. King-Kok Cheung. Honolulu: University of Hawaii Press, 2000. 270–280.

Lee, Li-Young. *The City in Which I Love You*. Rochester, NY: Boa Edition, 1990.

———. *The Winged Seed: A Remembrance*. Saint Paul, MI: Hungry Mind Press, 1995.
———. *Book of My Nights*. Rochester, NY: Boa Edition, 2001.
Levinas, Emmanuel. *Outside the Subject*. Trans. Michael B. Smith. Stanford: Stanford University Press, 1994.
Marshall, Tod. "To Witness the Invisible: A Talk with Li-Young Lee." *The Kenyon Review* 22.1 (Winter 2000): 129–147.
Miller, J. Innes. *The Spice Trade of the Roman Empire*. New York: Oxford at the Clarendon Press, 1969.
Milton, Giles. *Nathaniel's Nutmeg*. New York: Penguin, 1999.
Peter, John Durham. "Exile, Nomadism, and Diaspora." *Home, Exile, Homeland: Film, Media, and the Politics of Place*. Ed. Hamid Naficy. New York: Routledge, 1999. 17–41.
Rushdie, Salman. *Imaginary Homelands: Essays and Criticism 1981–1991*. London: Granta Books, 1991.
Said, Edward. *The Edward Said Reader*. Eds. Moustafa Bayoumi and Andrew Rubin. New York: Vintage, 2000.
———. "The Mind in Winter: Reflections on Life in Exile." *Harper's* 269 (September 1984): 49–55.
Vendler, Helen. *Part of Nature, Part of Us: Modern American Poets*. Cambridge, MA: Harvard University Press, 1980.
———. *Soul Says: On Recent Poetry*. Cambridge, MA: Harvard University Press, 1995.
West, Cornell. *The American Evasion of Philosophy*. Madison, WI: The University of Wisconsin Press, 1989.
Wilson, Rob. *American Sublime: The Genealogy of a Poetic Genre*. Madison, WI: The University of Wisconsin Press, 1991.
Wong, Sau-Ling Cynthia. *Reading Asian American Literature: From Necessity to Extravagance*. Princeton, NJ: Princeton University Press, 1993.
Xu, Wenying. "The Opium Trade and *Little Dorrit*: A Case of Reading Silences." *Victorian Literature and Culture* 25 (1996): 53–66.
Yao, Steven G. "The Precision of Persimmons: Hybridity, Grafting and the Case of Li-Young Lee." *LIT: Literature Interpretation Theory* 12 (2001): 1–23.
Zhou, Xiaojing. "Inheritance and Invention in Li-Young Lee's Poetry." *MELUS* 21.1 (Spring 1996): 113-32.
Žižek, Slavoj. *Tarrying With the Negative: Kant, Hegel, and the Critique of Ideology*. Durham, NC: Duke University Press, 1993.

PART III

POPULAR CULTURE

Chapter 8

Canon-Openers, Book Clubs, and Middlebrow Culture

June Dwyer

It is the twenty-first century but neither the controversy between highbrows and middlebrows that started in the 1920s, nor the debate over the legitimacy of ethnic, gay, and women's studies that started in the 1970s is over. In fact, the latter seems to have re-ignited the former. Both have raised the same questions: Who determines literary merit? What is the level of intellectual involvement of a given reading audience? And perhaps most importantly, What is the nature of the relationship between the book, the author, and the reader? The highbrows and the modernist keepers of the canon answer the questions one way. The so-called middlebrows (whom I see as represented by members of grass roots book clubs, organizations such as the Book-of-the-Month Club, and the academic advocates of a broader literary canon) have a different set of responses. The purpose of this article is threefold. My first concern is to connect book clubs to the opening up of the traditional literary canon. The canonical legitimacy now accorded to popular culture and to gay, women's, and ethnic literature has usually been linked to efforts from advocates in academic settings. However, the role played by the nonacademic middle classes in opening up the canon to these fields is just beginning to be understood. My article's second aim is to explore briefly the nature and the cultural implications of book clubs, for they provide an interesting alternative to the two accepted sites of highbrow reading: the classroom and the solitary study. From the start, they suggested that there are other sites for serious reading and other ways of learning. The final aim of this article is to explore the shifting allocation of power between the author, the reader, and the text. In the highbrow world, the author creates the text and then, like God, passes it down to the readers. Production and reception in the middlebrow world look a little different. There, the reader with the assistance (but not the insistence) of a third party (a critic, teacher, or book club selection committee) chooses a text and develops a relationship with it. In essence, I will be arguing that book clubs (early and late) have helped to open the canon and in so doing have blurred the boundary between highbrow and middlebrow culture. Those academics who in the 1970s began the fight to open the canon have been doing similar cultural work: they should acknowledge and welcome the partnership.

Although we tend to think of the traditional literary canon opening up (or being assaulted, depending on your point of view) in the 1970s, sparked by campus activism, postmodern criticism, and the post-Watergate distrust of authority, the first salvo against it actually came several decades earlier. And it came quietly—when an economic and cultural enterprise called the Book-of-the-Month Club (created in 1926) encouraged the middle classes to believe that they had a stake in the field of literature and that they should enter into the enterprise by buying and reading preselected books. The Club, whose rationale has been carefully chronicled in Janice Radway's *A Feeling for Books: The Book-of-the-Month Club, Literary Taste, and Middle-Class Desire*, excited a backlash among the intelligentsia. Oddly enough, instead of being gratified that more people were being encouraged to read, many intellectuals felt threatened by the Club's existence. They looked askance at the purveying of what they considered to be less-than-great books to the bourgeoisie. They held the Club accountable for the diminution of the dignity of literature because it "either inspired consumers to purchase the mere signs of taste or prompted them to buy a specious imitation of true culture" (Radway 11). In particular, they seemed concerned about the questioning of their authority, about incursions into their carefully demarcated preserve. In 1960 Dwight Macdonald attacked the Club for pretending to respect the standards of high culture "while in fact it waters them down and vulgarizes them" ("Masscult and Midcult: II" 592).

The aims of the Club, as Radway observes, were multiple. It was an economic enterprise, which also tapped into the middle-classes' desire for status and their wish to rise in the world. But it also fostered a more open attitude toward reading. It consciously avoided the academic kind of reading that approaches "only a few sacralized books as objects to be revered or fetishized," and instead it encouraged the consumption of "all sorts of books as different and distinct occasions for reflection, meditation, contemplation, or pleasure" (360). This broad view of reading does not precisely anticipate what the radical scholars of the 1970s had in mind as they pried open the canon, nor did the middle classes and the Book-of-the-Month Club think they were dismantling a tradition. Nevertheless, their actions began to do just that. In their own businesslike way, the Book-of-the-Month Club and their customers, like the radical 1970s academics, were endorsing a broader view of why we read, what we read, and how we learn.

Of course, the Book-of-the-Month Club was not a club that had meetings. Its aim was to stimulate the desire to own and to read books; discussions were not part of the program. Nevertheless, at the time of its inception, reading groups, which had modestly dotted the American cultural landscape since the nineteenth century, began to grow in importance. As early as 1927, the American Library Association worked with John Erskine of Columbia University to print reading guides for library groups that wanted to discuss classics ("The Great Ideas"). The University of Chicago-inspired Great Books Foundation, a tightly structured organization that promoted community reading and discussion of "literature worth talking about" (*Great Books* 1) was established in 1949. In its heyday in the 1950s there were seven thousand adult education Great Books courses around the country ("The Great Ideas"). Although the interest in such prescribed and traditionally academic readings has greatly diminished, there are still, according to a recent Foundation brochure, more than eight hundred Great Books discussion groups in the United States (*Great Books* 16). Although they are not as well-documented, other less structured groups had also begun to form.[1] Joan Shelley Rubin suggests that part of the impetus to designate the Book-of-the-Month Club a "club" stemmed from already extant "women's study clubs, those locally based groups dedicated to perpetuating genteel formulations of culture by learning about the classics" (108). By the early 1990s there was sufficient interest in community book clubs that a self-styled reading group organizer named Rachel Jacobsohn, who had been directing local Chicago book groups for two decades, came out with a how-to book called *The Reading Group Handbook*. At the time, she estimated that 250,000 Americans were members of book groups (Jones 55). All of this was before Oprah Winfrey, another Chicagoan, came up with the idea of using her television show to promote reading and discussion on a truly mass scale through her own book club. At present Jacobsohn thinks there are perhaps 750,000 Americans in reading groups (Jones 55).

What interests me more than the proliferation of these different groups is the cultural message that they bear. Different though they each may be (without getting into highbrow, middlebrow, and lowbrow labeling), they share several important elements. It is, of course, tempting to say that the difference between the Great Books "reading and discussion programs" and the more informally designated "reading groups" and "book clubs" associated with Rachel Jacobsohn and Oprah Winfrey replicates the split between the traditional and the wide-open canon. But in terms of their joint impact, this difference seems only marginally important. Granted, there is a gender divide between them. The Great Books Foundation at its inception was male-inspired and even today seems largely male-run.[2] And the authors included in the original Great Books Reading and Discussion Program of seventy-five "classic" Western texts, which is still available today, are all dead white men. In contrast, the lists at the back of Jacobsohn's book (which are only samples, as opposed to preset syllabi) are generally contemporary, at least fifty percent female, and representative of authors of color. Oprah Winfrey's selections (until she decided to turn to established "classics" in 2003) are even more heavily female- and minority-authored.[3]

Nevertheless, I would like to suggest that, for a number of reasons, the Great Books groups, like the other two, have worked to subvert elitism, empower the middle classes, and open the canon. First of all, none of these groups is exclusive: they welcome anyone as a member. Although the Great Books curriculum itself originated at the extremely selective University of Chicago, the Great Books discussion groups have always practiced open admission. Furthermore, the participants are almost always adults rather than eighteen to twenty-two-year-old students. They may not have the IQs of Chicago's elite students, but like most adults in continuing education situations, although initially reticent, they invariably bring seriousness, insight, and subversive questioning to their groups. Another important point that aligns the Great Books groups with other book clubs is that although the former's texts may be intimidating, the atmosphere of the discussion is not. The discussion leaders in all of these clubs are not experts (professors with PhDs) but instead members of the group. The following paragraph from a sheet in the Great Books packet on "How to Start a Great Books Discussion Group" reflects not the old-style lecture or expert-led discussion of the traditional university (like Chicago) but instead the student-centered classroom that has come into vogue in the last several decades:

> Who leads the discussion? Make sure your group has at least two members who are willing to lead discussion; this will ensure a long life for your group. We have found that the most successful groups are those in which participants take turns leading. Some groups use co-leading, a process in which two people lead a discussion together. [. . .] [B]ecause each person will bring a different point of view to the reading, two people working together can prepare better discussion questions than either could alone. ("How to Start")

Yes, the Great Books groups may still be reading the "classics" but at a different venue, in a different way, with a different audience from the traditional classroom.

And over the years, the Great Books syllabus has been modified. In response to requests for more diversity and more contemporaneity, the Great Books Foundation has brought out a "50th Anniversary Series" of nine thematic anthologies (e.g. "Love and

Marriage," "Identity and Self-Respect"), which now include living authors, women, and writers of color. Furthermore, the Foundation, responding to "a community-based initiative" ("Great Books" 12), published a syllabus and reader in 2001 called *A Latino National Conversation*. What these developments strongly suggest is that even the most conservative book groups, because of the way they are organized, not only cater to, but also reflect the middle-class desires of their members, and that those desires are expansive rather than exclusive.

If the relatively quiet incursions of both the Book-of-the-Month Club and of neighborhood book clubs into canon-formation annoyed certain members of the elite, those elite sensibilities became more obviously inflamed with the assault on academic departments that began in the 1970s. Yet despite publication of irate books and articles, the withholding of monies by angry older alumni, and the formation of conservative organizations like the Association of Literary Scholars and Critics decrying the takeover of higher education by fuzzy thinking and narrow-minded radicals, curriculum changes have occurred in virtually every college and university in the country. According to the 2004 *PMLA Directory*, there are over six hundred colleges and universities with Women's Studies programs and over 180 with Ethnic Studies programs (1077–82, 1071–73). The fighting was ugly, but the war, at the end of the twentieth century, seemed to have been won.

However, the success of another book club—in this case, Oprah Winfrey's—rekindled the animosity in several highbrow quarters, further underlining the convergence between the cultural work being done by book clubs and that of academics who would expand the canon. Therefore, I would like to turn for a moment and look in detail at the contemporary highbrow attacks on both the newly opened canon and on Oprah's Book Club during the first seven years of its existence (1996–2002). The attacks on both are so startlingly similar that it seems clear they were doing parallel cultural work. Highbrows perceived both as a common enemy, upstarts who would seize authority about what should be read, how it should be read, and by whom. Both were trying to reach a larger and heretofore nontraditional audience.

When each began their enterprises, they were condescended to by the establishment. They were said to be dismissing the classics; they were asked if the material they were pushing really merited any attention at all. Wasn't it obvious that the works they selected did not measure up to the aesthetic criteria of great literature? Both were told that they picked a lot of texts with limited literary value, and they were accused of getting stuck on certain themes—victimology in particular. Furthermore, their audiences were thought to be less intelligent than the norm. Nevertheless, both groups succeeded. Now gay, women's, and ethnic studies advocates have their own organizations, academic programs, conferences, journals, and sessions at the MLA. Many of the works they have championed are back in print, in anthologies, and on syllabi other than their own. Oprah, too, achieved some legitimacy in the book world. In 1999 she was recognized at the National Book Awards for her contribution to reading and literature (Kirkpatrick E1).

Nevertheless, a rather spectacular skirmish occurred in the fall of 2001 between author Jonathan Franzen and Oprah's Book Club, raising questions in particular about the intelligence, and therefore the authority of various reading audiences. When his much-touted book *The Corrections* was chosen as an Oprah selection, Franzen demurred. And in so doing, he reminded cultural observers that there is still in the minds of many a divide out there between the "high-art literary tradition" where he situates his work, and those like Oprah, whom he called "a literary populist" (Scott E4). According to Margo Jefferson in her article "There Goes the Neighborhood," Franzen wanted his "like-minded admirers to be men" (35). He was worried that Oprah's mostly female audience would alienate male readers, who were scarce already. Franzen himself in his 1996 *Harper's* article "Perchance to Dream . . ." noted that seventy percent of all fiction readers are women. What he didn't say, but seemed to imply with respect to Oprah, was that her middle- and lower-class, less educated women readers would cheapen his efforts. And of course, they wouldn't understand or appreciate what he was doing. He then backpedaled, saying "Both Oprah and I want the same thing and believe the same thing, that the distinction between high and low is meaningless" (Kirkpatrick E1). Nevertheless, he also admitted to being "bombarded by questions" at bookstore readings, "mostly from the anti-Oprah camp" (Kirkpatrick E1). In other words, he continued to acknowledge that there was an anti-Oprah camp, without publicly saying he was part of it, or that this camp housed the embattled highbrows who were carrying on the fight for him.

Not all established authors felt as Franzen did. Joyce Carol Oates's reaction, when her book *We Were the Mulvaneys* was selected by Oprah, was totally different. In an interview with Recorded Books, she seemed pleased that Oprah had chosen her novel. The phone call came, she said, "out of the blue" and she praised the "wonderful young people" on Oprah's staff whom she met on her visit to Chicago to tape the show. She, like Franzen, differentiated between Oprah and the literary establishment but in a very different way. The Recorded Books interviewer, Denise Lanctot, asked her if the choice had changed her life as an author. This was not a dumb question, as *Times* reporter David Kirkpatrick has noted that being selected by Oprah generally boosted a book's sales by 500,000 copies and earned an author about $1.5 million (E1). Oates replied, tellingly, that with Oprah, it's not about authors; it's about books. She said that the literary establishment cares about the author and his personality, but that Oprah was, in contrast, trying to establish a *relationship* between her viewers and a *book*. This approach, according to Oates, is "more populist and democratic." Or, to put it another way, Oprah cares more about the reader than about the author. Oates accepted this perspective without difficulty, and voiced no worries about any audiences having trouble relating to *We Were The Mulvaneys* or indeed to any of her books. In fact, she noted in the interview that her aim in writing was to have her readers experience what her characters were experiencing—in other words, to have a relationship not with her but with her book. I would note here that Oates must be considered part of the literary establishment because she is an award-winning author, teaches at Princeton, and often writes for *The New York Times Book Review* and the *New York Review of Books*. Nevertheless, I have always felt that the establishment looks down on her because she is so prolific and perhaps also because she writes romances under a pseudonym. In any case, she certainly did not have an establishment view about Oprah.

Franzen, when he talked about audiences sounded very different from Oates. He still seemed to believe, as he did in his 1996 *Harper's* essay, that there is such a thing as a "serious" audience, which, of course, means that there are nonserious audiences as well. I don't think that anyone would disagree that there are indeed nonserious audiences,[4] but my sense is that the canon-openers (and Oates as well) are much more suspicious of demarcation lines in general and of where they have been traditionally drawn. Franzen, in his *Harper's* essay, was very much interested in the work of former MacArthur fellow, Shirley Brice Heath, who teaches at Stanford. Heath has studied the audience for serious fiction in America. Franzen seemed fascinated by this work, probably because he seeks that serious audience. His fascination bespeaks definition and exclusion. The subtext seems to be: "Who are these people and how can I reach them?" His rejection of Oprah and the idea of appearing on her show were a reflection on *her* audience and an unspoken assertion that they were not the group he was trying to reach. Like Dwight Macdonald fifty years ago, Franzen seemed to dismiss both the mass and the middlebrow audience as passive consumers rather than engaged and intelligent readers ("A Theory" 2). While Oprah, Oates, and book clubs see the experience of reading books as democratic, open, horizontal—indeed as a club, Franzen seems to view it as a hierarchy, a class to be taught, and not a discussion class, either. For him it's a lecture. For Franzen, the author is above the audience; the book exists without the audience, as (to use Radway's terminology) a sacralized object. If the audience wants to worship it, it must be initiated; it must be instructed.

When we think about the work that popular cultural entities perform, Paul Lauter has suggested that we need to ascertain how they "help construct the frameworks, fashion the metaphors, create the very language by which people comprehend their experiences and think about their world" (11). Using Lauter's categories helps to further connect book clubs to the opening of the canon and to the transformation of the college classroom as well. For book clubs are not only actual entities; they have, over the years, become metaphors as well. A club is an affinity group, an amalgamation of like-minded people, and though some clubs may be exclusive, their internal organization is by and large democratic. One person does not call the shots. A club is a community whose members jointly decide on issues that are important to them. This organizational structure differentiates clubs from solitary activities performed by an individual and from activities where an individual sits in an audience and is instructed. Simply by calling the Book-of-the-Month Club a *club*, even though it was not technically one that met, its founders were suggesting reading as an experience held in common.[5] If not literally, then at least metaphorically, the Book-of-the-Month Club was a club. Although it did not explicitly encourage discussion groups (unlike Oprah's club, which did so by having both televised and online discussions), the word itself planted the seed. It encouraged the middle classes to talk to others about books jointly read. The power of this metaphor to generate discussion makes middlebrow reading a particularly interesting cultural phenomenon, since books in America have traditionally been associated with solitary reading or with lectures in college classrooms and public forums. But these traditional sites of reading have shifted, or to be more precise, they have broadened to include areas where groups discuss books.

Both the number of book clubs and their mode of organization are important to my argument, for book-club formation, given the numbers, could, in the first decade of the twenty-first century, fairly be called a mass movement. Publishers cater to book clubs by putting discussion questions online or at the backs of their books, and bookstores and libraries organize and house book clubs. A sizeable segment of the literate public in the United States now is engaged in group discussions of books. Other than being a boon to book publishers and booksellers, book clubs have been a boon to members, empowering them to both make choices about what they want to read and then to speak with authority about these selections. If the majority of the country's book clubs either opted to or felt it incumbent upon themselves to read only canonical literature, they would tend toward an informal replication of the college classroom—at least the college classroom of the first three quarters of the twentieth century. And if all book clubs had paid experts leading discussions, they would be even more like the old college classroom. But this is not what is happening. The members have the power of selection, and, except with Great Books groups, there is no parent organization. While some clubs do hire facilitators to help them organize and choose books, those facilitators do not dictate.

This does not mean that book club members root around in libraries to make their selections or that they wade through the many unheralded books that are published each year. They listen to suggestions from national and local newspapers, from businesses like Amazon.com, and from librarians. But they have a much wider range of choice than traditional readers and students of literature have had in the past. And, more importantly, they understand that they have the license to say, "No, we don't trust that reviewer," or "Let's read something from a small press." The result is that thousands of readers feel empowered to make their own judgments and their own mistakes. Yes, their choices are still influenced by the media and the book business, but they also listen to one another and make commonsense decisions. They pick books that they think will be of interest to themselves, and they bring their own experiences to bear on what they read.

If this pattern sounds familiar to academics, it is because it mimics to some degree what has been happening in English and American literature departments for the last three decades. Both new works and new ways of teaching have transformed the literature classroom from a stage whereon a professional performs, to—need I say it?—a club where conversations between members take place. I am not about to suggest that since book clubs came before canon- and classroom-renewal that they have made them possible. Nevertheless, the clubs, the canon expansion, and the transformation of the college classroom are all part of the postmodern moment, where accepted authority has been undermined and voices from the margins have gained authenticity. Middle-class book club participants may now be included with women, people of color, gays, and college students, as people whose opinions matter. All of these once-disenfranchised groups now have some influence and some respect. I think that it is particularly important to include book clubs in the mix that has brought about the dramatic change in what is read in this country and how it is discussed, because they are a middle-class rather than an elite or "highbrow" phenomenon. Although changes in literature departments were brought about by the traditionally disenfranchised (that is, people of color, gays, women, and those with working-class backgrounds), these individuals had moved into the elite by dint of their garnering intellectual capital in the form of their PhDs. Book club participants, on the other hand, have remained middle class, encompassing a much broader cross section of the reading population.

What does this mean culturally? Something very important, I think. It means that the middle classes, without moving into the intellectual elite, are allied with them (or at least with the canon-opening branch of them). This is a cultural milestone, because for a good part of the twentieth century, the intelligentsia have looked down on the bourgeoisie. They have often embraced the folk or the working classes but found the middle classes bland and dronelike. In 1923 T. S. Eliot, manifesting what David Chinitz calls the "modernist antagonism toward the middle class," decried the art favored by the middle classes as full of "sham ideas, sham emotions, and even sham sensations" (239). And in his 1960 essay attacking what he dubbed "masscult" and "midcult" (that is, mass culture and middle-class culture), Dwight Macdonald singled out the Book-of-the-Month Club as the embodiment of middle-class culture. Both Eliot and Macdonald attacked the "passivity" (Chinitz 239; Macdonald, "A Theory" 2) of the middle classes, suggesting that they did not want to enter into the American cultural conversation. If we in academic departments today believe that the middle classes are indeed capable of discernment and judgment (which I certainly think they are), we are according yet another silenced group, its legitimate voice.

And in that voice are contained not only insights and ideas, but also implicit critique. Although no one actually comes out and says so, those being criticized are not only the traditionalists but also the radical academics. For, alas, members of the intelligentsia (both traditionalists and radicals) have always been loath to admire the middle class *as the middle class*. Either they have tried to exclude them, in the manner of Dwight Macdonald, or improve them, in the manner of the canon-openers and the purveyors of the Great Books. To hail book-club members as a legitimate voice *as they are* and to value the book club as a legitimate site of learning is for many no easy task. For it asks those who have moved into the intelligentsia from the middle classes to come to terms with their own bourgeois roots. Janice Radway, by admitting in *A Feeling for Books* that "I still liked the books I read at night [that is, Book-of-the-Month type books] a lot more than the books I read for my classes" (3), gives us all license to do the same. We not only like these books, but we also learn from them. And if we listen to the middle-class members of the book clubs (as we have learned to listen to our students), we may learn even more.[6]

Notes

1. Because the Great Books Foundation has always been highly structured and centralized, it has the best statistics on club numbers. Membership in decentralized reading groups sponsored by local libraries and other civic organizations is harder to estimate.

2. The founders, Mortimer Adler and Robert Hutchins and their followers, were all men, and in the 2001 material sent out by the Foundation, both the Adult Program Director and the Adult Program Coordinator are men; twelve of the eighteen regional council presidents and regional representatives are men. This is striking because membership in most other book clubs is, by all accounts, overwhelmingly female.

3. See Jacobsohn, *Reading Group*, 141–96 and the appendix to this article. Even Oprah's turn to the classics shows her inclination toward diversity. In 2003 and 2004, she chose one male and one female American author (John Steinbeck and Carson McCullers), one European (Leo Tolstoy), one Latin American (Gabriel García Marquez), and one South African (Alan Paton).

4. The Reading With Ripa Book Club, for example, cites as a criterion for its choices books that have "no message." See http://tvplex.go.com/buenavista/livewith regis/bookclub/.

5. Joan Shelley Rubin points out that as early as the 1880s, mail-order advertisers had organized "clubs" for housewives to pool orders of household goods. She also mentions that the term conjures up "the tradition of women's study clubs," but suggests that by the beginning of the twentieth century, "the 'club idea' had an overarching meaning—the desire of Americans to band together in a world grown uncomfortably anonymous and diverse" with the idea of "achieving a feeling of community, based on shared interests" (108–9).

6. After this essay was submitted to the publishers, Oprah Winfrey reconstituted her book club in September 2005 to include contemporary works, once again, in a wider variety of genres like memoir, history, and biography. See Hughlett and Wyatt. Also see Rooney and Farr, who have recently published full-length books on Oprah's book club.

Works Cited

Chinitz, David. "T.S. Eliot and the Cultural Divide." *PMLA* (March 1995): 236–47.

Farr, Cecelia Koncher. *Reading Oprah: How Oprah's Book Club Changed the Way America Reads*. Albany, NY: State University of New York Press, 2004.

Franzen, Jonathan. "'Perchance to Dream . . .'" *Harper's* (April 1996): start 35 (20 pages), retrieved from ProQuest online.

Great Books Reading and Discussion Programs: Literature Worth Talking About. Chicago: The Great Books Foundation, November 2001.

"Great Books Councils." Great Books Foundation, February 2001.

"How to Start a Great Books Discussion Group." The Great Books Foundation, May 2001.

Hughlett, Mike. "Authors, Sellers Welcome Boost from Book Club." *Chicago Tribune*, 24 September 2005: sec. 2: 1+.

Jacobsohn, Rachel. *The Reading Group Handbook*. New York: Hyperion, 1994.

Jefferson, Margo. "There Goes the Neighborhood." *New York Times Book Review* 24 November 2001: 35.

Jones, Malcolm. "Reading All About It." *Newsweek* 29 July 2002: 54–56.

Kirkpatrick, David D. "'Oprah' Gaffe By Franzen Draws Ire And Sales." *New York Times* 29 October 2001:E1, E5.

Lauter, Paul. *From Walden Pond to Jurassic Park*. Durham, NC: Duke University Press, 2001.

Macdonald, Dwight. "A Theory of Mass Culture." *Diogenes* (Summer 1953): 1–7.

———. "Masscult and Midcult II." *Partisan Review* (Fall 1960): 589–631.

Oates, Joyce Carol. Interview with Denise Lanctot on Recorded Books Audiotape of *We Were the Mulvaneys*, 2001.

"Oprah's Book Club Archive." *Oprah's Books*, http://www.oprah.com/obc/pastbooks/.

"Philosophy: Great Books Discussions and Shared Inquiry." *The Great Books Foundation*. http://greatbooks.org/printer/programs/gb/sharinq/index.shtml.

PMLA Directory. New York: Modern Language Association of America, 2004.

Radway, Janice. *A Feeling For Books: The Book-of-the-Month Club, Literary Taste and Middle-Class Desire*. Chapel Hill, NC: University of North Carolina Press, 1997.

Rooney, Kathleen. *Reading with Oprah: The Book Club that Changed America*. Fayetteville, AR: University of Arkansas Press, 2005.

Rubin, Joan Shelley. *The Making of Middlebrow Culture*. Chapel Hill, NC: University of North Carolina Press, 1992.

Scott, A. O. "Seizing the Literary Middle." *New York Times* 4 November 2001: E4.

"The Great Ideas: The University of Chicago and the Idea of Liberal Education." University of Chicago Research Center. http://www.lib.uchicago.edu/e/spcl/excat/.

Wyatt, Edward. "Oprah's Book Club Reopening to Writers Who'll Sit and Chat." *New York Times*. 23 September 2005: A1+.

Appendix:
List of Selections of Oprah's Book Club
1996–2004

1996   *The Book of Ruth* by Jane Hamilton
Song of Solomon by Toni Morrison
The Deep End of the Ocean by Jacquelyn Mitchard

1997   *The Meanest Thing to Say* by Bill Cosby
The Treasure Hunt by Bill Cosby
The Best Way to Play by Bill Cosby
Ellen Foster by Kaye Gibbons
A Virtuous Woman by Kaye Gibbons
A Lesson Before Dying by Ernest Gaines
Songs in Ordinary Time by Mary McGarry Morris
The Heart of a Woman by Maya Angelou
The Rapture of Canaan by Sheri Reynolds
Stones from the River by Ursula Hegi
She's Come Undone by Wally Lamb

1998   *Where the Heart Is* by Billie Letts
Midwives by Chris Bohjalian
What Looks Like Crazy on an Ordinary Day by Pearl Cleage
I Know This Much Is True by Wally Lamb

Breath, Eyes, Memory by Edwidge Danticat
Black and Blue by Anna Quindlen
Here on Earth by Alice Hoffman
Paradise by Toni Morrison

1999 *A Map of the World* by Jane Hamilton
Vinegar Hill by A. Manette Ansay
River, Cross My Heart by Breena Clarke
Tara Road by Maeve Binchy
Mother of Pearl by Melinda Haynes
White Oleander by Janet Fitch
The Pilot's Wife by Anita Shreve
The Reader by Bernhard Schlink
Jewel by Brett Lott

2000 *House of Sand and Fog* by Andre Dubus III
Drowning Ruth by Christina Schwarz
Open House by Elizabeth Berg
The Poisonwood Bible by Barbara Kingsolver
While I Was Gone by Sue Miller
The Bluest Eye by Toni Morrison
Back Roads by Tawni O'Dell
Daughter of Fortune by Isabel Allende
Gap Creek by Robert Morgan

2001 *A Fine Balance* by Rohinton Mistry
The Corrections by Jonathan Franzen
Cane River by Lalita Tademy
Stolen Lives: Twenty Years in a Desert Jail by Malika Oufkir
Icy Sparks by Gynn Hyman Rubio
We Were the Mulvaneys by Joyce Carol Oates

2002 *Sula* by Toni Morrison
Fall on Your Knees by Ann-Marie MacDonald

2003 *East of Eden* by John Steinbeck
Cry, the Beloved Country by Alan Paton

2004 *One Hundred Years of Solitude* by Gabriel García Márquez
The Heart is a Lonely Hunter by Carson McCullers
Anna Karenina by Leo Tolstoy

Chapter 9

From the Boardroom to Cocktail Parties

"Great" Books, Multiethnic Literature, and the Production of the Professional Managerial Class in the Context of Globalization

Sarika Chandra

Present Day Context of the Canon Debates

The fact that university courses include the study of texts by ethnic writers such as Toni Morrison, Frank Chin, and Leslie Silko may lead us to believe that we have done the work of challenging the canon so that we can teach courses in, say, Chicano literatures alongside courses that feature the more mainstream and canonical texts. Although there is much work to be done in this area, we can safely say that texts that fall under the major categories of multiethnic literary scholarship such as African American and Asian American literatures have become an important part of American literary study. In addition, theoretical scholarship in cultural studies has challenged the notion of high and low cultures, to the effect that television advertisements make as interesting an object of study as Herman Melville's novels. Ethnic as well as other approaches to literary study such as feminism and queer theory have established their own categories of texts and also read rebelliously within the canon. But the perception that the value of mainstream and canonical works exceeds those of multiethnic texts is still far from displaced. In fact, this perception is being consolidated in unexpected ways in a globalized context.

Cocktail Parties: Cultural Capital and the Professional Managerial Class

Various publishing companies, among them Random House, have established a list of the one hundred "best" or "great" books that include mostly what are considered to be Western or Euro-American classics such as James Joyce's *Ulysses*, F. Scott Fitzgerald's *The Great Gatsby*, and just a few ethnic and non-Western texts by highly recognized authors such as Toni Morrison (*Beloved*) and Salman Rushdie (*The Satanic Verses*). InteliQuest has a similar list of World's Greatest Books that includes one or two multiethnic titles. These reading lists are part of marketing strategies employed by publishing companies and other booksellers to secure a reading public that falls into the American professional managerial class or PMC.[1] For example, InteliQuest markets a condensed audiocassette version of the World's Greatest list to corporate professionals who do not have time to read but want to be well read. Their advertisement claims to offer "A Lifetime of Learning in a Fraction of the Time . . ." (InteliQuest Learning Systems). Another company, All Things Family, markets its 100 Greatest Books CD collection as a "great educational resource." It claims: "Great literature can transport you to imaginative worlds full of romance, struggle and excitement. The World's 100 Greatest Books provides biographical information about each writer and details about the plots and characters of their classic works" (skymall.com). The company also suggests how busy professionals can find time to listen to this information, for instance in their car driving to and from work. The marketing language here is an indication of the fact that professionals are mostly interested in literature as a form of cultural capital, which they can acquire by learning a few facts about literary texts that they can perhaps drop in conversations at cocktail parties. In fact, their "appreciation" of "great" literary works can be likened to their "appreciation" of fine wines at receptions. Both indicate culture in the sense of "culturedness" and sophistication.

At first glance it might hardly seem that the desire on the part of business professionals to acquire cultural capital through literary texts is worth our attention. Nor is it surprising that their interest in literature does not go beyond a few facts about each text. More importantly, we as literary and cultural critics see literary production and scholarship as opposing corporate interest. But if we are indeed to oppose corporate interest then we must pay attention to the function of literary texts for corporate managers and what implications this has for the existing curricula as well as for its potential to shape it in the future.

In *Distinction* (1984) Pierre Bourdieu has shown that accumulation of cultural capital through products such as works of art and literature is based on social class and is designed to maintain class divisions. "Cultural Nobility" deeply connected with the bourgeoisie, for example, is cultivated by the association of refinement and distinction to acquisition of products. But the fact that the PMC does indeed appear interested in acquiring capital at present in the form of literature runs counter to conventional assumptions such as those voiced by John Guillory. In *Cultural Capital* (1993), he asserts that the PMC "no longer requires the cultural capital of the old bourgeoisie"—meaning, cultural capital in its "traditional," literary and artistic form. (45). In a discussion of how the positioning of ethnic literature in opposition to the "great" works is problematic, Guillory shows that this opposition is just as often mobilized by the right as it is by the leftist multiculturalists. In Guillory's view, the PMC has assessed that "as far as its future profit is concerned, reading great works is not worth the investment of money or time" (45). The members and aspiring members of this class, according to Guillory's argument, tend to desire technical skills instead. But then how do we account for the seeming fact that professionals do indeed think literature to be worth the investment of their money if not their time? And more importantly, in what ways can we expect the perceptions of business professionals to affect university curricula?

The idea that professional demands have already begun to affect university courses is explored by Evan Watkins. In *Everyday Exchanges* (1998) he states, "positions in English studies are already affiliated with specific publics depending on how claims for professional status are made and realized in specific ensembles of practices" (186). Both Watkins and Guillory advance the idea that composition studies are a good example of how professional interests are instrumental in shaping university curricula. Indeed, composition studies are just as much focused on technical writing as on critical writing.

Guillory suggests that the "professional-managerial class . . . many of whose members have only recently attained to middle- and upper-middle class status, depends entirely on the acquisition of technical knowledge" (47). He makes such apt observations to show that the opposition between "Western culturalism [and] multiculturalism" that has fueled canon debates works much more in the interest of the right than the left, and that harms the study of literary texts in general. But as book lists such as those cited above and, as we shall see shortly, the "literary" concerns of management theory itself show, literary texts are becoming extremely crucial to management professionals. It may not be so far-fetched to think that universities might return increasingly to courses in "great" works as they become conscious of a demand for this from the PMC. In fact management curricula in universities across the country are already beginning to reflect the way in which literary fiction is becoming important to management practitioners. One such example is a course offered at the Harvard Business School entitled "The Moral Leader" in which students read classics such as *Macbeth* and *The Secret Sharer* alongside *The Last Tycoon*, and *Remains of the Day*. They also study the philosophy of "Aristotle, Confucius, and Machiavelli, to clarify the issues of personal character and sound, practical judgment" (*Elective Curriculum MBA Courses 2001–02, Harvard Business School*). This list seems to be fairly typical of such courses, in which students read an older set of canonical texts with one or two contemporary or lesser-known works. These courses are offered through many other management programs such as those at New York University, Columbia University, and many more. And the fact that very few multiethnic works make it on to the lists and courses geared toward business professionals is indicative of the fact that some of the ideas that arose during the culture wars are operational in the production of these lists. Specifically, the notion that great Western texts carry wisdom unmatched by the literary production of either U.S. ethnic or non-Western writers seems particularly poignant here.[2]

"Great" Books, Multiethnic Fiction, and the Global Firm

Neverthless, an awareness of a changed, global context is reflected in the modest degree to which U.S. multiethnic and more recent world fiction does find its way onto such reading lists. One of the leading American management theorists, Tom Peters, for example, recommends that business practitioners read books by Gabriel García Márquez along with those by Paul Bowles and Norman Mailer (*Liberation Management* 1992). Nevertheless, the inclusion of names such as García Márquez, Ralph Ellison, Toni Morrison, and Salman Rushdie on the reading lists for the PMC does not simply reflect the fact that we live in a world that has become interconnected. Rather it also speaks to the fact that whether or not corporate management likes it, issues of cultural diversity are becoming extremely crucial to corporations in the context of globalization[3]

The idea of culture has long been of importance to the corporate world, mostly in the ethnographic sense of learning factual cultural information for the purposes of managing employee diversity and of selling products to consumers from diverse cultures. But in the context of globalization, cultural issues have become even more paramount for corporations. While literary and cultural studies fear the loss of "culture" as corporatization becomes more pronounced, business and management theorists emphasize its importance in helping them realize profit. In his book, *Selling Globalization* (1998), Michael Veseth points out "international marketing textbooks are filled with studies of global strategies defeated by language, culture, or local practice" (53). These cases of international failure have led management theorists to think that it is not simply enough to have knowledge about the cultural patterns of the people in their markets. Theorists are realizing that management practitioners have to change the way they think.

Tom Peters begins one of his books, *The Circle of Innovation* (1997), with quotes from CEOs who claim that corporate practices must change to meet the needs of a rapidly emerging new era. Lew Platt, Chairman and CEO of Hewlett Packard, declares: "Whatever made you successful in the past *won't* in the future." Peter Georgescu, chairman and CEO of Young & Rubicam, claims: "It's the end of the world as we know it." Making further, similar pronouncements, such as "distance is dead" and "destruction is cool," *The Circle of Innovation* joins a long list of books on globalization that declare the emergence of a new world order and the death of an old one.

Consequently, rather than merely accumulating cultural capital for the sake of appreciating "great" literature, management theorists are turning to literary fiction to help them negotiate corporate problems that arise in the context of globalization. For example, in ways similar to those of other management theorists, Peters employs literature and culture in order to think about this new world order. In *Liberation Management*, he states—in a notably "un-businesslike" way—that

> To read Max Frisch, Paul Bowles, Gabriel García Márquez, Anton Chekhov, Jane Smiley, Malcolm Lowry, or Norman Mailer is to consume a rich diet of relationships, chance, interconnectedness, songlines, things large within small, small within large, things within things that nonetheless encompass things that are beyond them. (375)

For Peters, attention to such "interconnections" and "chances" in organizational life is crucially required to succeed in what he calls "a knowledge economy." He goes on to claim that "the richness of life, which we accept as private selves and when we turn to novels or poetry, seems abandoned at the front door of the business or public agency establishment" (375). He further urges business practitioners to adopt novels and poetry as pedagogical tools, and implies that the "richness of life" (that is, cultural matters) seems at once necessary and difficult for members of corporations to understand because thus far these issues have been "abandoned at the front door." Therefore, business practitioners are looking for help from literary fiction to solve administrative problems. As Peters says: "If fiction and poetry (drama, opera, etc.) capture life better than other cultural media, then why not think of fiction as a model for organization?" (375).

In a large measure, particular texts turn out to be canonical—the "great works" as well as books by "great" Western thinkers. For instance, Peter Drucker, another influential management theorist, suggests that the history of Western thought has much to teach management practitioners. In *The Executive in Action* (1996), Drucker enlists Kierkegaard to support his ideas on individuality and individual freedom. Applying such ideas to contemporary conditions, Tom Peters asserts that the way in which organizations are run have "more in common with convolution within convolution in Norman Mailer's *Harlot's Ghost* than with [management theory's latest pronouncements]" (379). This turn toward fiction, along with questions such as whether organizations "really" do exist, seems also to emerge from the theoretical underpinnings of postmodernism. In fact Peters says: "[L]et's hold applause for chaos theory. Instead of the frantic pursuit of total comprehension (via central-control schemes) let's revel in our very lack of comprehension!" (*Liberation Management* 491). Although Peters himself draws upon scientific versions of chaos theory, notions of chaos and apparent synonyms such as "conundrum," "convolution," and "ambiguity" would, one presumes, lead him more towards postmodernist fiction with its emphasis on the dissolution of metanarratives, fragmentation and, indeed, chaos. More importantly, the pressing issues of cultural diversity that make management practitioners turn to literary fiction in the first place, assuming it is not mere self-indulgence on the part of idiosyncratic management theorists, would lead them toward contemporary U.S. multiethnic and world fiction. However, to complicate matters further, Peters and others choose a list of authors and titles that for the most part do not make for an easy fit into these categories. Why might this be?

In *The Condition of Postmodernity* (1990), David Harvey defines two significant features of the present world financial system as follows: (1) the formation of financial conglomerates such as the World Bank and the IMF which, since their inception in 1944 and 1945 respectively, have come to command tremendous global powers; (2) the creation of new financial instruments and markets which in turn produce a proliferation and decentralization of financial activities and flows. Consequently the global financial system has become "so complicated that it surpasses most people's understanding. The boundaries between distinctive functions like banking, brokerage, financial services, housing finance, consumer credit, and the like have become increasingly porous at the same time that new markets in commodity, stock, currency, or debt futures have sprung up, discounting time future into time present in baffling ways" (161). In other words, the seeking of profit has become baffling and chaotic even for those business theorists and practitioners who have been responsible for studying and disseminating ways to understand financial systems. Along these lines, might we not speculate that the reasons certain leading business theorists have begun to ponder the fictive nature of their organizations stem from the fact that it is not exactly clear to them how to go about understanding the nature of the present system as a whole. Consequently we see a turn to culture and the cultural and even to literary fiction because, in the absence of a convincing or comprehensible social or economic theory, they can be presented as new ways of understanding globalization.

However, since it is not clear how one is to go about understanding contemporary conditions in order to earn a profit, the endeavor to understand cultural diversity or to rethink practices for monetary profit from the standpoint of writers such as Toni Morrison and Gabriel García Márquez can itself only go so far before it too turns baffling. Such texts often illustrate the problems associated with corporate expansion and contraction. While the rhetoric of newness that is part of American corporate enterprise—witness Tom Peters—is heady and exciting, ethnic works tend to show current problems arising from cultural differences and do not necessarily portray an exciting disposition towards the present state of affairs. Ultimately, it would seem, such texts cannot be good guides for selling to a diverse public, managing employees from different cultures, or navigating through complex economic/financial systems. For example, consider a recent use of Toni Morrison's fiction. In "The Trader: Stocks Gain Ground Through [sic] Corporate Woes Grow" published in *Barron's*, Michael Santoli writes: "There's a novel by Toni Morrison that takes place in a town's poorer, black neighborhood, known as The Bottom even though it rests in the unfertile hills high above a river. The area's earliest residents were duped into moving there by a dishonest slave-owner who assured them it was desirable 'bottom land'" (MW 2). Santoli uses this description to warn against mistakes in stock trading. He goes on to say that the Bottom

> could be a metaphor for the kind of enduring, painful mistake that investors are desperate to avoid right now- being led by hope and misplaced trust to believe they're at an attractive bottom. Analysts are quick to plead impotence in declaring definitively that stocks have reached their lows. After all, bottoming is a process, not a moment in time, and the trough is clear only in hindsight. (MW 2)

The use of Morrison's novel (I assume he means *Sula*) to think through issues in financial securities and exchange seems odd to say the least. Nevertheless, he does acknowledge that stocks can reach the bottom and employs *Sula* to show that living in such a bottom, thinking one is perhaps at the "top," is indeed not a desirable thing. But structurally, the goal for making a profit by managing the stock market does not allow for something other than buying low and selling high. This is only a caution against "bad" bottom stocks rather than good ones, for Santoli will not argue against the system of stock brokerage itself.

Morrison's novels, however, illustrate the problems with capitalism in general. *Sula* opens with a description of the Bottom that is actually on the hills. The first thing we hear about the Bottom is that its trees such as oaks, maples, and chestnuts along with the nightshade and blackberry patches have been torn "from their roots" to build a golf course (3). The people of the Bottom share a similar fate as they have also been uprooted. This aspect of the novel serves to remind us of the systemic violent uprootings of African Americans at many different levels. In Morrison's illustration, the problem isn't so much that those people duped into living in the infertile Bottom would be better off if they had been able to claim a piece of fertile land for themselves; rather, Morrison shows the problems with the entire structure that sytematically produces the hierarchies between top and bottom, white and black. By examining the continuous uprooting of African Americans, the novel not only exposes the greed and hierarchies in society, but also critiques the premise of the system in which people and plants are torn violently from their roots as their death and agony becomes normalized.

Morrison's other novels also portray the problems with capitalism. For example, Valerian, a character in *Tar Baby*, is a man who has accumulated considerable wealth in the candy business. The story connects present-day capitalism with plantation slave labor since the ingredients for the candy—sugar and cocoa—have a history of being harvested on plantations in the Caribbean. His relationship with his employees is similar to that of a master with his slaves. In addition, the building of the house in which he lives not only resembles a scene out of plantation life, but also destroys much of the natural surroundings. Read in this way, Morrison's work can hardly be made to function as models for corporate organizations! It shows the crushing problems of capitalism, intertwined with issues of racism and sexism. Perhaps this explains why, despite a certain noblesse oblige on the part of "gurus" like Peters and Drucker, there is a paucity of multiethnic texts on the various PMC reading lists.

It is true, as Guillory argues, that the opposition between older canonical works and minority literatures can be a false one. Nor can it be denied that writers like Morrison have gained a stable presence in American literary curricula. Notwithstanding this, however, she continues to be placed in opposition to writers considered canonical and mainstream by both literary and management theorists. An article published by *Fortune* that profiles four businessmen, authored by Thomas Stewart and others, states: "To select one man to be the Businessman of the Century is to look back upon almost unimaginable change. The world of Henry Ford . . . and the world of [Bill] Gates . . . are as different from one another as Henry James from Toni Morrison, high tea from happy hour, or Queen Victoria from Bill Clinton" ("Henry Ford, Alfred P. Sloan, Tom Watson Jr., Bill Gates" 108). Leaving aside for the moment that this casually evoked opposition between James and Morrison is not based on careful reading of their work, the opposition itself, as between "black" and "white" literature in general, reproduces an idea that has been endemic to the culture wars and the canon debates: that ethnicity and race form the basis of culture and the cultural. But, while Morrison's writing style and subject matter differ from that of James, and James can be taken to task for racism, associating James with the "good old days" of American business is itself a piece of myth-making and shows how desperate the PMC seems to have become for literary capital, "blue chip" and otherwise. For in James's work, as in Morrison's, there is ample literary basis from which to critique corporate enterprise. In *The American Scene*, a collection of his late works, James, for example, laments the loss of culture to "money in the air, ever so much money—grossly expressed," and to the "triumphant payers of dividends" (192). Here James is not so much evoking the hackneyed opposition between culture and material wealth as he is questioning, out loud, whether anything but the latter remains at the heart of American "culture." According to James,

> that of active pecuniary gain and of active pecuniary gain only—that of one's making the condition so triumphantly pay that the prices, the manners, the other inconveniences, take their place as a friction it is comparatively easy to salve, wounds directly treatable with the wash of gold. What prevails, what sets the tune, is the American scale of gain, more magnificent than any other, and the fact that the whole assumption, the whole theory of life, is that of the individual's participation in it, that of his being more or less punctually and more or less effectually "squared." To make so much money that you won't, that you don't "mind," don't mind anything—that is absolutely, I think, the main American formula. (236–37)

The tone of James' words ("wounds directly treatable with the wash of gold") hardly suggests that PMC will find endorsement of corporate practices much less solutions to contemporary problems associated with the crisis of accumulation. No doubt the America of James' day differs radically from Morrison's, but this difference, though it makes James a reference point for the PMC "cultural" (and perhaps racial) nostalgia, scarcely makes of him a source of literary legitimation for the once simpler pursuit of financial gain. James is objecting to the basis of financial activity, not so much as an opposition to business in favor of culture and the cultural but more so to the nature of the system that produces the pursuit of pecuniary gain as a single basis for culture. Therefore the nature of critique in the works of *both* Morrison and James operates in a similar manner and questions the systemic nature of uprooting and violence in relationship to the pursuit of profit.

The curious (but perhaps not so curious) fact is that only those multiethnic and non-Western writers that have become highly recognized appear on the reading lists for the PMC—even while still being differentiated from their Euro-American counterparts. One suspects here that these books, even more than their canonical "business partners," are being read simply to enhance their readers' cultural capital and that "book appreciation" takes on an added significance here. The urge for accumulating cultural capital comes to stand in here, in an unmitigated way, for critical engagement with the texts. In effect, while appearing to attend to issues of cultural diversity by advocating the reading of literary texts, the PMC assimilates these books to an older form of cultural capital, and seeks to maintain status quo with ever-recurring appeals to the "great works." While arguing for new and fresh ways of dealing with corporate problems, management practitioners consistently suggest the reading of older canonical texts, in effect bestowing a quality of timelessness on these works of literary fiction. In this way management theory attempts to situate its concerns in a realm that, in appearance, does not itself change with the passage of time and history, an idea that has been a significant aspect of the canon debates. What else but to hold onto something that seems timeless? In this way business professionals seek out continuity when discontinuity seems to rule the day. Ideas of culture and great literary texts in effect help the PMC to circumvent the kinds of issues they otherwise proclaim the need to address. Such circumvention is, in effect, reproducing the necessity for the canon debates of past decades, perhaps even replicating them, albeit for different reasons in the present context of globalization.

Notes

1. The professional managerial class according to critics such as John Guillory (*Cultural Capital*, 1993) and Bruce Robbins (*Secular Vocations*, 1993) is comprised of that group of people who are different from

the older bourgeoisie but have gained entry into the middle or the upper middle class through professionalization in relationship to their career building.

2. While many argue that globalization has existed in some form or other since the 1400s, the term itself describes the more contemporary conditions, which are in part created by the uneven expansion and detraction of capital around the world. See David Harvey's *Spaces of Hope* (Berkeley, CA: University of California, 2000).

3. Scholarship on globalization shows that however incomplete the processes of globalization may be, they are presented as inevitable and coercive, affecting and erasing certain cultural practices. See for example, Fernando Henrique Cardoso's *Charting a New Course* (Lanham, MD: Rowman & Littlefield Publishers, 2001); and Kenichi Ohmae's *The End of the Nation State* (New York: The Free Press, 1995).

Works Cited

Bourdieu, Pierre. *Distinction: A Social Critique of the Judgement of Taste.* Trans. Richard Nice. Cambridge, MA: Harvard University Press, 1984.

Cardoso, Fernando Henrique. *Charting a New Course: The Politics of Globalization and Social Transformation.* Lanham, MD: Rowman & Littlefield Publishers, 2001.

Drucker, Peter Ferdinand. *The Executive in Action.* New York, NY: HarperBusiness, 1996.

Guillory, John. *Cultural Capital: The Problem of Literary Canon Formation.* Chicago: University of Chicago Press, 1993.

Harvey, David. *The Condition of Postmodernity: An Enquiry into the Origins of Cultural Change.* Cambridge, MA: Blackwell, 1990.

———. *Spaces of Hope.* Berkeley, CA: University of California Press, 2000.

James, Henry. *The American Scene.* London: Chapman and Hall, Ltd., 1907.

Jay, Gregory S. *American Literature and the Culture Wars.* Ithaca, NY: Cornell University Press, 1997.

Lauter, Paul. *Canons and Contexts.* New York: Oxford University Press, 1991.

"The Moral Leader." Elective Curriculum MBA Courses 2001–02, General Management Course 1562. Harvard Business School, Cambridge, MA. Winter 2001. October 1, 2002. <http://www.hbs.edu/mba/admin/acs/1562.html>.

Morrison, Toni. *Sula.* New York: Plume, 1996.

———. *Tar Baby.* New York: A. A. Knopf; Random House, 1981.

Ohmae, Kenichi. *The End of the Nation-State: The Rise of Regional Economies*. New York: The Free Press, 1995.

"100 Greatest Books CD." SkyMall.com. September 13, 2002. <http://www.skymall.com/cgibin/WebObjects/Store.woa/wa/>.

Peters, Thomas J. *The Circle of Innovation: You Can't Shrink Your Way to Greatness*. New York: A. A. Knopf, 1997.

———. *Liberation Management: Necessary Disorganization for the Nanosecond Nineties*. New York: A. A. Knopf, 1992.

Robbins, Bruce. *Secular Vocations: Intellectuals, Professionalism, Culture*. New York: Verso, 1993.

Santoli, Michael. "The Trader: Stocks Gain Ground Through Corporate Woes Grow." *Barron's* (July 29, 2002): MW2–MW4.

Stewart, Thomas A., Alex Taylor III, et. al. "Henry Ford, Alfred P. Sloan, Tom Watson Jr., Bill Gates: The Businessman of the Century." *Fortune* (November 22, 1999): 108–28.

Veseth, Michael. *Selling Globalization*. Boulder, CO: Lynne Reinner Publishing, 1998.

Watkins, Evan. *Everyday Exchanges: Marketwork and Capitalist Common Sense*. Stanford, CA: Stanford University Press, 1998.

"The World's 100 Greatest Books Audiocassette Collection." InteliQuest Learning Systems Main Product Page. http://www.4iq.com/main.html (September 12, 2002).

Chapter 10

It's Just Beginning

Assessing the Impact of the Internet on U.S. Multiethnic Literature and the "Canon"

Patricia Keefe Durso

Tussling con remolinos (whirlwinds) of different belief systems [. . .] calls you to retribalize your identity to a more inclusive one, redefining what it means to be *una mexicana de este lado*, an American in the United States, a citizen of the world, classifications reflecting an emerging planetary culture. In this narrative, national boundaries dividing us from the 'others' (*nos/otras*) are porous, and the cracks between worlds serve as gateways.

—Gloria E. Anzaldúa[1]

Statements by theorists concerned with literature, like those by theorists concerned with computing, show a remarkable convergence. [. . .] [They] argue that we must abandon conceptual systems founded upon ideas of center, margin, hierarchy, and linearity and replace them with ones of multilinearity, nodes, links, and networks.

—George P. Landow[2]

Defining the "canon" of American literature has never been easy, and it just (relatively speaking) got harder. The advent of the Internet—the migration of existing literary texts to it, the birth of new literary genres within it, the growth of cyberculture studies from it—is changing the study of American literature in immeasurable ways, not the least of which is the way in which we define and think about the "canon." While we could argue that the "canon" of American literature—as a stable, uncontested body of "great" works—does not exist, there are certainly those core texts (by authors such as Whitman, Emerson, Hawthorne, Hemingway, Faulkner, etc.) that have been "canonized" through, for example, long-standing inclusion in anthologies, integration into curricula, and attention from scholars. Such canonical authors have, ironically, gained strength as the traditional canon has been challenged by the addition of multiethnic literature. Their position as *"the"* canon, as the "center" of American literature—as that against which other texts are measured and judged for inclusion—has been reinforced as the ranks in the margins have continued to swell. But the borders still stand. There is still *"the"* (largely white male) canon on the one hand, and the "multiethnic" canon (often broken down further, of course, into the African American canon, and Asian American canon, etc.) on the other hand. But now there is another force in canon formation, something that has the power and potential to change all that, to move multiethnic literature to the "center" not only by improving access and availability of texts, but also by changing the way we read, think, and write about literature. And that force is the Internet.

As a "global network connecting millions of computers" linking and facilitating exchanges between more than one hundred countries,[3] the Internet is dramatically reshaping literary studies, from the literary and critical texts to the contexts in which we read them to the ways in which we write and imagine them. As Stephen Pulsford points out in *Literature and the Internet* (2000), "[m]any commentators have suggested that we are in the early stages of a revolution as profound as that once initiated by the development of [. . .] print culture" (170). Just as the advent of print culture in the mid-fifteenth century irrevocably—if slowly—changed not only the publication and dissemination of books, but also the ways in which books were written and read, so too has the advent of electronic culture and hypertext unquestionably changed—and will continue to change—all of this in the twenty-first century. As Pulsford continues (and as many leading scholars in electronic textual theory have suggested), "we can anticipate changes in the ways we think as we move away from the 'linear' and hierarchical arguments privileged by print technologies towards postmodern, 'multivocal' networks of meaning" (170). The Internet, in other words, has engendered a significant shift away from traditional notions of linearity, hierarchy, and individuality and towards multilinearity, nonhierarchicality, and multivocality.

In *Hypertext 2.0: The Convergence of Contemporary Critical Theory and Technology* (1997), George Landow argues that this "paradigm shift" "marks a revolution in human thought," and he focuses on the convergence—the unexpected "shocks of recognition"—between hypertext and poststructuralist theory, suggesting that the similarities between these two areas are significant for many reasons, not the least of which is that "critical theory promises to theorize hypertext and hypertext promises to embody and thereby test aspects of theory, particularly those concerning textuality, narrative, and the roles or functions of reader and writer" (2). What this focus has resulted in is a reification of "high" poststructuralist theory and postmodernist prose through the study of electronic textualities. And what this focus ignores is the fact that the "paradigm shift" Landow points to is not a shift in *"human* thought" (my emphasis) but a shift in Western, Eurocentric (and, dare I say, patriarchal) thought.

Many women and minority writers have been living on the nonhierarchical, multilinear, multivocal side of the binary divide that has underwritten that paradigm shift for a long time. While there is indeed a convergence between poststructuralist theory and hypertext, I would suggest that there is also a striking and significant convergence that has gone unremarked—and that is the convergence between Internet-based paradigms of multilinearity, nonhierarchicality, multivocality, and collaboration and cultural- and text-based paradigms found in the work of many U.S. multiethnic writers and theorists. The fact that this convergence has gone unremarked, while that between cyberculture and "high" postmodernist and poststructuralist texts has been emphasized, brings to our attention a number of issues and concerns regarding canon formation in the age of the Internet.

As the epigraph from Gloria Anzaldúa at the beginning of this essay suggests, many "minority" writers have struggled against the constraints of Western, Eurocentric "belief systems" and the ways in which these belief systems have negated non-Western cultural systems. Looking towards an "emerging planetary culture," Anzaldúa emphasizes the breakdown of binaries and the liberatory potential of "cracks between worlds"—spaces that can serve as "gateways" to new narratives, new ways of thinking and defining the self and others—spaces that can be found, I would suggest, on and through the Internet. For minority writers, the shift engendered by the Internet is not a revolution in terms of modes of thought, but a revolution in terms of avenues for change. In *Cyberspace Textuality: Computer Technology and Literary Theory* (1999), Marie-Laure Ryan observes that "beyond—or perhaps on—the computer screen lies a 'New Frontier'" (1). And the Internet is truly a "New Frontier," a new "gateway," for women and minority writers—not just a place of potential, of opportunity, of growth—but a place that, ultimately, they can call "home."

But to what extent are multiethnic writers finding a "home" on the Internet? Is the Internet in fact providing these writers with a "gateway," with a virtual door through which to enter the "canon" of American literature as well as the broader "emerging planetary culture"? In this essay I seek to answer questions such as these, beginning with some of the basic ones—that is, with practical questions about how electronic tools and resources are (or are not) being used to support the study and dissemination of U.S. multiethnic literature. After addressing some of the main practical questions—and thereby broadly establishing the literary climate on the Internet as we enter the twenty-first century—I will then return, in the second part of this essay, to discuss and illustrate my assertion of the symbiotic relationship between multiethnic and electronic textuality and theory, and, particularly, the lack of recognition of this relationship in contemporary hypertext and related literary theory. For this lack, as I suggested above, leads us to significant questions about canon formation in an age of electronic texts and technologies, including related questions of the exclusion and inclusion of authors from the "canon," of the Internet's purported democratizing powers, and of the many sides of the "digital divide."

Using the Internet: Researching, Teaching, and Reading Multiethnic Literature

One of the broadest, and perhaps most difficult, questions to answer regarding the impact of the Internet on U.S. multiethnic literature and the "canon" is whether the Internet has affected—and continues to affect—our sense of "literary value," and, if so, how. Might a student, for instance, conclude that an author with the most websites—or the most "hits" to that website, or the most listings in a major search engine—has the most literary value? A search on Henry James using Google's search engine, for example, results in approximately 161,000 listings, while a search on Zora Neale Hurston results in approximately 32,200 listings—certainly a great deal, but less than one-fifth of the listings for James. Faced with such statistics, will students interpret technological quantity as literary quality? And might quantity in this instance actually reflect a text's "canonical" or "noncanonical" status, given the fact that at this point traditionally "canonical" authors do indeed have a stronger web presence? Does the availability and accessibility of Internet resources for a given author signal an author's canonicity? Can a marginalized author or work with a strong Internet presence enter the canon of American literature through that virtual door? Or will one's place in the "canon" continue to be secured only through admittance to print anthologies? All of these questions speak to the ways in which the Internet may impact our sense of literary value; however, in order to get a better idea of what the answers to such questions may be, we need to look at the current tools and resources available on the Internet and the ways in which they are being used in connection with U.S. multiethnic literatures.

Electronic tools and resources most relevant to literary studies—such as search engines, institutional and individual websites, hypertext, e-mail discussion lists, online journals and essays, electronic syllabi, bibliographies and webliographies, literary directories, online texts, digital archives, forums/bulletin boards, images, and even streaming audio and video—have indeed, as Randy Bass observes in "New Canons and New Media: American Literature in the Electronic Age" (his introduction to the online resources for *The Heath Anthology of American Literature*) "enhanced and transformed" the study of American literature.[4] Furthermore, as Jerome McGann points out in "The Rationale of Hypertext," "electronic tools in literary studies don't simply provide a new point of view on the materials, they lift one's general level of attention to a higher order."[5] Electronic texts, for example, allow the reader, as Bass points out, to "do something with them: to search them, manipulate them, annotate them, to make them into hypertexts, to write productive connections between them, to make visible (through electronic linkages) connections between them."[6]

Electronic texts—whether online texts or simply informative websites—also, at their best, enable the reader to jump from hyperlinks in the text to related texts, documents, or audio or video files that serve to contextualize and enrich a reader's understanding of the work. Again, Bass's discussion of online resources for *The Heath Anthology* is instructive here: "In order to help students understand texts as part of a 'field of historically discursive practices' we need new strategies for helping students place a text in a field of other texts. Electronic archives provide an unusual opportunity for that to happen." While studying a work such as Anzia Yezierska's *The Bread Givers*, to use one of Bass's examples, resources such as the online archives in the Library of Congress's National Digital Library, or "the 25,000 images of the Detroit Publishing Company's collection of views of American life from 1890–1925" might be used to offer "a visual guide to urbanization and immigration around the turn of the century."[7]

The immense variety of resources available on the Internet for contextualizing literature is particularly significant in the case of U.S. multiethnic literatures, which must be placed in the appropriate cultural, historical, political, and (sometimes) linguistic context in order to be fully understood and appreciated. In "'Border' Studies: The Intersection of Gender and Color," Paula Gunn Allen suggests, for example, that "without a critical apparatus that enables a variety of literatures to be explored within their relevant contexts, the works of las disappearadas are doomed to obscurity. Yet, given the prevailing ethnocentric cultural climate, devising such a system and finding it applied by a great number of critics seems a hopeless task" (38). David Palumbo-Liu likewise emphasizes the necessity of contexualization in *The Ethnic Canon: Histories, Institutions, and Interventions* (1995) as he calls for a truly "*critical* multiculturalism" (2). The Internet clearly offers a framework that welcomes and invites the type of critical approach Allen calls for and the critical multiculturalism that Palumbo-Liu advocates, as hyperlinked primary works, essays, biographies, and other materials facilitate the exploration of literatures "within their relevant contexts." There is, of course, the issue of human agency behind the hyperlinks—the decisions made about what to contextualize and how to contextualize it, what to include and exclude from the links for any given work or author—but there is also the fact that the Internet offers an immense variety of resources to anyone who types a word or phrase in a search engine, so readers of electronic texts on the Internet can follow the hyperlinked paths established for them or they can define and follow their own paths. At the same time as it offers a system of links for contextualizing literary works, then, the Internet—through its very structure—reinforces and supports the nonhierarchical, multilinear paradigms found in so many works by "las disappearadas," or marginalized writers. If "hypertext," as Landow rightly suggests, "offers a means for a novice reader to learn the habit of multisequential reading necessary for the use of both educational technologies and scholarly apparatuses" (225), then it also familiarizes and trains readers with ways of reading much non-Western literature which shares its multilinear, nonhierarchical tendencies.

There are countless other practical issues one might consider in assessing the impact of the Internet on U.S. multiethnic literature and the "canon," and while it is beyond the scope of this essay to assess them all, I would like to look more closely at the question of electronic texts and digital archives, as this issue speaks directly to the formation of what is essentially an electronic "canon." To return, then, to a question I posed earlier: Does the fact that a text has been put online—or an author's body of works "digitally archived" and fully contextualized—confer upon the work or author greater literary value in the Internet age? As Jerome McGann points out, a "computerized edition" of a print book "can store vastly greater quantities of documentary materials, and it can be built to organize, access, and analyze those materials not only more quickly and easily, but also at depths no paper-based edition could hope to achieve."[8] The digital preservation of texts, and the preparation of the electronic equivalents of scholarly editions, complete with hyperlinks to related historical, political, cultural, and other relevant electronic, audio, or video files, is one of the most significant endeavors of literary scholars on the Internet, and the single most significant factor, perhaps, in the Internet's impact on canon formation. It is in fact through its own "storehouse of works" (that is, digital archives, e-texts, e-books), as Stephen Pulsford observes, that the Internet "challenges the power of the anthology" (185). But what works are being put in this virtual "storehouse"? Who decides what gets digitally archived?

While copyright restrictions largely govern what texts may be converted to online format, there are clearly choices being made—choices that are shaping the content of the "canon" of American literature both online and off. Associate Director of the University of Virginia's Electronic Text Center, Matthew Sweegan Gibson—a leader in the field with more than 70,000 online texts collected since their inception in 1992—explains that in the case of UVA's Etext Center (and this also seems true of many other university-based Electronic Technology Centers),[9] much of what gets put online is determined by grants funding and scholarly interests. Gibson explains:

> [M]uch of our collection development is project and user-driven. The texts we actually create from scratch—i.e., from codex bound form to electronic version—are dictated by grant funds [. . .]. [W]e create very few e-texts from the ground up primarily because we do not have the funds to do that. We take contributions from e-text donors from other universities who have taken the time and energy to digitize a corpus of material.[10]

Like UVA's EText Center, Project Gutenberg, which currently offers approximately six thousand online texts, depends primarily on voluntary contributions, with the texts that make it into electronic form there determined almost completely by the interests of "volunteers": "Simply, a volunteer decides that a certain book should be in the archives, obtains the book and does the work necessary to turn it into an e-text."[11] In some ways, then, electronic publishing decisions are determined by the same market forces—economics and individual interests—that shape print publishing decisions. But "[f]or a *text* to be excluded from hypertext," as Silvio Gaggi suggests in *From Text to Hypertext: Decentering the Subject in Fiction, Film, the Visual Arts, and Electronic Media* (1998 ed; 1997) "is likely to be even more crippling than its being excluded from the 'canon' as presently constituted. The ease and speed of navigating among texts embedded in hypertextual networks has as its flip side a tendency to ignore texts that are not included, as if they did not exist at all" (117). According to this logic—which I believe is not entirely true at this point in time but certainly will be in the future—texts that are not digitally archived will drop out of the "canon," while those that are put online will remain in—or become part of—the canon.

A brief survey of existing online texts and digital archives suggests a strong African American and, to lesser extent, Native American collection of online texts—but the electronic holdings in these areas do not begin to compare with those in "traditional" American literature. Most of the initial, "groundbreaking," "landmark" literary e-text projects on the Internet, for example, have been based on the work of canonical authors ("The Walt Whitman Archives" and "The Dickinson Archives" are the two most prominent in American Literary studies).[12] And Bartleby.com, which was voted "Best Literary Resource" on the web in 2002 by *Yahoo! Internet Life* magazine, clearly defines its literary holdings as the "classics." As you browse through the listings on the "fiction" page at Bartleby.com,[13] for example, you'll find a fairly traditional representation of canonical authors with a sidebar reminding you that "Bartleby.com provides the best works of fiction from a wide range of classic authors." Even texts by those U.S. multiethnic writers who have made it into the print canon (e.g., Toni Morrison, Maxine Hong Kingston, W. E. B. Du Bois, James Baldwin, Leslie Marmon Silko) are not represented in the fiction section of Bartleby.com, a site which, in many ways, one might consider the first, or at least most widely known, electronic analogue to the print anthology. If the "Internet dissemination of alternative voices" is, as Pulsford observes, "a force [. . .] in the revision of the literary canon," one must ask, then, what the absence of those voices in popular literary resources, such as Bartleby.com, means in terms of their place in the canon: is the dissemination of marginalized voices on the Internet a force in canon revision only if those voices make themselves heard at the most widely used websites?

Canon formation is affected not only by *what* works get digitally archived and *where* they get archived, but also by *how* the works get digitally archived, a consideration which raises the question of the quality of online texts. The Text Encoding Initiative (TEI),[14] a collaborative effort established in 1987 by four major universities, has established guidelines that have become standard for creating online texts in the humanities in order to ensure that the texts are widely accessible (e.g., not specific to a proprietary software program, such as MS Word), and in order to ensure that the texts are created in a way that will allow, for example, for advanced searches and research. Of the print texts that are converted to electronic text, then, we must ask whether they are being created carefully, in accordance with TEI (or other) guidelines, or whether they are being created in a less careful manner and thus essentially relegated to the "temporary" virtual shelves. The approximately six thousand online texts in Project Gutenberg, for example, are all created in the "simplest, easiest to use forms available," but at the same time they contain acknowledged and allowed levels of error, for the mission of Project Gutenberg is not to create scholarly "authoritative" editions but to create e-books for the general reading public.[15] While Project Gutenberg's electronic texts are indeed invaluable resources for the general reading public, then, their usefulness in terms of an electronic "canon"—in terms of their validity as subjects of research and teaching—is questionable. On the Internet, then, considerations of a work's "staying power" aren't just about "universal" appeal throughout time and for generations of readers—they are also about the digital quality, structure, and accessibility (present and future "readability") of online texts.

Theorizing the Internet: Thoughts on the Convergence of Contemporary Multiethnic Literature and Technology

As noted at the beginning of this essay, in *Hypertext 2.0*, George Landow calls attention to the striking similarities between poststructuralist literary theory and hypertext, "apparently unconnected areas of inquiry" which converge in their shared argument that "we must abandon conceptual systems founded upon ideas of center, margin, hierarchy, and linearity and replace them with ones of multilinearity, nodes, links, and networks" (2). The association between computer technology and poststructuralist theory, and the lack of recognition of a similar association of the former with the writing and theory of marginalized communities (as I illustrate below), raises a number of issues regarding the relationship between U.S. multiethnic literatures and the Internet. In an effort to call attention to these issues, I will first examine the politics behind the convergence of poststructuralism and hypertext, and the implications of this for canon formation. I will then briefly point to a few texts from various ethnic traditions that might be used to illustrate the parallels between hypertextual and multiethnic textualities (a full discussion of these texts is clearly beyond the scope of this essay—my intention here is to point to possible texts with which to begin to study the links between the conceptual and textual characteristics of multiethnic literature and cyberspace).

The print texts that Landow and other hypertext theorists most frequently offer as testimonies to this "paradigm shift," as print "precursors" of hypertext (and here we are primarily talking about hypertext fiction, such as Michael Joyce's seminal 1987 work "Afternoon, a story"), are primarily (though not exclusively) texts from the "high" postmodernist, and sometimes modernist, canons. For example, a well-known project in the study of hypertext and nonlinear fiction, "The Electronic Labyrinth," looks at hypertext in the "context of the literary tradition of non-linear approaches to narrative," and focuses on works such as Julio Cortázar's *Hopscotch*, Vladimir Nabokov's *Pale Fire*, Milorad Pavic's *Dictionary of the Khazars*, and Laurence Sterne's

Tristram Shandy.[16] James Joyce's *Ulysses* and *Finnegan's Wake*, Alfred, Lord Tennyson's *In Memoriam*, and John Fowles's *The French Lieutenant's Woman*, as well as the work of authors such as Robert Coover and Jorge Louis Borges are examples of other authors and texts commonly offered as precursors of hypertext. Examining hypertext in conjunction with such print precursors, as Landow observes, "suggests that this new information technology has roots in prestigious canonical texts," and this has at least two implications: first, it has "the political advantage of making the [electronic/hypertext] medium seem less threatening to students of literature and literary theory," and second, it "makes those canonical texts appear especially forward looking, since they can be seen to provide the gateway to a different and unexpected literary future" (182–183).

What is happening here, then, is that hypertext theory is calling upon an association with high canonical texts as a way of familiarizing hypertext and legitimizing itself as a serious object of study—at the same time, this has had the effect of reinforcing the canonicity of the "precursor" print texts and of even raising their canonical status, adding another notch to their canonical belts. Similarly, emphasizing the connection between contemporary French poststructuralist theorists and hypertext serves to reify the canon of "high" literary theory in the same way. I am not saying that poststructuralist theory does not comment tellingly on hypertext and electronic technologies, for I believe it does; what I am saying is that a great deal of U.S. multiethnic fiction, like the modernist and postmodernist texts mentioned above, may also be read as precursors of hypertext, and this possibility speaks directly to the ways in which U.S. multiethnic literature may—or may not—find heightened "canonical" status on the Internet.

We might look, for example, at Native American fiction, with its overwhelming emphasis on community rather than the individual, on circular rather than linear structures, and on binaries as collaborative rather than hierarchical entities. Much Native American literature, as Gerald Vizenor observes in *Narrative Chance: Postmodern Discourse on Native American Indian Literatures* (1989), is characterized by features associated with postmodernism and poststructuralism (and, I would add, with hypertext), such as fragmentation, intertextuality, decentralization, multilinearity, multivocality, and multiplicity. Leslie Marmon Silko's *Almanac of the Dead* (1991) provides just one example of this, with its expansive, fragmented, nonlinear, multivoiced narrative. This is a work in which Silko, in her own words, was "consciously trying to expand what the genre 'novel' can mean"[17]—that is, trying to break the boundaries of the "novel" as established by Western discourse and theory, and the result is a narrative that is, in many ways, "hypertextual."

Just as Vizenor identifies postmodernist (and again, I would add, hypertextual) features as indigenous elements of Native American literature, Ramón Saldivár observes similarities between postmodernism and Chicano American writing, specifically the "bifurcated, interstitial" "border writing" found, for example, in Américo Paredes's *Between Two Worlds*. This collection of poetry, Saldivár writes, "might well emblematize the features of [. . .] postmodern border writing were it not for the fact that it predates the notion [of postmodernism] by more than a half a century" (1995, 73). Contemporary writing by Chicana American writers also illustrates a striking invocation of elements such as fragmentation and multilinearity, with Ana Castillo's *The Mixquiahuala Letters* (1986), perhaps, offering the most obvious example, as it explicitly invites multiple readings, multiple approaches and orderings of the material. Castillo numbers, but does not date the letters in this epistolary novel, and she provides three different tables of contents (one "For the Conformist," another "For the Cynic," and a last "For the Quixotic"). Furthermore, she prefaces the novel with the following note to the reader: "It is the author's duty to alert the reader that this is not a book to be read in the usual sequence. All letters are numbered to aid in following any one of the author's proposed options." Castillo's work could obviously be included, for example, as one of those "print texts with multiple reading sequences" which serve as "the embryo of an electronic genre" that Marie-Laure Ryan points to in *Cyberspace Textuality* (7). Furthermore, Castillo's work invites shifting and multiple centers and, as such, it clearly anticipates hypertext, where "readers move through a web or network of texts" and "continually shift the center—and hence the focus or organizing principle—of their investigation and experience" (Landow 36).

Finally (and this is not to say that there are not *many* more examples from other ethnic American traditions—particularly the African American tradition—that could be called upon here), we might look at Asian American literature, such as Theresa Hak Kyung Cha's *Dictée* (1982). As Lisa Lowe points out in "Canon, Institutionalization, Identity: Contradictions for Asian American Studies" *Dictée* "refuses to provide either a linear, unified development of the writing subject or an aesthetic synthesis or ethical resolution at the text's conclusion" (60). Furthermore, "[i]n combining autobiographical and biographical fragments, photographs, historical narrative, calligraphy, and lyric and prose poems in a complex multilingual piece, *Dictée* blurs conventions of genre and narrative authority, troubling the formal categories upon which canonization depends" (Lowe 60). As hypertexts increasingly become an object of study in American literature (and Norton's latest anthology of *Postmodern American Fiction* includes, in fact, two online hypertext fictions),[18] the "formal categories upon which canonization depends" may well shift to categories more receptive to multiethnic, multilinear, multimedia works such as *Dictée* and the others I have mentioned here that anticipate and demonstrate a pronounced hypertextuality. Whether this shift in the formal categories of canonization will occur as a result of the entry of hypertext into literary studies—or, if it does, whether it will translate to multiethnic fiction, particularly if the affinities between multiethnic fiction and hypertext continue to go unrecognized and untheorized—remains to be seen.

Calling for recognition of the affinity between U.S. multiethnic literatures and hypertext may also, as I briefly mentioned earlier, result in increased attention to the modes of reading most amenable to multiethnic fictions. The Internet is fostering a new generation of readers, schooled on the Internet and fully accustomed to navigating multilinear, nonhierarchical, fragmented environments and texts. For such readers, opening novels such as Ana Castillo's *The Mixquiahuala Letters* or Theresa Hak Kyung Cha's *Dictée* will not result in disorientation but in familiarity. But for other readers (i.e., those not schooled on the Internet), we might look to works such as Alice Walker's *The Temple of My Familiar* (1989) for a lesson in reading both multiethnic and electronic literature. In this novel, a nineteenth-century British white woman finds the designs on African huts (erected in a British museum) somehow "wrong," as she writes in her diary:

> It was so completely what one was not used to that it was hard to take it in. In the same way one takes in a painting, say, by an English or European artist, no matter how odd. It was as if the reference point was missing; I could not grasp either the feeling tones of the work or the meaning. It seemed natural, somehow, to begin thinking of all that was "wrong" with it. (222)

Here, Walker provides her (white) reader with a reminder of the necessity of reading "differently from Westerners" (267) in order to avoid misreading and misinterpretation of multiethnic texts. It is precisely this skill of reading "differently from Westerners" that electronic literature calls for and, in the process, paves the way for increased accessibility of multiethnic texts.

Overall, the lack of recognition of the convergence between hypertext and multiethnic literature suggests that the latter is in danger of once again being pushed aside, marginalized in cyberspace. Even as the conceptual paradigms that are inherent to much multiethnic literature—as a literature of resistance against Western oppression and domination—make their way (ironically) to the "center" of cyberspace, that literature is neglected while more "canonical" (and primarily male) authors are pushed to the front. "Technology," as Landow observes, "always empowers someone, some group in society, and it does so at a certain cost" (275). Are we witnessing yet another type of "digital divide"—one internal to cyberspace, specific to literature, and arranged according to hierarchies of the print canon? Ron Eglash, an "ethnomathematician," points out that "[w]e seem to have no problem celebrating the culture of the have-nots [. . .] but we usually assume that we have nothing to learn from them technologically."[19] Is this sort of attitude at work in literary and hypertext theory as well? Has multiethnic fiction and theory— the literary production of minority and immigrant writers, those typically associated with the "have-nots" side of the digital divide—been overlooked in the discussion of electronic textualities because it's been assumed that "we have nothing to learn from them technologically"? There is, as Eglash emphasizes, a "two-way bridge across the digital divide." Anzaldúa similarly emphasizes multiple crossings between cultures: "[a] bridge is not just about one set of people crossing to the other side; it's also about those on the other side crossing to this side. And ultimately, it's about doing away with demarcations like 'ours' and 'theirs'" (4). "Diversity of perspective," Anzaldúa further reminds us, "expands and alters the dialogue, not in an add-on fashion but through a multiplicity that's transformational" (4). Examining the points of convergence of U.S. multiethnic literatures and the Internet enriches our understanding of both, and suggests that looking at both together allows us to see increased transformational possibilities that have the power to (re)shape the ways we read, write, and think about literature in the twenty-first century.

It's Just the Beginning

The Internet is clearly transforming the ways in which we study and teach American literature and, by extension, the ways in which the canon of American literature is formed. This has particular implications for the study of U.S. multiethnic literature and its inclusion—or exclusion—from the canon. The Internet can, indeed, be "celebrated as an opportunity for marginalized voices" (Pulsford 184), and it does offer an unprecedented opportunity to increase the availability and accessibility of U.S. multiethnic literature and, by extension, the entry of that literature into the American literary canon. The question of "availability" and "accessibility" is, however, a multifaceted one in this context. It speaks, first, for example, to the question of content. Anyone with the literary knowledge and technological skills and resources can "publish" a website on a particular author or work. While market constraints clearly affect the conversion of print texts into high-quality, long-lasting electronic texts, as I have discussed, there are no substantial constraints stopping teachers, institutions, independent scholars, or the general public from publishing information about particular authors and works on the Internet and making that information accessible to others through listings in search engines and literary directories. Anyone seeking to further knowledge, discussion, and exchange about a particular author or work, then, can easily do so on the Internet. In this way, U.S. multiethnic writers—particularly those who still stand outside the American literary canon—may find a way into classrooms and scholarly discussions and, eventually, into the canon.

In addition to speaking to the issue of content—of the presence (or absence) of information about an author or work on the Internet—the issue of "availability" and "accessibility" speaks to the question of contextualization of literary works. As I have discussed in this essay—and as Randy Bass illustrates so well in his introduction to the online resources for *The Heath Anthology of American Literature*[20]—the Internet offers endless and rich opportunities for placing literary works within specific historical, political, cultural, racial, social, and other contexts. Websites focusing on specific authors or works can use the Internet's hypertext capabilities to support and encourage an understanding of U.S. multiethnic literature in the appropriate context(s) by linking to relevant online resources that speak directly to that author or work. In this way, as I have suggested, the Internet offers a structure through which to build and promote that truly "*critical* multiculturalism" David Palumbo-Liu calls for—a multiculturalism that "explores the fissures, tensions, and sometimes contradictory demands of multiple cultures, rather than (only) celebrating the plurality of cultures by passing through them appreciatively" (5). As Palumbo-Liu observes, while certain texts "deemed worthy of representing the 'ethnic experience'" have made their way into the "canon," "the critical and pedagogical discourses that convey these texts into the classroom and present them to students and readers in general may very well mimic and reproduce the ideological underpinnings of the dominant canon, adding 'material' to it after a necessary hermeneutic operation elides contradiction and smooths over the rough grain of history and politics, that is, those very things that have constructed the 'ethnic' in the United States" (2). The Internet's hypertextual, nonhierarchical structure encourages and facilitates active interaction with a text's history and politics. Furthermore, its multilinear, nonhierarchical, decentered structure interrogates those very "ideological underpinnings of the dominant canon" that threaten to homogenize ethnic literatures.

This interrogation leads me to my final point about the ways in which the Internet increases the "accessibility" and "availability" of U.S. multiethnic literature. As I have discussed in this essay, the "paradigm shift" represented by the Internet—a shift towards multilinear, multivocal, and nonhierarchical modes of thought and away from linear, univocal, and hierarchical belief systems—is, as many critics have observed, engendering a change in the way we read, write, and think about literature. Insofar as U.S. multiethnic literature—in its narrative forms, its cultural contexts, and its literary subjects—converges with the modes of thought that support hypertext and characterize the Internet, we can predict an increase in the "accessibility" of multiethnic literature in terms of the ways in which it may be read and understood. The Internet is educating new generations of readers in multilinear, nonhierarchical modes of reading and understanding the world, and, as it does so, it is paving the way for an appreciation of, and clearer understanding of, multiethnic literatures with similar "poststructuralist" and "postmodern" features. As the convergence between multiethnic and electronic textualities becomes clearer, as the Internet's influence on the study and teaching of American literature grows (as it surely will), and as both multiethnic literatures and hypertext interrogate "the formal categories upon which canonization depends" (Lowe 60), we may even witness a shift of U.S. multiethnic literatures to the literary "center" of the decentered, constantly shifting space of the Internet, perhaps the first "New Frontier" that truly welcomes, rather than oppresses, minority voices.

Notes

1. Gloria E. Anzaldúa, "now let us shift . . . the path of conocimiento . . . inner work, public acts," *this bridge we call home: radical visions for transformation*, eds. Gloria E. Anzaldúa and AnaLouise Keating (New York: Routledge, 2002), 561.

2. George P. Landow, *Hypertext 2.0: The Convergence of Contemporary Critical Theory and Technology*, 2nd ed. (Baltimore: Johns Hopkins University Press, 1997), 2.

3. *Webopedia.com.* "Internet." 9 Sept. 2002 <http://www.pcwebopaedia.com/TERM/I/internet.html>.

4. Randy Bass, "New Canons and New Media: American Literature in the Electronic Age," *Heath Anthology of American Literature Online Instructor's Resource Manual*, 12 Sept. 2002 <http://college.hmco.com/english/heath/editorintro.html>.

5. Jerome McGann, "The Rationale of HyperText," *General Publications of the Institute for Advanced Technology in the Humanities*, Charlottesville: IATH, 1994, 15 Sept. 2002 <http://jefferson.village.virginia.edu/public/jjm2f/rationale.html>.

6. Randy Bass, "New Canons and New Media: American Literature in the Electronic Age," *Heath Anthology of American Literature Online Instructor's Resource Manual*, 12 Sept. 2002 <http://college.hmco.com/english/heath/editorintro.html>.

7. Randy Bass, "New Canons and New Media: American Literature in the Electronic Age," *Heath Anthology of American Literature Online Instructor's Resource Manual*, 12 Sept. 2002 <http://college.hmco.com/english/heath/editorintro.html>. Also see The Library of Congress's National Digital Library at <http://lcweb2.loc.gov/ammem/> and the Detroit Publishing Company's website at <http://lcweb2.loc.gov/ammem/detroit/dethome.html>.

8. Jerome McGann, "The Rationale of HyperText," *General Publications of the Institute for Advanced Technology in the Humanities*, Charlottesville: IATH, 1994, 15 Sept. 2002 <http://jefferson.village.virginia.edu/public/jjm2f/rationale.html>.

9. Additional Electronic Text Centers with holdings related to American literature include the *Center for Electronic Texts in the Humanities (CETH)*, a joint project of Rutgers and Princeton Universities (<http://www.ceth.rutgers.edu/>); *Yale's Electronic Text Center Project* (<http://www.library.yale.edu/etc/>); the *New York Public Library's Schomburg Center for Research in Black Culture* (<http://www.nypl.org/research/sc/sc.html>); the University of Michigan's and Cornell University's *Making of America* project (<http://www.hti.umich.edu/m/moa.new/>); and *Project Gutenberg* (<http://promo.net/pg/>). There are also a number of directories of electronic texts, including the *Electronic Literature Directory* (<http://directory.wordcircuits.com/>), the University of Washington-based *The English Server* (<http://eserver.org/>); the University of Pennsylvania's *Online Books Page* (<http://digital.library.upenn.edu/books/>); the Internet Public Library's *IPL Book Collection* (over 20,000 titles, <http://www.ipl.org/div/books/>); the *Voice of the Shuttle* (<http://vos.ucsb.edu/>).

10. Personal e-mail correspondence with Matthew Gibson, 3 October 2002.

11. See *Project Gutenberg* at <http://www.promo.net/pg/index.html>. Information about the volunteer process taken from the "Help and FAQ" page at <http://www.promo.net/pg/helpex.html#Whatbooks>.

12. See *The Walt Whitman Archive* at <http://www.iath.virginia.edu/whitman/> and *The Dickinson Archives* at <http://www.iath.virginia.edu/dickinson/>.

13. See <http://www.bartleby.com/fiction/>.

14. More information about The Text Encoding Initiative (TEI) is available at their website, <http://www.tei-c.org/>.

15. See more information on Project Gutenberg at <http://promo.net/pg/>. The "History and Philosophy" page (<http://promo.net/pg/history.html>) provides further information regarding their more "bang for the buck" philosophy of online text creation. Note, however, that they do "intend to release many editions of Shakespeare and the other classics for the comparative study on a scholarly level."

16. Christopher Keep, Tim McLaughlin, and Robin Parmar, "The Electronic Labyrinth," 1 Oct. 2002 <http://eserver.org/elab/> and <http://jefferson.village.virginia.edu/elab/elab.html>.

17. Personal telephone conversation with Leslie Marmon Silko, January 1993.

18. See *Postmodern American Fiction: A Norton Anthology* at <http://www.wwnorton.com/pmaf/welcome.htm>.

19. Ron Eglash, "A Two-Way Bridge Across the Digital Divide," *The Chronicle of Higher Education* 21 June 2002 <http://chronicle.com>.

20. Randy Bass, "New Canons and New Media: American Literature in the Electronic Age," *Heath Anthology of American Literature Online Instructor's Resource Manual*, 12 Sept. 2002 <http://college.hmco.com/english/heath/editorintro.html>.

Works Cited

Allen, Paula Gunn. "'Border' Studies: The Intersection of Gender and Color." *The Ethnic Canon: Histories, Institutions, and Interventions.* Ed. David Palumbo-Liu. Minneapolis, MN: University of Minnesota Press, 1995. 31–47.

Anzaldúa, Gloria E. "now let us shift . . . the path of conocimiento . . . inner work, public acts." *this bridge we call home: radical visions for transformation.* Eds. Gloria E. Anzaldúa and AnaLouise Keating. New York: Routledge, 2002. 540–78.

Bartleby.com. 6 Sept. 2002. <http://www.bartleby.com/fiction/>.

Bass, Randy. "New Canons and New Media: American Literature in the Electronic Age." *Heath Anthology of American Literature Online Instructor's Resource Manual.* Georgetown University 12 Sept. 2002. <http://college.hmco.com/english/heath/editorintro.html>.

Browner, Stephanie, Stephen Pulsford, and Richard Sears. *Literature and the Internet: A Guide for Students, Teachers, and Scholars.* New York: Garland Publishing, Inc., 2000.

Castillo, Ana. *The Mixquiahuala Letters.* 1986. New York: Doubleday, 1992.

Cha, Theresa Hak Kyung. *Dictée.* New York: Tanam Press, 1982.

Cortázar, Julio. *Hopscotch.* 1962. New York: Pantheon Books, 1966.

The Dickinson Archives. Ed. Martha Nell Smith. University of Virginia. 5 Oct. 2002. <http://www.iath.virginia.edu/dickinson/>.

Eglash, Ron. "A Two-Way Bridge Across the Digital Divide." *The Chronicle of Higher Education.* 21 June 2002. <http://chronicle.com>.

Fowles, John. *The French Lieutenant's Woman.* Boston: Little, Brown, and Company, 1969.

Gaggi, Silvio. *From Text to Hypertext: Decentering the Subject in Fiction, Film, the Visual Arts, and Electronic Media.* Philadelphia: University of Pennsylvania Press, 1998.

Hooks, bell. "Postmodern Blackness." *Yearning: Race, Gender, and Cultural Politics.* Boston: South End Press, 1990. 23–31.

Joyce, James. *Finnegan's Wake.* 1939. New York: Penguin, 1999.

———. *Ulysses.* 1922. New York: Modern Library, 1992.

Keep, Christopher, Tim McLaughlin, and Robin Parmar. *The Electronic Labyrinth.* University of Virginia. 1 Oct. 2002. <http://eserver.org/elab/> and <http://jefferson.village.virginia.edu/elab/elab.html>.

Landow, George P. *Hypertext 2.0: The Convergence of Contemporary Critical Theory and Technology.* 2nd ed. Baltimore: Johns Hopkins University Press, 1997.

Lowe, Lisa. "Canon, Institutionalization, Identity: Contradictions for Asian American Studies." *The Ethnic Canon: Histories, Institutions, and Interventions.* Ed. David Palumbo-Liu. Minneapolis, MN: University of Minnesota Press, 1995. 48–68.

McGann, Jerome. "The Rationale of HyperText." *General Publications of the Institute for Advanced Technology in the Humanities.* Charlottesville: IATH, 1994. University of Virginia. 15 Sept. 2002. <http://jefferson.village.virginia.edu/public/jjm2f/rationale.html>.

Nabokov, Vladimir. *Pale Fire.* New York: Putnam, 1962.

Palumbo-Liu, David, ed. *The Ethnic Canon: Histories, Institutions, and Interventions*. Minneapolis, MN: University of Minnesota Press, 1995.

Paredes, Américo. *Between Two Worlds*. Houston: Arte Publico Press, 1991.

Pavic, Milorad. *Dictionary of the Khazars*. New York: A. A. Knopf, 1988.

Project Gutenberg. 12 Sept. 2002. <http://www.promo.net/pg/index.html>.

Pulsford, Stephen. "Literature and the Internet: Theoretical and Political Considerations." *Literature and the Internet: A Guide for Students, Teachers, and Scholars*. New York: Garland Publishing, Inc., 2000. 169–86.

Ryan, Marie-Laure, ed. *Cyberspace Textuality: Computer Technology and Literary Theory*. Bloomington, IN: Indiana University Press, 1999.

Saldivár, Ramón. "The Borders of Modernity: Américo Paredes's *Between Two Worlds* and the Chicano National Subject." *The Ethnic Canon: Histories, Institutions, and Interventions*. Ed. David Palumbo-Liu. Minneapolis, MN: University of Minnesota Press, 1995. 71–87.

——. *Chicano Narrative: The Dialectics of Difference*. Madison: University of Wisconsin Press, 1990.

Silko, Leslie Marmon. *Almanac of the Dead*. New York: Simon & Schuster, 1991.

Sterne, Laurence. *Tristram Shandy*. 1760–1767. New York: The Modern Library, 1950.

Tennyson, Alfred, Lord. *In Memoriam*. 1850. New York: W. W. Norton & Company, Inc., 2003.

The Text Encoding Initiative (TEI). 6 Sept. 2002. <http://www.tei-c.org/>.

Vizenor, Gerald. *Narrative Chance: Postmodern Discourse on Native American Literature*. Albuquerque: University of New Mexico Press, 1989.

Walker, Alice. *The Temple of My Familiar*. San Diego: Harcourt Brace Jovanovich, 1989.

The Walt Whitman Archive. Eds. Ed Folsom and Ken Price. University of Virginia. 3 Oct. 2002. <http://www.iath.virginia.edu/whitman/>.

Webopedia.com. "Internet." 9 Sept. 2002. <http://www.pcwebopaedia.com/TERM/I/internet.html>.

Yezierska, Anzia. *The Bread Givers*. 1925. New York: Persea Books, 2003.

Contributors

Mary Jo Bona is Associate Professor of Italian American Studies and English at SUNY—Stony Brook. She is author of *Claiming a Tradition: Italian American Women Writers* and editor of *The Voices We Carry: Recent Italian American Women's Fiction*. Bona's work has been published in *Encyclopedia of Multiethnic American Literature*, *A Companion to Postwar American Literature and Culture*, *The Lost World of Italian American Radicalism*, and *New Ethnic American Literature and Arts: A Literary Encyclopedia*.

Sarika Chandra is Assistant Professor of English at Wayne State University. She teaches courses in globalization studies and contemporary American literary and cultural studies. Currently, she is working on a book manuscript focusing on the convergence of concepts such as mobility and migration with theories of globalization.

Kristin Czarnecki is Visiting Assistant Professor of English at University of Louisville, where she teaches multiethnic American literature, British literature, and first-year composition. Her research concerns primarily transatlantic modern women's fiction, and she is currently at work on a comparative study of women writers of the Harlem Renaissance and the Bloomsbury Group.

Aureliano Maria DeSoto was born and raised in Los Angeles and is a product of its public schools. His research interests encompass a broad range of topics concerning race, gender, and sexuality, visual and textual representation, and the role of the intellectual. He currently serves as Assistant Professor in the Department of Ethnic Studies at Metropolitan State University in Minneapolis.

Patricia Keefe Durso joined Fairleigh Dickinson University in Fall 2005 where she teaches required online courses such as "The Global Challenge" and will develop and teach online courses on women and literature. She has published essays on a variety of contemporary women writers and recently edited a special issue of *Modern Language Studies* on "The 'White Problem': The Critical Study of Whiteness in American Literature" (Spring 2002). Current projects include designing and developing a website devoted to Irish American women writers.

June Dwyer is Professor of English at Manhattan College in New York City. She has written two books, *John Masefield* and *Jane Austen*, articles on women and patriotism for *Studies in Short Fiction, Modern Language Studies*, and *The Faulkner Journal*, and articles on immigration and ethnic American literature for *Proteus, MELUS, LIT* and *VIA*.

Joe Kraus teaches at the University of Scranton. He is the co-author of *An Accidental Anarchist* (Academy Chicago, 2000), and his work has appeared in *The American Scholar, MELUS, Callaloo, The Centennial Review* and elsewhere.

John Lowe is Professor of English and Comparative Literature, Associate Chair of English, and Director of the Program in Louisiana and Caribbean Studies at Louisiana State University, where he teaches African American, Southern, and ethnic literature and theory. He is author of *Jump at the Sun: Zora Neale Hurston's Cosmic Comedy* (Illinois, 1994), editor of *Conversations with Ernest Gaines* (Mississippi, 1995); *Bridging Southern Cultures* (LSU Press, 2005); and *The Future of Southern Letters* (Oxford, 1996). He is currently completing *The Americanization of Ethnic Humor*, a cross-cultural, multidisciplinary examination of changing patterns in American comic literature.

Irma Maini is Assistant Professor of English at New Jersey City University, where she teaches courses in Ethnic American literature, Postcolonial Narratives, Women's literature, and Adolescent literature. Her articles on Maxine Hong Kingston, Jhumpa Lahiri, Toni Morrison, Anita Desai, and others have been published in *MELUS, Families: A Journal, The Literary Criterion, Modern Language Studies*, and *The Commonwealth Quarterly*.

Veronica Makowsky is Professor of English and Women's Studies and Interim Vice Provost for Academic Affairs at the University of Connecticut. Her authored books are *Caroline Gordon: A Biography* and *Susan Glaspell's Century of American Women*, both published by Oxford University Press. She also has published some editions and is the author of numerous articles on American women and southern writers. She is the editor of *MELUS* (Multi-Ethnic Literature of the United States).

Stephen Spencer is Associate Professor of English and Area Coordinator of Humanities and Modern Language at Wilmington College of Ohio. He has published articles on teaching, race, Pearl Buck, Eric Jerome Dickey, and Zora Neale Hurston. He recently taught at Universidad de Complutense in Madrid, Spain, where he was a Senior Fulbright Scholar in American studies.

Wenying Xu is Associate Professor of English at Florida Atlantic University. She teaches and researches American literature and Asian American literatures. She is the author of *Ethics and Aesthetics of Freedom in American and Chinese Realism*, as well as numerous articles published or to be published in *Modern Language Studies, boundary 2, Victorian Literature and Culture, MELUS, LIT: Literature Interpretation Theory, Paintbrush*, and *Philosophy and Social Action*.

Index

A.A. Knopf publishers, 4
Abrahams, Roger, 96
The Academy
   changes in constituencies of, 2
   dismissal of minority writing
      by, 61
   gender in, 2
   social function of, 8
Achievement in American Poetry
   (Bogan), 62
Acosta, Oscar Zeta, 45
Acuña, Rudy, 45
Adler, Mortimer, 179n2
Affirmative action, 52, 115
African American literature, 33,
   111–123. *See also* Writers and
   writing, African American
   contemporary, 121
African American Review (journal), 5
Afro-American Literature: The Reconstruction of Instruction (Fisher, Stepto), 5
"Afternoon" (Joyce), 207
Ahearn, Carol Bonomo, 91
Aiiieeeee! An Anthology of Asian American Writers (Chin), 3
Alberti, John, 13
Aleandri, Emelise, 92
Alexie, Sherman, 37, 78, 139
Allen, Paula Gunn, 5, 12, 202

Amerasia Journal, 5, 151
American Anthology (Stedman), 62
American Indian Fiction (Larson), 4
American Indian Literature: An Anthology (Velie), 3
American Indian Movement, 68
American Library Association, 169
American Life in Literature (Hubbell), 65
American Literature: A Study and Research Guide (Leary), 69
American Literature (journal), 67
American Poetry and Prose: A Book of Readings (Foerster), 63
American Quarterly (journal), 67
American Renaissance (journal), 67
American Scene, The (James), viii, 193
American Tradition in Literature, The (Bradley), 68
American Tradition in Literature (Stripes), 70
"An Accidental Murder" (Vannucci), 101
Anaya, Rudolfo, 4, 45, 77
An Introduction to the Study of American Literature (anthology), 62
Anthologies, 4, 198
   absence of Native American
      literature in, 15
   American frontier life in, 63
   changes in syllabi and, 3

of Chicano literature, 45
concentration on Anglo male
 writing, 62, 63
of essays, 4
importance of, 3
inclusion of writers of color, 63
Italian American writing, 92
moral criteria in, 62
multiethnic works in, 61
Native American, 61–79
Puritan emphasis in nineteenth-
 century, 62
regional, 63, 64
revamping of, ix
specialty, 11
Antin, Mary, 97
Anzaldúa, Gloria, 11, 12, 49, 50–55,
 122, 197, 200, 212
Apess, William, 72, 75, 77
Appiah, K, Anthony, 111
Aristotle, 63
Armstrong, Paul, 12
Art and Lies (Winterson), 102
Ashcroft, Bill, 11
Asian American literature, 3.
 See also Writers and writing,
 Asian American
poetry, 145–162
Assimilation
 African American literature and, 114
 Chicano Movement and, 43, 44, 47,
  51, 52, 53
 seeming, 158
Association for Asian American
 Studies, 5
Association of Literary Scholars and
 Critics, 172
Autobiography of a Brown Buffalo
 (Acosta), 45
Autobiography of Miss Jane Pittman,
 The (Gaines), 3, 4
Awkward, Michael, 116
Aztlán: An Anthology of Mexican
 American Literature (Valdez), 3
Aztlán (journal), 44, 45

Bak, Hans, 74
Baker, Houston Jr., 4, 5, 121
Bakhtin, Mikhail, 122
Baldwin, James, 12, 25, 69, 205
Bambara, Toni Cade, 121
Baraka, Amiri, 3, 68
Barolini, Helen, 85, 90, 91–93, 101,
 103, 104, 105n3
Barrio, Raymund, 45
Barrio Boy (Galarza), 45
Bass, Randy, 202
Batinich, Mary Ellen Mancina, 94
Baym, Nina, 77, 78, 79
Beck, Evelyn Toron, 11
Beloved (Morrison), 10, 14, 184
Bennett, Edward, viii
Bennett, William, 6
Bercovitch, Sacvan, 139
Berry, Wendell, 12
Bevilacqua, Winifred Farrant, 94, 95,
 96, 97
Bhabha, Homi, ix, 11, 122
Black Aesthetic (Gayle), 4
Black Aesthetics, 121
Black Elk, 71, 77
Blacker the Berry, The (Thurman), 116
Black-Eyed Susans: Classic Stories
 by and about Black Women
 (Washington), 3
Black Madonna, The (Ermelino),
 101, 103
Black studies programs, 121
Bless Me, Ultima (Anaya), 4, 45
Bloom, Allan, 6, 12, 105n2
Bloom, Harold, 153, 154
Blues, Ideology, and Afro-American
 Literature: A Vernacular Theory
 (Baker), 4, 121
Bluest Eye, The (Morrison), 3
Boas, Franz, 112
Boelhower, William, 105n6
Bogan, Louise, 62
Bona, Mary Jo, 1–17, 37, 85–104
Bonnin, Gertrude Simmons
 (Zitkala-Sa), 71, 72, 77

Index

Book clubs, x, 12, 16, 111, 167–179
  as alternative to classroom/solitary study, 167, 175–179
  attacks on, 168, 169
  Book-of-the-Month Club, 168, 169, 172
  broad view of reading in, 169
  choices and, 176, 177
  cultural implications of, 167, 170–175
  desire for status and, 169
  gender divides in, 170
  goals of, 169
  intelligentsia backlash and, 168
  as mass movement, 176
  as metaphor, 176
  opening of traditional literary canon and, 167, 168, 169, 170
  Oprah's Book Club, 170, 172–175, 179$n3$, 180$n6$, 181, 182
  Reading with Ripa, 179$n4$
  role of, 16
  subversion of elitism by, 170, 171
  threats to intellectuals from, 168
Booker prize, 11
Book lists, 184–187
Borderlands
  brutal aspects of, 54
  centralizing, 11
  gender politics and, 54
  theory, 53, 54
Borderlands—La Frontera: The New Mestiza (Anzaldúa), 11, 49, 53, 54, 55
Borges, Jorge Louis, 208
Boudinot, Elias, 72, 77
Boundaries
  breaking down, 44
  preoccupation with, 37
  of privilege, 133
  revision of, 148
  to self-reinvention, 131
  social, 64
  traditional, 44
  university-community, 44

Bourdieu, Pierre, 16, 185
Bowles, Paul, 187
Bradley, Sculley, 68
Bridge of Leaves, A (Cavallo), 104
Broadside Press publishers, 4
Brooks, Gwendolyn, 69
Brown, Sterling, 112
Brown v. Board of Education, 115
Bruce-Novoa, Juan, 56
Bruns, Gerald, 7
Bryant, Dorothy, 99, 105$n3$
Bulosan, Carlos, 77
Bush, Mary Bucci, 100
Butler, Octavia, 37

Cahan, Abraham, viii
Cain, William, 2
Calcagno, Anne, 101
Caleb the Degenerate (Cotter), 29
Callaloo (journal), 5
Camarillo, Albert, 45
Cane (Toomer), 3
Canon, American literary, x
  biblical, 7, 87
  breaking into, 153
  Chicano, 45
  creation of, 87
  critique of, 11
  cultural, 7, 9
  debates, 7, 8, 14
  decentering, 5, 127–141
  decisions on categories in, 8
  decolonization of, 10
  defining, 85–91, 88, 197
  development, 74
  discourse of, 153
  dominant, 87
  electronic, 203
  entrance to, 88
  exclusions from, 88
  expansion of, x, 10
  formation, 17, 55, 64, 65, 73, 198, 199, 206, 207
  imaginary, 13
  impact of Internet on, 197–214

literary, 7, 8, 9, 16, 24, 28, 85, 87, 94
multiethnic, 62, 64, 72, 73, 77, 78
omission from, 88
opening, 7, 8
pedagogical, 13
power of, 25
present context of debates, 183–184
reevaluating, 9
reform, 14
reinterpreting, 4
revision of, 85
traditional, 73
wars, vii
will to, 145, 146, 151–155
Capital, cultural, x, 13, 15, 64, 184–187
Caponegro, Mary, 101, 102
Cappello, Mary, 103
Carby, Hazel, 114
Carilli, Theresa, 105n6
Carlson, Scott, 1, 2
Caroli, Betty Boyd, 105n5
Cassettari, Rosa, 94–98, 104
Castillo, Ana, 49, 209
Cather, Willa, 86, 95, 104
Cavallo, Diana, 104, 105n3
Century Readings for a Course in American Literature (Pattee), 89
Ceremony (Silko), 3
Cervantes, Lorna Dee, 49
Cha, Theresa Hak Kyung, 210
Chandra, Sarika, 16, 38, 183–195
Chapman, Abraham, 3
Chase, Richard, 65, 66
Cheney, Lynne, viii, 6, 9
Chesnutt, Charles, viii, 69
Chiaroscuro (Barolini), 92
Chicana/o literature, x, 3, 4, 41–56. See also Writers and writing, Chicana/o
foundational articles in, 29
fragmentation in, 209
multilinearity in, 209
sexual outlaws in, 50–55
Chicana/o studies, 41–56, 42
in bilingual/bicultural education, 44

Chicana Critique and, 42
feminist intervention in, 46–50
feminist views ignored by male scholars in, 49
future of, 55–56
gender and, 49
left wing of, 51
mestizaje and, 43
mixed parentage and, 51, 52
Movement activism and, 42, 43–46
poststructuralist theory and, 42
sexuality in, 49
Chicanismo, 43, 44, 51
"Chicano Big Three," 4
Chicano Manifesto (Rendon), 45
Chicano Movement, 43–46
access to education and, 41
accommodation and, 43, 53
acculturalization and, 51
assimilation and, 43, 44, 47, 51, 52, 53
contesting foundations of aesthetics of, 53
cultural nationalism and, 43, 44, 46
economic opportunity and, 41
feminist conflict in, 46, 47
focus on male experience, 46
gender and, 51
gendered hierarchies in, 46–50, 56n1
identification with indigenous roots in, 43
patriarchy and, 48
radicalism of, 44, 53
representation of Mexican American culture and identity in, 41, 42
sexism in, 47
sociopolitical development and, 43–46
view of family in, 47
Chicanos in a Changing Society (Camarillo), 45
Chicano Student Movement, 44
Chin, Frank, 3, 25, 26, 183

Chinaberry Tree, The (Fauset), 116
Chinitz, David, 178
Christian, Barbara, 121
Christ in Concrete (di Donato), 104n1
Chua, C. Lok, 38
Ciresi, Rita, 99, 100, 103
Cisneros, Sandra, 49, 50
Citizenship, 148
"City in Which I Love You, The" (Lee), 148, 155–162
Clarke, Donald Henderson, 142n5
Class
    connections and, 129, 130, 133, 136
    divisions, 185
    exclusion and, 129
    middle, 167–179
    mobility, 98, 130
    social, 11, 100, 185
    system, 96
    working, 95, 96, 100
Cleaver, Eldridge, 5
"Cleaving, The" (Lee), 155–162
Closing of the American Mind, The (Bloom), 6, 12, 105n2
Cofer, Judith Ortiz, 77
Colonialism, 147, 148
Color Purple, The (Walker), 10
Commodification, x
Conferencia de Mujeres por La Raza (anthology), 46–50
Conservatism, 9, 13
Cooke, Rose Terry, 89
Cook-Lynn, Elizabeth, 73
Coover, Robert, 208
Copway, George, 77
Córdova, Teresa, 47, 56n1
Corkin, Stanley, 112, 114
Cortázar, Julio, 207
Cotter, Joseph, 29
Country of the Pointed Firs, The (Jewett), 85, 86, 87, 104n1
Courtyard of Dreams, The (Monardo), 101
Covello, Leonard, 105n5
Cowley, Malcolm, 137, 138, 139

Criticism
    function of critic in, 93
    postmodern, 168
Cullen, Countee, 69
Cultural
    aesthetics, 42
    Afro-American domains, 121
    canon, 7, 9
    capital, x, 13, 15, 64, 184–187
    co-existence, 25
    cohesion, 102
    conflict, 71
    constructions, 119
    corruption, 46
    criticism, 121
    differences, 4, 190
    differentiation, 161
    diversity, viii, 187, 189, 190, 194
    exchange, 25
    existence, 151
    expression, 32
    heritage, 69
    history, 93
    hybridity, 12, 14, 38, 90, 153
    identity, 11
    information, 187
    institutions, 120
    literacy, 7, 12
    nationalism, 43, 44, 46, 54
    nobility, 185
    order, 64
    politics, 15, 41, 42, 43, 56n2
    preservation, 55
    production, 44, 49, 50, 51, 52
    relativism, 119, 122
    resistance, 47
    snobbery, 26
    stereotypes, 90
    studies, 26, 111
    survival, 61
    systems, 200
    traditions, 157
    traits, 120
    values, 44
Cultural Capital (Guillory), 13, 64, 185

228 Index

Cultural Literacy (Hirsch), 6, 12, 105n2
Cultural Revolution (Wong), 11
Culture
  agrarian, 45
  ancestral, 145
  black, 113, 120, 121
  debates, 9
  feminist, 12
  folk, 120, 121
  food in, 149, 150, 151
  high, 115, 168, 169, 183
  immigrant, 93
  literary, 7, 10, 72
  Mexican American, 44
  middlebrow, 167–179
  peasant, 96
  popular, 175
  print, 198
  wars, 7
  white, 115, 116, 120, 121
Curriculum/syllabus
  classics in, 12
  collegiate, 9
  construction, vii
  decision-making on, 87
  ethnic writing not seen as part of, 6
  exclusion of women and minorities from, 89
  inclusion of easily available materials in, 95
  involvement of government in, vii, viii
  legitimate debates on shaping, 139
  literature in, 89
  pluralistic, 6
  professional interests and, 186
  restoration of "classics" to, viii, 6
  selection in, 64
Czarnecki, Kristin, 15, 61–79

D'Acierno, Pellegrino, 105n6
Davis, Rebecca Harding, 2, 104
Davis, Rocio, 38
Days of Obligation: An Argument With My Mexican Father (Rodriguez), 52

Deconstruction, 32
  identity, 33
"Degrees of Blue" (Lee), 155
De Rosa, Tina, 98, 99, 100, 104
Desai, Gaurav, 37
DeSalvo, Louise, 99, 102, 103, 104, 105n3
DeSoto, Aureliano Maria, 15, 41–56
Devereux, Georges, 143n8
de Vries, Rachel Guido, 100
Diaspora, 146
  memories and, 149
Dickinson, Emily, 64, 69, 71
Dictée (Cha), 210
Dictionary of the Khazars (Pavic), 207
di Donato, Pietro, 104n1
di Prima, Diana, 102
Discourse
  of canon, 153
  colonial, 11
  critical, 11
  dominant, 118
  literary, 93
Distance
  ironic, 146
Donofrio, Beverly, 102
Dove, Rita, 10
Dream Book, The (Barolini), 90, 91–93, 104
Drucker, Peter, 189, 192
Du Bois, W.E.B., viii, 71, 76, 93, 113, 118, 205
Dunne, Finley Peter, 138
Durso, Patricia Keefe, 17, 197–214
Dwyer, June, 16, 167–179

Eakin, Emily, 1
East India Company, 147, 162n4
Eastman, Charles Alexander, 72, 75, 77
Edwards, Jonathan, 68
Eglash, Ron, 211, 212
Elder, Arlene, 34
El Grito del Norte (newsletter), 48
El Grito (journal), 45
Eliot, T.S., 68, 178

Elizondo, Virgilio, 122
Ellison, Ralph, 69, 112, 113, 114, 187
El Movimiento Estudiantíl Chicano de Aztlán (MEChA), 44
Emerson, Ralph Waldo, 28, 29, 68, 153, 154, 159
Empire Writes Back, The (Ashcroft), 11
Emplumada (Cervantes), 49
Encuentro feminil (journal), 46–50
Enríquez, Evangelina, 45, 46
Erdrich, Louise, 10, 38, 71, 72, 77, 78
Ermelino, Louisa, 100, 101, 102, 103
Erskine, John, 169
Essentialism, 119, 120, 129
Estampas del valle y otras obras: Sketches of the Valley and other Works (Hinojosa), 4
Ethnic
  authenticity, 157, 162n8
  cuisine, 155, 156, 157, 159
  differences, 4
  diversity, 73
  empowerment, 78
  groups, 28
  humor, viii, 34
  hybridity, 38
  identification, 145
  identified with race, 33
  identity, 28, 30, 99, 100, 149
  literary study, ix
  markers, 155
  neighborhoods, 98
  oppositional groups, 33
  outsiderness and, 132
  poetry, 34, 35
  revival, x
  self, 160
  signifiers, 146
Ethnicity, 35
  ambiguities of, 10
  embrace of, 158
  erasure of, 130
  in *The Great Gatsby*, 127–141
  markers of, 16
  modified by authors, 30
  origin of term, 10
  rejection of, 145, 149
  tension with transcendentalism, 155–162
Ethnocentrism, 78
Ets, Marie Hall, 94–98
Exile, 146–151
  access to community in, 149
  arrested state of, 150
  citizenship and, 148
  diaspora and, 146
  as freedom, 146
  politics of, 148
  as process of discovery, 146
  seed trope in, 147, 148
  violence and, 148
Experience(s)
  complexity of, 119
  gendered, 53
  immigrant, 94–98
  life, 54
Experimentalism
  narrative, 12

Fama, Maria, 101
Fanning, Charles, 33
Far, Sui Sin, 77
Faulkner, William, viii, 75
Fauset, Jessie, 116
Feminism
  black, 121
  Chicana, 48, 49, 50, 54
  equated with Anglo women, 47
  second-wave, 46–50, 102
  white, 48
Feminist
  challenges to literary canon, 8
  criticism, 111, 121
  culture, 12
  identity, 54
  intervention in Chicano Movement, 46–50
  literary criticism, 87
  literature, 12
  politics, 46

Feminist Press publishers, 4, 99, 104, 105*n*3
Fences (Wilson), 10
Ferguson, Otis, 112
Festa (Barolini), 101
Fetterley, Judith, 13, 14, 103, 104
Finnegan's Wake (Joyce), 208
First Convocation of American Indian Scholars (1970), 68
First National Chicano Student Conference (1969), 47
Fisher, Dexter, 5
Fitzgerald, F. Scott, 127–141, 184
Fliegelman, Jay, 78
Foerster, Norman, 63
Fools Crow (Welch), viii
Fowles, John, 208
Franklin, Benjamin, 62, 68
Franzen, Jonathan, 173, 174, 175
Freeman, Mary Wilkins, 89
French Lieutenant's Woman (Fowles), 208
Freud, Sigmund, 159
From Behind the Veil: A Study of Afro-American Narrative (Stepto), 4
Frost, Robert, 68
Frus, Phyllis, 112, 114

Gadamer, Hans-Georg, 158, 161, 163*n*9
Gaggi, Silvio, 205
Gaines, Ernest, 3
Galarza, Ernesto, 45
Gallagher, Susan, 13, 17
García, Alma, 47
García, Mario, 50, 56*n*1
García Márquez, Gabriel, 179*n*3, 187, 190
Gardaphé, Fred, 92, 93, 95, 96
Gates, Henry Louis Jr., 4, 93, 111, 121
Gayle, Addison, 4, 69, 121
Gender
  differences, 4
  hierarchies, 46
  identity, 99, 100
  politics, 54, 56*n*2
  relations, 32
Georgescu, Peter, 188
Ghost Dance (Maso), 12, 100
Gibson, Matthew Sweegan, 204
Gilbert, Sandra, 7, 101
Gillan, Maria, 101
Gilman, Charlotte Perkins, 2
Gioia, Dana, 90
Giunta, Edvige, 105*n*6
Glancy, Diane, 77
Globalization, 195*n*2, 195*n*3
  multiethnic fiction and, 187–194
Gomez, Anna Nieto, 48
Gómez-Peña, Guillermo, 53
Gonzales, Rodolfo "Corky," 45, 56*n*1
González, Deena, 56*n*4
Gottesman, Ronald, 69, 70, 71
Graywolf Annual, 12
Great Books programs, 1, 13, 16, 169, 170, 171, 172
  non-Western writers in, 2
Great Gatsby, The (Fitzgerald), 127–141, 184
Green, Rose Basile, 105*n*5
Griffiths, Gareth, 11
Gubar, Susan, 7
Guillory, John, 8, 13, 16, 64, 89, 185, 186, 192, 194*n*1
Gutiérrez, Ramon, 56*n*1

Hall, Stuart, 150
Harjo, Joy, 72, 77, 78
Harlem Renaissance, 69, 111, 113, 114, 115, 116
Harris, Wendell, 7, 8, 87, 94, 95
Harvey, David, 189
Hassan, Salah, 11
Hawthorne, Nathaniel, 62, 65, 68, 86, 87
Heath, Shirley Brice, 175
Heath Anthology of American Literature, The, ix, 10, 13, 14, 71, 72, 73, 74, 75, 76, 77, 78, 112, 202

Hegemony
  of colonial discourse, 11
  ideological, 74
  institutional, 44
  literary, 91
Hemenway, Robert, 3, 111, 119, 120, 121
Hemingway, Ernest, 75, 138
Hendin, Josephine Gattuso, 99, 105*n*3, 105*n*6
Heroes and Saints and Other Plays (Moraga), 51
Hesford, Walter, 158
Hicks, D. Emily, 53
Higonnet, Margaret, 37
Hijas de Cuauhtemoc (newsletter), 48
Hinojosa, Rolando, 4
Hirsch, E.D., 6, 12, 105*n*2
History of American Literature, A (Tyler), 67
Hopscotch (Cortázar), 207
House Made of Dawn (Momaday), 71
House on Mango Street (Cisneros), 49, 50
Howe, Florence, 5
Huang, Yibing, 151
Hubbell, Jay, 65
Hughes, Langston, viii, 69, 111, 114
Hull, Gloria, 121
Hunger of Memory: The Education of Richard Rodriguez (Rodriguez), 52, 53
Hurston, Zora Neale, 1, 2, 14, 15, 16, 71, 111–123, 201
Hutchins, Robert, 179*n*2
Hwang, David, 10
Hybridity, 122, 123, 153

I Am Joaquin/Yo Soy Joaquin (Gonzales), 45
Identity
  as act of continual production, 121
  affirmation of, 120
  American, 17, 139, 143*n*7
  black, 116, 120
  Chicana/o, 48, 49, 52, 54, 56
  construction, 122
  cultural, 11
  deconstruction, 33
  denial of, 158
  double, 151
  essentialist, 53
  establishing, 131
  ethnic, 28, 30, 99, 100, 149
  experience and, 119
  female, 96, 102
  feminist, 54
  gender, 99, 100
  group constructions of, 138
  homogeneous ethnic, 30
  increased discussion of, 11
  Italian American, 90
  lesbian, 11, 51, 54, 56*n*4
  marginalized, 11
  markers of, 16
  mestizo, 56*n*2
  Mexican American, 41, 42, 43
  multiple, 11
  national, 12, 148
  politics, 15, 23, 33
  racial, 11, 116
  reconstruction of, 119
  retribalization of, 197
  sexual, 11, 14
  theories, 122, 150
  white, 38
Ifkovic, Edward, 34
Immigrant(s)
  attempts to enter mainstream, 140
  culture, 93
  deportation and, 141*n*1
  in ethnic conclaves, ix
  outsiderness and, 16
Immigration, 35, 94, 100
  American Legion and, 141*n*1
  ethnic writing and, viii
  narratives of, viii
  oral histories and, 94, 95
  reform, 141*n*1

Incidents in the Life of a Slave Girl, Written by Herself (Jacobs), 2, 14, 97, 98, 104
Individualism, 120
  neoliberal, 52
Inge, Thomas, 26
InteliQuest, 184
Internet
  Bartleby.com, 205, 206
  digital archives on, 202, 203, 204, 205
  dissemination of multiethnic literature and, 17
  hyperlinks and, 202, 203
  hypertext theory and, 208
  ssues in, x
  multiethnic literature and, 197–214
  as "New Frontier," 200
  online texts, 204, 205
  Project Gutenberg, 204, 205, 206
  research on, 201–206
  reshaping literary and critical texts on, 17
  resources on, 201, 202
  search engines, 201
  Text Encoding Initiative, 206
  theorizing, 207–212
  using, 201–206
  as virtual "storehouse," 204
  websites on, 201, 202
Irving, Washington, 62
Italian Americana (journal), 105*n*4
Italian American Literature, x, 85–104. *See also* Writers and writing, Italian American
  abandonment by Italian and American cultures, 93
  creation of, 85–91
  features of *italianità* in, 100
  recurring themes in, 94
Italian Signs, American Streets: The Evolution of Italian American Narrative (Gardaphé), 92, 93

Jackson, Helen Hunt, 89
Jacobs, Harriet, 2, 14, 97, 104
Jacobsohn, Rachel, 170
Jacobson, Matthew Frye, 141*n*2
James, Henry, viii, 65, 68, 192, 193, 194, 201
Jay, Gregory, 14
Jefferson, Margo, 173
Jewett, Sarah Orne, 85, 86, 87, 89, 104*n*1
Johnson, E. Pauline, 77
Johnson, James Weldon, 115
Jones, Howard Mumford, 89
Jones, LeRoi. *See* Baraka, Amiri
Jordan, June, 120
Journal of Ethnic Studies, 5
Joyce, James, 184, 208
Joyce, Michael, 207
Joy Luck Club (Tan), 10

Kampf, Louis, 5
Kaplan, Carey, 9
Keenan, Ruth, 26
Kierkegaard, Soren, 189
Kimball, Roger, 10
Kingston, Maxine Hong, 3, 14, 33, 35, 139, 162*n*7, 205
Kirkpatrick, David, 174
Kirschenbaum, Blossom, 105*n*6
Kitchen, Judith, 151
Knowledge
  dissemination, viii
  distribution of, 3, 8
  hegemonic control of, 3
  technical, 186
  visceral, 156
Kraus, Joe, 16, 127–141
Kreymborg, Alfred, 63
Krupat, Arnold, 62, 63, 64, 65, 66, 75, 76, 79

Lacan, Jacques, 159
La Chicana:The Mexican American Woman (Mirandé, Enríquez), 45
Lanctot, Denise, 174
Landow, George, 197, 199

Language
  African American, 118
  literary, 29
  marketing, 184
  of power, 155
La Nueva Chicana, 48
Larsen, Nella, 77, 116
Larson, Charles, 4
Last Generation, The (Moraga), 51
Lauter, Paul, 5, 6, 7, 9, 17, 61, 62, 63, 68, 71, 72, 73, 75, 76, 77, 78, 79, 85, 88, 175
Leary, Lewis, 69
Lee, Charles, 63, 64
Lee, Li-Young, 16, 145–162
Leisy, Ernest, 89
Levinas, Emmanuel, 161
Liberalism, 9
Library of Congress
  National Digital Library, 202
"Life in the Iron Mills" (Davis), 2, 104
Like Lesser Gods (Tomasi), 99, 104n1
Lincoln, Kenneth, 69
Literacy
  cultural, 12
  school history and, 8
Literary
  canon, 28, 85, 87, 94
  criticism, 87
  culture, 72
  discourse, 93
  hegemonies, 91
  landscape, 26
  languages, 29
  production, 64
  studies, 27
  tradition, 93
Literature, African American. *See* African American literature
Literature, Asian American. *See* Asian American literature
Literature, Chicana/o. *See* Chicana/o literature
Literature, multiethnic. *See* Multiethnic literature
Literature, Native American. *See* Native American literature
Literature, women's. *See* Women's literature
Lloyd, Susan Caperna, 101
Lo chicano, 41
Locke, Alain, 113, 115, 116
Lorde, Audre, 121
Los Angeles Times, 52
Love Medicine (Erdrich), 10, 71
Loving in the War Years: lo que nunca pasó por sus labios (Moraga), 49, 51
Lowe, John, vii–xi, 34
Luedtke, Luther, 28
Lyons, Mary, 111
Lyric America (Kreymborg), 63

M. Butterfly (Hwang), 10
Macdonald, Dwight, 168, 175
Madonna of the Rocks (Leonardo), 100
Maggio, Theresa, 101
Mailer, Norman, 187, 189
Maini, Irma, 1–17
Major American Writers (Leisy), 89
Major Writers of America (Miller), 67
Makowsky, Veronica, x, 14, 15, 23–39
Manfredi, Renée, 94
Mangione, Jerre, viii, 35, 105n5
Mannino, Mary Ann, 105n6
Marshall, Tod, 145, 151, 153, 160
Maso, Carole, 12, 100, 102
Masterpieces of American Literature (anthology), 62
Mathews, John Joseph, 71, 78
Mattanza (Maggio), 101
Mazza, Chris, 103
McCovey, Shaunna, 61
McCullers, Carson, 179n3
McGann, Jerome, 202, 204
McKay, Claude, 114
McKay, Nellie, 10
McNickle, D'Arcy, 3, 71, 77, 78
Means, Russell, 68

MELUS (journal), x, 5, 14, 15, 23–39, 69
  authoritative status of, 32
  digitalization of, 36
  founding, 23–27
  future of, 36–39
  initial criticisms of, 24
  Miller years, 30–31
  Newman years at, 27–30
  nurturance of women's writing in, 31
  Skerrett years, 32–36
  specialty issues, 33, 34, 36, 37
  support for multicultural education, 36
Melville, Herman, 64, 65, 68
Memoirs of a Beatnik (di Prima), 102
Middleman and Other Stories, The (Mukherjee), 10
Midnight's Children (Rushdie), 11
Miller, Perry, 67
Miller, Wayne, 30–31
Milton, Giles, 147
Minority Language and Literature (Fisher), 5
Mirandé, Alfredo, 45, 46
Miss Giardino (Bryant), 99, 105n3
Mixquiahuala Letters, The (Castillo), 49, 210
Modern Chicano Writers: A Collection of Critical Essays (Sommers, Ybarra-Frausto), 4
Modernism, 138
  in Italian American women's writing, 101, 102
Modern Language Association
  Commission on the Status of Women in, 5
  Committee on Minority Literature, 5
  founding of MELUS and, 23–27
  JStor project, 36
  repression of authors by, 5
  seminars in African American literature, 5
  silencing of "radical" membership by, 5
Momaday, N. Scott, 71, 72, 75, 77, 78
Monardo, Anna, 101
Moraga, Cherríe, 11, 49, 50–55, 56n3, 56n4
Morrison, Toni, 1, 3, 10, 14, 65, 112, 183, 187, 190, 191, 192, 193, 194, 205
Moths and Other Stories, The (Viramontes), 49
Mount Allegro (Mangione), viii, 35
Mourning Dove, 71, 72, 78
Movements
  American Indian, 68
  Chicano, 15, 41
  civil rights, 23, 68
  feminist, 11
  political, 68
  social, 2, 68, 76, 89
  women's, 70
Mukherjee, Bharati, 10, 139
Mules and Men (Hurston), 112, 119, 121
Multiculturalism, 12
  advent of, 14
  critical, 203
  criticism against, 2
  crusades against, 1
  literary studies and, 27
  Western culturalism and, 186
Multiethnic literature. *See also* Writers and writing, multiethnic
  "Americanness" of, 65, 66
  Anglo-domination of, 27, 28
  attempts to imitate life by, 63
  availability of, 13, 14
  Caribbean, 37
  children's, 37
  contemporary, 2
  development of, 15, 23–39
  disabilities and, 38
  distribution of, 15
  elimination of programs in, viii
  exclusion from Great Books programs, 2

Filipino American, 38
as form of cultural capital, 184–187
humorous, viii, 34, 73
impact of Internet on, 197–214
imperialism of, 66
inclusion of Anglo male writers
 only in, 65, 66
influence of European predecessors
 on, 65
Internet dissemination of, 17
literary value of, 17
marketing of, 16
moral values in, 62, 65
in new millennium, 1–17
not seen as part of mainstream
 curriculum, 6
pedagogical intent in, 62
pedagogical strategies in
 teaching, 13
political ideologies and, 1
professionalization of teaching
 of, 88
professional managerial class and,
 183–195
protest, 29, 30
racial identification in, 28
reception and dissemination of, 14
redefining, 5
redefining teaching of, 139
relation of law to, 37
relation to audiences, 34
religious, 73
reprints, 14
republishing, 3
seen as protest literature, 29, 30
significance of study of, 14
social inequities and, 37
social justice and, 37
as "specialty" program, 6
teaching, viii
teaching focus on periods and
 themes, 89
technology and, 207–212
textbooks, 26
Thai American, 37

theoretical approaches to, 23–39
value of teaching, ix
viewed as uncomplicated, 30
white colonial responses in, 65
Munns, Jessica, 17

Nabokov, Vladimir, 207
Nair, Supriya, 37
Narratives. *See also* Stories
 ancestral, 98
 competing, 12
 elegiac, 98
 fragmented, 209
 gateways to, 200
 historical, 72
 of immigration, viii, 29
 Italian American, 98–104
 multivoiced, 209
 neo-colonialist, 123
 nontraditional, 95
 slave, 29, 97, 115
 theorizing on, 4
 traditional, 29
National Association for Chicano
 Studies, 49
National Association of Scholars, 1
National Book Awards, 173
National Book Critics Circle Award,
 10, 71
National Council of Teachers of
 English (NCTE), 89
National Endowment for the
 Humanities, 6, 9
Native American literature, 3, 15, 31,
 33, 37, 61–79. *See also* Writers and
 writing, Native American
 anthologizing, 15, 61–79
 poststructuralism and, 208, 209
Native American studies, 68, 69
Native Son (Wright), 111
Naval, Uday, 24
Nelson, Marilyn (Waniek), 28
*New Black Voices: An Anthology of
 Contemporary Afro-American
 Literature* (Chapman), 3

New Criterion (journal), 10
New Criticism, 24, 38
Newman, Katharine, 24, 27–30, 38, 39
Newshour with Jim Lehrer (television), 52
New York Times best seller list, 10
Nice Jewish Girls: A Lesbian Anthology (Beck), 11
Night Bloom (Cappello), 103
No-No Boy (Okada), 3
No Pictures in My Grave (Lloyd), 101
North, East, South, West: A Regional Anthology of American Writing (Lee), 63, 64
Norton Anthology of American Literature, 3, 13, 14, 15, 69, 70, 71, 72, 75, 77, 78, 104, 210

Oates, Joyce Carol, 174, 175
Occupied America:The Chicano's Struggle Toward Liberation (Acuña), 45
Okada, John, 3
Olsen, Tillie, 104
Orientalism (Said), 11
Ortiz, Simon, 72, 77, 78
Oskison, John Milton, 71, 72, 75, 77
Ostendorf, Berndt, 78
The Other
  racial, 132, 135, 159
Outsiderness, 16, 132, 148

Pacific News Service, 52
Page, Thomas Nelson, viii
Pale Fire (Nabokov), 207
Palumbo-Liu, David, 203
Paper Fish (De Rosa), 98, 99, 100, 104
Paredes, Américo, 45
Paredes, Raymond, 28–29
Parker, Hershel, 72, 73
Passing (Larsen), 116
Patee, Fred Lewis, 89
Paton, Alan, 179*n*3
Patriarchy, 4, 48
Pauly, Thomas, 134, 135
Pavic, Milorad, 207

Paz, Octavio, 5, 56*n*2
Peragallo, Olga, 105*n*5
Perkins, George, 70
"Persimmons" (Lee), 153, 157
Peter, John Durham, 146
Peters, Tom, 187, 188, 190, 192
Pinsker, Sanford, 24
Pipino, Mary Frances, 105*n*6
Place of Light, A (Bush), 100
Plato, 63
Platt, Lew, 188
Playing in the Dark: Whiteness in the Literary Imagination (Morrison), 65
Plum Bun (Fauset), 116
Plum Plum Pickers, The (Barrio), 45
Pocho (Villarreal), 3, 45
Poe, Edgar Allan, 1
Poetry
  ethnic signifiers in, 146
  identification with canonical figures in, 155
  sublime in, 154, 155
  transcendentalist, 145–162
Politics
  academic, 41
  cultural, 15, 41, 42, 43, 56*n*2
  of exile, 148
  feminist, 46
  gender, 54, 56*n*2
  identity, 15, 23, 33
  racial, 23, 111–123
  sexual, 3
  social, 3
Pope, Alexander, 1
Portales, Marcos, 31
Postcolonial studies, 10, 11
Postmodernism, 189, 208, 209
Poststructuralism, 52, 53, 54, 209
  Chicana/o studies and, 42
Pound, Ezra, 68
Power
  in academia, 9
  author-reader-text, 168
  canonical, 25

extremes of, 137
institutional, 123
language of, 155
literary canon and, 8
Pray for Yourself and Other Stories (Calcagno), 101
Primitivism, 116
Professional managerial class, 183–195
  cultural capital and, 184–187
  illustration of problems in capitalism through literature, 191, 192
  reading as investment for, 185
  reading lists for, 184–187
Project Gutenberg, 204, 205, 206
Promised Land, The (Antin), 97
Provisions: A Reader from 19th Century American Women (Fetterley), 104
Publishing
  academic, vii
  trade, vii
Pulitzer Prize, 10, 71
Pulsford, Stephen, 198, 204, 206
Purdy, James, 28

Quick, The (Rossi), 100
Quicksand (Larsen), 77, 116
Quinn, Roseanne, 105n6
Quinney, John Wannuaucon, 77
Quinto Sol publishers, 4

Racial
  categorization, 120
  conflict, 78
  construction of culture, 119
  divides, 78
  health, 120
  hostility, 159
  identification, 33
  identity, 11, 116
  indeterminacy, 141n2
  justice, 115
  liberation, 120
  oppression, 35
  othering, 159

otherness, 132, 135
politics, 23, 111–123
provenience, 137
purity, 132
stereotypes, 112, 113, 117
supremacy, 132
Radway, Janice, 168, 169, 179
Random House publishers, 4, 184
Readers' Guide to the Great Books of the Western World, 1
Reading. *See also* Book clubs
  academic, 169
  community, 169
  deficiencies, 12
  global strategies and, 187–194
  groups, 169
  lists, 184–187, 187
  organization of practices of, 8
Reagan, Ronald, 6
Reed, Ishmael, 25
Regeneracion (newsletter), 48
Reilly, John, 29, 30
Relativism, 119
  cultural, 119, 122
Rendon, Armando, 45
Revista Chicano-Riqueña (journal), 5
Ridge, John Rollin, 72, 77
Right Thing to Do, The (Hendin), 99, 105n3
Rincón, Bernice, 48
Rivera, Tomás, 4, 45
Robbins, Bruce, 194n1
Robeson, Paul, 113
Robinson, Edwin Arlington, 68
Robinson, Lillian, 8, 9, 87
Rodriguez, Richard, 50–55
Rölvaag, O.E., 95
Romano, Rose, 101
Romanticism
  European, 154
Rosa: The Life of an Italian Immigrant (Ets), 94–98
Rose, Ellen Cronan, 9
Rose, Wendy, 78
Rossi, Agnes, 100

Rothstein, Arnold, 134, 135, 142*n*4, 142*n*5
Rubin, Joan Shelley, 169, 179*n*5
Ruland, Richard, 65, 66, 67, 68, 73, 74
Runyon, Damon, 142*n*3
Ruoff, A. LaVonne Brown, 71, 75
Rushdie, Salman, 11, 150, 184, 187
Russo, John Paul, 105*n*6
Ryan, Marie-Laure, 200, 209

Said, Edward, 11, 146, 148
Saldivár, Américo, 209
Salt, 150, 151
Santoli, Michael, 190, 191
Satanic Verses, The (Rushdie), 184
Scarlet Letter, The (Hawthorne), 86, 87
Schiavo, Giovanni, 105*n*5
Schoolcraft, Jane Johnston, 77
Schweninger, Lee, 78
Seattle, 77
Seed trope
  exile and, 147, 148
  violence and, 148
Self
  creating, 97
  definition, 121
  deification, 155
  ethnic, 160
  history of, 153
  individual sense of, 96
  reinvention, 132, 133
  reliance, 154
Sexual
  difference, 12, 51, 52
  identification, 14
  identity, 11, 14
  mores, 97
  outsiders, 53
  politics, 3
  preference, 4, 52
Sexuality
  increased discussion of, 11
  lesbian, 102

Signifying Monkey: A Theory of African American Literary Criticism (Gates), 4
Silko, Leslie Marmon, 3, 71, 72, 77, 78, 183, 205, 209
Simonson, Rick, 12
Singh, Amritjit, 5, 38
Sisters Mallone, The (Ermelino), 100
Skårdal, Dorothy Burton, 31
Skerrett, Joseph, 28, 31, 32–36
Slavery, viii, 35
Smith, Barbara, 121
Smith, Felipe, 37
Smith, Katharine Capshaw, 37
Smyth, Gerry, 122, 123
Social
  boundaries, 64
  change, 2, 89
  class, 11, 100, 185
  crises, 114
  difference, 137, 138
  hierarchies, 25
  inequities, 37
  justice, 2, 37
  mobility, 135
  mores, 49
  movements, 2
  order, 130
  politics, 3
  protest, 114, 120
  radicalism, 43
  reform, 43
  relevance, 73
  revolution, 37
  rights, 41
  tolerance, 78
Society for the Study of Multi-Ethnic Literature of the United States. *See* MELUS (journal)
Sollors, Werner, 10, 138, 143*n*7
Sometimes I Dream in Italian (Ciresi), 99, 100
Sommers, Joseph, 4
Song of Songs, 146
Spencer, Stephen, 15, 16, 111–123

Spices, 147, 162*n*3
Spiller, Robert, 66
Spirit of American Literature, The
   (anthology), 62
Spivak, Gayatri, 11
Standing Bear, 72, 77
Stedman, Edmund Clarence, 62
Stein, Gertrude, 138
Steinbeck, John, 179*n*3
Steiner, Stan, 3
Stepto, Robert, 4, 5
Sterne, Lawrence, 207
Stevens, Wallace, 68
Stewart, Thomas, 192
Stoddard, Lathrop, 132
Stories
   creation, 74
   emergence, 72
   folk, viii, 4, 62, 111
   generational, 86
   of immigration, 98
   myths, 4
   Negro spiritual, 62
   oral, 86, 98
   origin, 72
   plantation, viii
   of resettlement, 98
   "Simple," viii
   of slavery, viii
   telling of, 86, 96, 97, 149
   told in stables, 96
   trickster, 72, 119
   urban, 148
Stowe, Harriet Beecher, 62, 89
Stripes, James, 70
Studies, diasporan, ix
Studies in American Indian Literature
   (Allen), 5
Studies in American Indian Literature
   (journal), 5
Subjectivity
   Chicano, 43, 45
   community-based notion of, 43
   positivist, 46
Sula (Morrison), 191

Surrounded, The (McNickles), 3
Swift, Jonathan, 1

Taft, Robert, 115
Talese, Gay, 90, 105*n*4
Tamburri, Anthony Julian, 90, 93
Tan, Amy, 10
Tar Baby (Morrison), 192
Taylor, Edward, 68
Technology
   computer, 207
   contemporary multiethnic
      literature and, 207–212
   electronic, 200
   print, 199
Tedlock, Dennis, 75
Temple of My Familiar, The (Walker),
   210, 211
Tender Warriors (de Vries), 100
Their Eyes Were Watching God
   (Hurston), 2, 14, 15, 111–123
Theory
   aesthetic, 88
   borderlands, 53
   of double-consciousness, 71,
      76, 118
   electronic textual, 199
   hypertext, 208
   identity, 122, 150
   postcolonial, 11
   poststructuralist, 199, 208
   queer, 183
This Bridge Called My Back: Writings
   by Radical Women of Color
   (Moraga, Anzaldúa), 11
Thomas and Beulah (Dove), 10
Three American Literatures, Essays in
   Chicano, Native American, and
   Asian American Literatures
   (Houston), 5
Thucydides, 1
Thurman, Wallace, 116
Tiffin, Helen, 11
Timpanelli, Gioia, 104
Tolstoy, Leo, 179*n*3

Tomasi, Mari, 99, 104*n1*
Tony award, 10
Toomer, Jean, 3, 69
Tradition(s)
  American rhetorical, 139
  cultural, 157
  literary, 93
  oral, 4, 97, 98
  semantic, 159
  of the sublime, 154
  vernacular, 4
  Western, 7
Transcendentalism, 16, 145
  resistance to, 146
  tension with ethnicity, 155–162
  will to canon and, 151–155
Transnationalism, ix
Trefzer, Annette, 120
Tristram Shandy (Sterne), 208
TuSmith, Bonnie, 38
Twain, Mark, 1, 68, 86
Tyler, Moses Coit, 67

Ulysses (Joyce), 184, 208
Umbertina (Barolini), 91, 105*n3*
Universalism, 145
Uno, Roberta, 34

Valdez, Luis, 3, 45
Value, literary
  criteria for, 6
Values
  cultural, 44
  literary, 25
  middle-class, 43
  radical, 44
  transcendent, 155
Vannucci, Lynn, 101
Vasquez, Enriqueta Longeaux, 48
Vecoli, Rudolph, 94, 95, 99, 105*n5*
Velie, Alan, 3
Vendler, Helen, 153, 154
Vertigo (DeSalvo), 102, 103, 105*n3*
Veseth, Michael, 187
Vicinus, Martha, 11

Vico, Giambattista, 93
Vidal, Mirta, 48
Villarreal, Jose Antonio, 3, 45
Violence
  as male prerogative, 98
  narratives of, 103
  retention of privilege and, 137
  seed trope and, 148
Viramontes, Helena Maria, 49
Viscusi, Robert, 90, 93
Vizenor, Gerald, 29, 77, 208, 209

Waiting in the Wings (Moraga), 51
Wald, Priscilla, 118, 120
Walker, Alice, 10, 71, 91, 111, 120, 121, 210, 211
Waniek, Marilyn (Nelson), 28
Warren, Kenneth, 78
Washington, Booker T., 71
Washington, Mary Helen, 3, 121
Watkins, Evan, 185, 186
Watsonville: Some Place Not Here (Moraga), 51
Way to Rainy Mountain, The (Momaday), 75
Weber, Brom, 26, 27
Welch, James, viii, 72, 75, 78
Where Love Leaves Us (Manfredi), 94
Whitecloud, Thomas, 72, 78
Whitman, Walt, 30, 62, 71
Williams, William Carlos, 68
Wilson, August, 10
Wilson, Rob, 154, 161
Winfrey, Oprah, 12, 16, 170. *See also* Book clubs
Winged Seed, The (Lee), 146–151
Winnemucca, Sarah, 77
Winter in the Blood (Welch), 75
Winterson, Jeanette, 102
With His Pistol in His Hand (Paredes), 45
Woman Warrior: Memoirs of a Childhood Among Ghosts (Kingston), 3, 14, 33, 35, 159

Women: New Voice of La Raza (anthology), 46–50
Women's literature. *See also* Writers and writing, women and feminist
  canonization in, 86
  reiteration of existence of, 2, 3
  republishing, 3
Wong, Norman, 11
Wong, Sau-Ling Cynthia, 159
Wright, Richard, 69, 111, 112, 113, 114, 119
Writers and writing
  canonical, viii
  colonial, 65, 66, 67, 68
  conservative, 9
  creative, 31
  cultural credence of, 13, 14
  regional, 73
  Southern, viii
Writers and writing, African American, 111–123
  assimilationism and, 114
  construction of blackness in, 116
  criticisms of, 113
  defining color in, 119, 120
  marginalization and, 118
  racial politics and, 111–123
  social crises in, 114
  social protest and, 113, 114
  understandings of race from, 116
  visions of black life in, 114
Writers and writing, Asian American, 16
  poetry, 145–162
Writers and writing, Chicana/o, 15, 41–56
  assimilation in, 43, 44, 47, 51, 52
  figure of the traitor in, 48
  indigenismo in, 54
  lesbian, 56n4
  Malintzín/Malinche in, 48
  mestizaje in, 54
  mother-daughter relationships in, 48
  notions of family in, 47, 48
  politicized, 51
  sexual outlaws in, 50–55
  views on family in, 51
Writers and writing, gay and lesbian, 10, 56n4
  cultural and sexual identities and, 11
Writers and writing, Italian American, 15, 85–104
  culinary references in, 101
  cultural cohesion in, 102
  emergence of, 91–93
  features of *italianità* in, 100
  festa in, 101
  genres of, 98
  on immigration experiences, 94
  increasing recognition of, 105n3
  recurring themes in, 94
  reversal of portrayals of Italy in, 101
  sibling solidarity in, 100
  spirituality in, 101
  themes and influences on, 98–104
Writers and writing, multiethnic, 3, 23–39
  dismissal of, 66
  excellence of, viii
  freedom to write on other groups, 27, 28, 29
  immigration and, viii
  impact of Internet on, 197–214
  technology and, 207–212
Writers and writing, Native American, 61–79
  creation stories, 74
  emergence stories, 72
  Ghost Dance Songs, 72
  historical narratives, 72
  origin stories, 72
  trickster tales, 72
Writers and writing, women and feminist, 8, 10, 12, 31
W.W. Norton Company, Publishers, ix

Xu, Wenying, 16, 145–162

Yao, Steven, 153
Ybarra-Frausto, Tomas, 4
Yekl (Cahan), viii
"Yellow Wallpaper, The" (Gilman), 2
y no se lo tragó la tierra/ And the Earth Did Not Part (Rivera), 4, 45

Young, Robert, 122
Yue Fei, 157

Zebrowski, John, 26
Zhou, Xiaojing, 152
Žižek, Slavoj, 149